CONTENTS

FLYING
THROUGH THE
RANKS

In them is plainest taught, and easiest learnt.
What makes a nation happy, and keeps it so.

John Milton, *Paradise Regained*

FLYING THROUGH THE RANKS

THE EXTRAORDINARY EXPERIENCES OF AIRMEN TO AIR MARSHALS FROM THE COLD WAR TO THE GULF

AIR MARSHAL
G.A. 'BLACK' ROBERTSON

GRUB STREET • LONDON

For all those from whom I learnt so much

Published by
Grub Street
4 Rainham Close
London SW11 6SS

Copyright © Grub Street 2024

Copyright text © G.A. 'Black' Robertson 2024

A CIP record for this title is available from the British Library

ISBN-13: 978-1-911714-10-1

Design by Myriam Bell Design, UK

Printed and bound by Finidr, Czechia

INTRODUCTION

I fell in love with flying at an early age. From the day I first took the controls of a light aircraft, as a teenager in the summer of 1962, I was hooked. But I was daunted too. There seemed so much to learn. And learning didn't come easily to a schoolboy for whom the sports field held more attractions than the classroom. With an RAF Flying Scholarship behind me and A level exams ahead, a contemporary report aptly summarised my precarious academic position: 'He knows very little about much of the ground covered.' In an apposite parallel with my classroom struggles, I went on to view flying much as Izaak Walton saw angling: 'so like the mathematics, that it can never be fully learnt.'[1] If three years at Cranwell taught me the value of application, no matter how hard I eventually worked, there was always something new to learn about flying.

As the Deputy Commander in RAF Germany during the early 1990s I found myself in a privileged position, with access to a number of types I'd not flown before, amongst them the Harrier and Tornado. There were helicopters too. With minimal previous rotary experience beyond the ritual winching from a cold and miserable North Sea during dinghy drills, I managed a few hours in the Chinook, Gazelle and Puma. One particular sortie during my Puma conversion, on 19 October 1992 under the watchful eye of Flight Lieutenant Neil Strevens, is etched indelibly in my memory. It involved the unnerving prospect of landing at a small site amongst a forest of pines. As we came to the hover overhead, the crewman, Sergeant Bob Mullen, began issuing a steady stream of commands. No sooner had I responded to his, "Right one – steady!" than it was "Left two ... back one – steady!" This airborne mazurka went on for what seemed an age, but probably lasted no more than a couple

---

1   *The Compleat Angler*, Epistle to the Reader.

of minutes, sapping my concentration. The crewman's commentary conveyed a real sense of urgency and I could feel myself tensing up under the pressure of responding to a drumbeat of firm, precise instructions. So it was a considerable relief when at last I heard, "Clear to descend."

Gently lowering the collective, I began to sink slowly into the abyss. There was still the odd correction as we descended, supplied in a tone that demanded an immediate response. But now there were other problems. The surrounding trees loomed perilously close and it was becoming noticeably dark. I was getting more tense by the minute. I'd never had to concentrate quite so hard on flying accurately (with the possible exception of a back-seat Master Green instrument rating in the Phantom), or so it seemed. I heaved a huge sigh of relief when at last we touched down in the clearing. I released the collective and finally prised loose my iron grip on the cyclic.

No surprise that after such a demanding exercise my flying helmet was soaked in perspiration. Rarely had I been so taxed. I sat back and tried to relax. Sergeant Mullen broke the ensuing silence with a hardly deserved, "Well done, Sir." A short pause, then, "Any questions?" It was a moment before I replied. "Just one. When you say left, right, back or forward one, what exactly is one?" He laughed. "It's whatever you make it, Sir. All that messing about is simply calibration. I need to know what 'one' and 'two' are to you, and I need to get the same response every time." After some 30 years' flying, I'd just spent a few short minutes – minutes that felt like hours – stretched to the limit. And I was still learning!

This brief incident also served as a reminder, not that I needed it, that the flying game is by no means the province of pilots alone. Without the support of related specialists – designers, engineers, manufacturers, servicing teams and a host of other trades – members of 'the two-winged master race' could never ply their trade. And if a pilot's compendium of knowledge is never complete, the same is equally true of these enablers: those upon whom all aircrew – passengers too – depend for their lives. The story also reinforces another truism: acquiring knowledge is a never-ending process.

The RAF has long recognised the importance of spreading knowledge across the aviation community – in its purest form by teaching, but teaching supplemented by experience. In an effort to expand aircrew experience, in the 1940s the service began including in Flight Safety magazines articles describing how 'I learnt about flying from that'. Never didactic, sometimes amusing and occasionally eye-opening, they were invariably a good read. Nearly a quarter-century after retiring and increasingly distanced from service life, paradoxically I found myself closer to it – closer to flying too – through writing. This realisation prompted the idea of tapping into others' experiences and putting together a collection of flying stories, broadly similar to the 'I learnt' tales I'd enjoyed all those years ago.

This sort of thing had been done before, of course. So what was needed was a twist, a different angle. What if it were possible to tap into a hitherto unprecedented breadth of retired air force experience, from top to bottom – every rank from five-star officer to the most junior airman? Expanding the catchment area beyond aircrew to ground crew as well would provide an additional, arguably unique perspective, not just on the development of RAF flying through the years, but also on the sort of characters who formed the service's post-war (and post-Cold War) backbone.

Once I settled on this approach, in the summer of 2023 I began to trawl for inputs. But as contributions started to arrive, it became clear that the concept was flawed. First, the distribution of stories was unbalanced. Their origins tended to mirror the RAF's pyramid rank structure, with a bias towards the more populous lower levels – obvious with hindsight, but something I'd failed to anticipate. Reluctant to discard any worthwhile inputs, the solution was simply to accept the resulting imbalance. If the chapters devoted to individual ranks varied in size, then so be it.

The second issue I hadn't foreseen was that inputs from near the lower end of the respective rank spectrums would prove hard to come by. Again, this was for good reason. Few officers or 'other ranks' retire at the lowest levels: respectively pilot officer and aircraftman 2nd class – air specialist (class 2) in current nomenclature. And those who do have only limited experience to draw upon. The solution was to deal with these two cohorts under a single, collective heading in each case: junior officers and non-commissioned officers (NCOs), the latter embracing other ranks' stories too.

One last problem remained: how best to deal with the pre-commissioning stories of those who later went on to earn their RAF wings? The answer was to add a final construct: a chapter featuring tales where the common factor, inevitably perhaps, is youthful indiscretion. Some of these individuals went on to enjoy full careers and reach the upper echelons of the service. Their stories could thus have featured elsewhere; but this seemed a more fitting approach.

Editing the various inputs proved an illuminating and rewarding experience. I'm immensely grateful to each and every contributor for the time and effort put into telling their fascinating tales, to Ray Deacon for his help with the illustrations, and to my publisher, John Davies, for his support and encouragement throughout. The exercise has left me with nothing but respect and admiration for all those individuals who helped make the RAF such an exhilarating environment in which to fly, to fight – as some necessarily did – and, importantly, to have fun.

It's no surprise that the theme of enjoyment echoes across this entire volume. There's a common thread of learning from experience too, of course. But it is the unprecedented range of contributors – from a junior technician to a marshal of the Royal Air Force – and the variety of their experiences that set this anthology apart. The stories they tell run the gamut of risk-taking during the Cold War – a Lightning first tourist succumbs to the 'press-on' spirit – to the Gulf conflicts. In between, figuratively speaking, lie the Falklands, where calculated wartime gambles put the lives of tanker and helicopter crews in danger. A Hunter pilot comes up with a brilliant, almost equally risky, piece of improvisation to avert a potential disaster, while for a split-second an experienced Harrier aviator stares death in the face. A Typhoon pilot meets some aggressive Russians and a Phantom flyer who tries the navy for size finds that he rather likes it, so much so that he eventually transfers his allegiance – unlike the Buccaneer navigator who happily returns to the fold after his own carrier experience. There are engineer stories too. In fact a Phantom engineer becomes the first woman to fly operationally in the RAF. And marrying the themes of risk and good fortune that accompany almost every narrative, from Kosovo comes a tale of the narrowest of helicopter escapes.

On the ground, there are accounts of unlikely escapades in Cyprus, fighting in the Dhofar campaign and a UK base apparently prone to serious accidents. Last but by no means least in this brief preview of some extraordinary stories, a seemingly inconsequential incident during the Suez crisis exemplifies the bond between those who fly and those who support them on the ground – a professional relationship central to so many of these tales.

To all the contributors with whom it has been such a privilege to work, and to everyone who has helped bring this book to fruition, I once again extend my sincere thanks.

Black Robertson
Cheltenham
February 2024

CHAPTER 1
A MARSHAL'S MEMORIES

MARSHAL OF THE ROYAL AIR FORCE THE LORD STIRRUP OF MARYLEBONE

After graduating from Cranwell in 1970, a first tour as a 'creamed-off' qualified flying instructor (QFI) on Gnats led Jock Stirrup to a tour with the Sultan of Oman's Air Force (SOAF). Thereafter, with the exception of a USAF exchange tour on the Phantom, all his operational flying was on the Jaguar. It included command of 2 Squadron, a recce unit in Germany and, later, a tour as station commander at Marham during the Gulf War. One of the RAF's most distinguished post-war officers, he went on to serve as both Chief of the Air Staff (CAS) and Chief of the Defence Staff (CDS).

A ONE-NIGHT STAND

Long ago in a galaxy far away – at least that is how it seems these days – I was a young loan service pilot in the Sultan of Oman's Air Force. The Dhofar War [1962–1976] was then in full swing, and most of my time was spent operating Strikemaster aircraft in the close-air-support and interdiction roles from Salalah, in the south of the country. The life was varied and exciting – I acquired my fair share of bullet holes during my tour – and it might be thought that one would have needed no further professional challenge beyond this. But those ground-attack sorties were only part of the story, and some of my most memorable experiences came in another role entirely.

For a reason that I never fully understood, my squadron was tasked with operating not just Strikemasters but also a small number of Beavers. This rather venerable type, built by de Havilland of Canada, had first flown on 16 August 1947, but it remained in use well into the 21st century. It was a single-engined, high-wing, propeller-driven aircraft that had been designed to take off from and land on short, rough airstrips. It was intended for utility transport roles and could carry up to six passengers or just under 1,000kg of freight. In Oman it was used for a variety of tasks: the transport of small numbers of personnel between remote locations; casualty and medical evacuation; and – particularly in Dhofar – photographic reconnaissance. The latter role did not involve much in the way of high technology; the aircraft would take off with one of the side doors removed, and at a suitable altitude an army liaison officer, fitted with an appropriate safety harness, would lean far out from the cabin and take photographs with a motor-drive-equipped 2½-inch Hasselblad camera. It was all very basic, but it worked. The great advantages of the Beaver were that it was robust, cheap to operate, and could fly into almost any location. The landing airspeed at a short strip was only about 45kts, so with a decent headwind the aircraft could be brought to a halt in a very short distance indeed. This made it ideal for operations in an undeveloped country such as the Oman of those days.

My conversion to the Beaver was a rather perfunctory affair: two dual sorties followed by a solo. I then flew a couple of further duals to familiarise me with the various rough strips around Dhofar, after which I was cleared for operations on the aircraft. I have always been a fast-jet pilot – a fighter pilot, in common parlance – at

A SOAF Beaver.

heart as well as in fact, but the hours that I spent in the Beaver provided me with some of the most interesting experiences of my career in the air. Just one month after starting to fly the aircraft, for example, I became the first pilot to land at Heiron, a newly cleared desert strip north of the Dhofar jebel which gave a whole new meaning to the term rough and ready. Apart from my sense of relief at having survived the experience in one piece, I was also left with the feeling of being a real pioneer.

Most of the locations we flew to were within about 30 minutes of Salalah (we cruised at around 130kts), but one was further away and always made for an exciting excursion. Makinat Shahan was a small army outpost in the middle of the desert, right on the border with Saudi Arabia. There was nothing else for miles around. The purpose of the army presence in such a desolate area was to make clear to the Saudis that Oman knew where the border was and meant to maintain it, just in case their neighbours to the north got any funny ideas. Needless to say, routine communication and resupply had to be done by air, and that often meant the Beaver.

The challenge lay in actually finding Makinat Shahan. For more than half of the trip you flew over featureless desert, with no distinguishable landmarks; nor were there any of the modern electronic navigation aids on which aircraft normally rely for ascertaining their position. You therefore had to fly an accurate compass heading and airspeed designed to take you to the destination at a certain elapsed time. But this took no account of wind, about which our meagre meteorological facilities could give us little accurate information, and which could blow your aircraft seriously off track. To add to the difficulty, the army camp was small and very difficult to spot until very close to it. The only thing in our favour was that the desert sand in the vicinity of the camp had a faint pink tinge to it. The trick was to fly as accurately as you could for an hour or so, and then to search desperately for a hint of pinkness; if this was spotted, you could then home in on the base. I flew many missions to Makinat Shahan, and I am pleased to say that I found it every time; but every time was an adventure, and each successful landing there came as something of a relief.

The greatest challenges, though, lay outside Dhofar. Soon after my conversion, I flew a Beaver on the nearly three-hour trip to Seeb in the north of Oman, and then a couple of days later took the aircraft up to Khasab on the Musandam Peninsula. Oman is bounded to the north-west by the United Arab Emirates (UAE), but one part of the country lies on a small peninsula – the Musandam – which forms the southern shore of the Straits of Hormuz. The Musandam is not contiguous with the rest of Oman – it is separated from it by a 60-mile stretch of the Emirates – but it is of enormous strategic importance.

The Straits of Hormuz constitute the gateway to the Persian Gulf, and much of the world's supplies of oil and gas flow through them. They are commanded by Iran to the north and by Oman to the south, and the Musandam was – and is – accordingly of great geopolitical significance, which only served to underline the risks of the communist-backed insurgency in the south. Should Soviet Russia have gained control of the Straits, the consequences for the West would have been severe. The Musandam is, however, a wild and mountainous peninsula, and in the days I flew there it was still undeveloped. The principal town (little more than a village) was Khasab, which sits on the western side of the northern tip of the Musandam; the other population centres were in settlements on either side of the peninsula. The army maintained small bases at each location, with a regional headquarters at Khasab, but movement between these places was something of a challenge. There were no roads, and sailing around the peninsula was a time-consuming process. The answer was to travel by air, and the best means of doing this was in a helicopter. Helicopters, however, were expensive to run, and the government was short of funds, particularly given the demands of the war in the south. The solution was a compromise: for one week out of every four, the army would have a helicopter at its disposal for command, control and communication tasks; for the other three, it would have a Beaver. Thus it was that each of us on my squadron would take it in turns to go to Khasab and operate a Beaver there for those three-week detachments.

Khasab today has a population of around 18,000, but It was much smaller then. It was essentially a fishing village with some date palms and a little livestock. There was a rudimentary school and hospital, and a little way outside the town lay the army base with its small dirt airstrip. The Musandam Military Region was commanded by a British loan service major, who lived in the small officers' mess with a civilian development official (again British) and whichever pilot happened to be detached there. There were no air force support personnel; we carried out routine maintenance checks on the Beaver ourselves, and local soldiers helped us to refuel it by hand-pumping petroleum into the aircraft out of large oil drums. We received tasking requests from the army commander, but the detached pilot was the first, last and only authority on what we actually did. It was a position of great responsibility, and enormous fun.

We flew principally to five different locations on a routine basis. The first of these was the village of Bukha, on the west coast of the peninsula. The main distinguishing feature of Bukha, from a pilot's viewpoint, was a large hill on the landing approach to the airstrip; this meant that the latter stage of the final flightpath to touchdown, while some height above the strip itself, was only 100–200ft above the ground below, which sloped downwards at roughly the same angle as the aircraft was descending. It also gave rise to some unpredictable wind effects, which could make the landing tricky. On one particular occasion, for example, a very nasty wind shear nearly took me off the side of the airstrip. I brought the aircraft under control almost without thinking – instincts and training invariably take over in such situations – but the army major in the seat next to me got very tense; I think it took the better part of an hour for the blood to return to his knuckles.

The second location was the village of Limah, on the east coast of the Musandam. The terrain around the strip was flat and undemanding, but what made Lima a popular destination for us was the presence of some young American Peace Corps personnel who always entertained us with iced coffee and chocolate brownies. Thirdly, there was al-Bayah, also on the eastern side of the peninsula but right by the border with the UAE. Along the route from the airstrip to the town lay an unusually large burial site; rumour had it that a couple of centuries earlier one of the chieftains in the hills had decided that the villagers were insufficiently assiduous with their prayers, and accordingly had descended on the settlement with his warriors and carried out a mass slaughter. Whether or not this gruesome tale was actually true I do not know, but the locals recounted it with relish. The fourth site was the village of Rawdah; this was an unusual location, as it was in the mountainous interior of the peninsula rather than on the coast. It was at an altitude of about 1,500ft, which reduced the power of the aircraft's engine, and the surrounding peaks meant that after take-off you had to circle within the valley containing the village until you gained sufficient altitude to clear the terrain. Our final – and by far our most popular – destination was Dubai, where we flew from time to time to replenish the more exotic elements of the officers' mess stores. Dubai in those days was nothing like the city it has become; to 21st century eyes it would seem small and undistinguished, but to us it was an oasis of civilisation, and we greatly enjoyed our brief sojourns there.

Apart from Dubai, which had an international airport – albeit on a much smaller scale than today's facility – the process of landing at these various locations followed a similar pattern. First, we would 'buzz', or fly low over, the nearby army fort to let the soldiers know we were coming. Then we would fly low over the strip, to ensure that it was in a satisfactory condition, and sometimes to scare off the odd wandering camel. Finally, we would make another low pass while tossing a smoke grenade out of the cockpit window, which would give us an idea of the wind conditions for landing. Once on the ground, we would shut down the aircraft and, leaving a soldier to guard it, we would accompany the army commander to the fort while he carried out his business. Most of the landings and take-offs were uneventful, but now and again we ran into something unusual. On one occasion, for example, a camel died halfway down the strip at Rawdah. The soldiers had no vehicles to tow it away, and there were too few of them to manhandle it off the strip until it had decomposed sufficiently. While waiting for that to happen, I was forced to circumnavigate the corpse on my landing and take-off runs!

But my most singular and certainly most nerve-wracking experience took place one evening back at Khasab. I was relaxing with my colleagues in the officers' mess after dinner, and just thinking about retiring to my room in order to continue Norman Mailer's classic war novel, *The Naked and the Dead*, which I was then much enjoying, when the Indian doctor who ran the local clinic appeared at the door. His facilities at Khasab were fairly basic, and in serious cases it was quite usual for him to request a medevac by Beaver to the much better appointed hospital in Dubai. That was indeed the purpose of his visit on this occasion, so I told him to have the patient at the airstrip by first thing in the morning, when I would be ready to take them on the short journey down the coast. At this he wrung his hands and explained that in his opinion the patient would almost certainly be dead by the morning if she did not receive expert care before then.

A local who was nearly nine months pregnant, the woman had developed a pelvic abscess; she absolutely had to get to hospital that night. This left me in something of a quandary. We did not operate the Beaver at night. I had never flown the aircraft in the dark; what is more, we had drunk a glass of two of champagne with our dinner, and there are very strict rules against flying with alcohol in the bloodstream. But what choice did I have? This woman would die if I could not help her, and no rules or regulations could alter that fact. I had to do something, but there were very real practical difficulties. Khasab was undeveloped and had almost nothing in the way of electric lighting. The army base had internal lights, but most of the village did not, and in any event it was some distance off. There was no external lighting of any kind, so it was pitch-black outside. The airstrip was simply a fairly level piece of ground delineated by whitewashed stones, with no other markings of any kind. It was clear that we were going to have to improvise in a big way.

I told the doctor to bring the patient and her husband to the Beaver in 30 minutes. Meanwhile, I asked the army commander to drive his Land Rover to the far end of the strip and point down it with his dipped headlights. I then groped my way through the darkness to the aircraft; I did not even have a torch, so I could see next to nothing. I felt around in the cockpit, flipping every switch I came to until I chanced on the battery control, and the internal lights came on. I then started the engine and waited until the doctor and his party were aboard. The poor woman with the abscess was clearly in agony, but her screaming, while entirely understandable, only added to the already febrile atmosphere in the cabin. I turned on the taxiing light which was set into the leading edge of the wing, and with its aid and a great deal of trial and error eventually found my way out to the strip without hitting anything. I then pointed the aircraft at the dipped Land Rover headlights some distance away, which were the only things I could see, ran the engine up to full power and released the brakes, keeping the Beaver pointed at the lights and hoping that this would ensure that I stayed on the strip and did not stray off into some of the obstacles that lay alongside it.

Fortunately, we made it safely into the air, and I set course for Dubai. Once we were a little distance south, cultural lighting started to appear along the coast, and I was able to find my way with no difficulty. Although I had never landed the Beaver at night, Dubai airport was lit up like a Christmas tree, so touching down was far less of a drama than the take-off had been. The doctor, patient and husband were unloaded and rushed off to hospital (the woman survived and gave birth successfully), while I repaired to a local hotel for a night's sleep before returning to Khasab the next day.

So ended my first and last night sortie in a Beaver. I had taken risks and broken several rules in the process, and had something gone wrong then the consequences for me (not to mention the patient) would probably have been distinctly unpleasant. But I felt that I had made the right decision, and I have not changed my view over the many years since. I was faced with doing something that I considered within my ability, but which was clearly unauthorised – or letting someone die. The choice seemed to me, and still seems, obvious. In the world of aviation, rules are generally derived from hard-won experience and are designed to make flying as safe and effective as possible. There is certainly no excuse for ignoring them or flouting them with insouciance. On the other hand, life is hardly ever free from risks, so you cannot entirely avoid them. Sometimes those risks call into question accepted – and usually sensible – rules and practices. The trick is to balance the risks you run with the benefits to be gained and see how the equation comes out; when a life is at stake, you sometimes have to hazard beyond the ordinary. My one-night stand with the Beaver was one of the most significant experiences in my flying career, and it has remained with me all of my life – not least because from it I learnt about so much more than just flying.

CHAPTER 2

FOUR-STAR FORUM – SOME CHIEFLY CHAT

AIR CHIEF MARSHAL SIR DAVID HARCOURT-SMITH

In a long and distinguished career, David Harcourt-Smith led two fighter squadrons, 54 and then 6, the RAF's first Phantom squadron. A station commander in Germany, at Brüggen, he later served as Commandant of the Royal Air Force College Cranwell, Air Officer Commanding-in-Chief Support Command and, finally, Controller Aircraft. He retired in 1989.

LESSONS IN LEADERSHIP

If I learnt anything about leadership it came from Squadron Leader 'Joe' Blyth. He was an amazing commanding officer (CO) and certainly left his mark on me as a young flight commander. He may well have been unique being awarded five decorations in a short period after the Second World War – two DFCs, two AFCs and the American Air Medal.

Colin Ian Blyth was known as Joe throughout a remarkable career that began when he bluffed his way into the RAF in 1940, aged only 15. He trained initially as a wireless operator/air gunner. After transferring to 161 (Special Duties) Squadron,[2] a unit flying operations into occupied Europe to drop agents and supplies, in September 1942 his Whitley was shot down and crash-landed in the Ardennes. Some of the crew were captured but Joe managed to escape on foot. Helped initially by French farmers, over 200 miles south in Lyon he was picked up by the local escape line and moved

---

2   Part of the RAF's Special Duties Service, created to provide air transport support for the resistance movement on the Continent.

to a safe house in Marseilles. Finally, together with other evaders, he was taken to a beach near Perpignan and thence by boat to Gibraltar. The signs were already there that this was a very special kind of man.

On his return to the UK, and still only a teenager, Joe trained as a pilot, initially in South Africa. Assessed as 'above average', he was promptly creamed off as a QFI and rapidly made his mark. He moved effortlessly from piston- to jet-engined aircraft, demonstrating the dynamism and innovative leadership that earned him the first of his AFCs.

I first came across Joe Blyth when 8 Squadron's Venoms were deployed from Aden to Akrotiri in Cyprus in preparation for the ill-fated Suez adventure. At this critical time the squadron was minus a squadron commander; he'd left for reasons I never did discover. Joe was promptly despatched to take over. A staff officer in the Cyprus Headquarters at the time but with previous Venom experience, his reputation was second to none.

In the meantime I had been on the Day Fighter Leaders' course at West Raynham and rejoined the squadron in Cyprus. I was told to report to the new boss in his caravan on the edge of the airfield (Akrotiri was still being developed when it was overwhelmed by three Venom squadrons and various visits from the French and Israel Air Forces). I knocked on the caravan door and opened it – to be greeted by a flying telephone and a burst of expletives from my new CO about the stupid staff officers at headquarters who had no idea what was going on at the 'sharp end'.

When Joe's obituary was written in 2012 it included my opening comment that anything I learnt about leadership came from him. I stand by this observation but have some difficulty in explaining why. He would never ask you to do anything that he would not be prepared to do himself; he would stand by you if you did something stupid, admitted to it and accepted that you had learnt a lesson. He would defend the squadron against unjustified outside comment, even if it

Refuelling David Harcourt-Smith's Venom at Salalah.

came from higher authority and, unlike some squadron commanders, he would never do anything just to impress a superior.

The answer to this leadership conundrum may perhaps lie in the breadth of Joe's experience and his appetite for action. As his decorations suggest, he had a thirst for operations. He'd served with 77 Squadron RAAF (Royal Australian Air Force) in Korea, initially on Mustangs and later flying Meteors, where he was part of an RAF team sent to convert the unit to their first jet fighter. Although not authorised to fly on operations, Joe persuaded his CO to allow him to fly a few sorties. In the event he completed more than 100, including one where his Mustang was hit by ground fire and several Meteor engagements with MiG-15s.

One final, rather naughty thought. During Suez, we were given strict instructions to fire only on the targets we were briefed to attack. On my second sortie into Egypt I was flying as number two to Joe. As we left, flying low over the Nile Delta (where there were a few boats!) I saw him firing his cannon. I thought what was good for the boss was OK for me, so I followed my leader's example. I queried this in the debrief only to be told, "It's simple. It makes for a faster and more straightforward job for the ground crew on the turnround." Joe Blyth saw things in strictly operational terms.

It was an immense privilege to serve with such an outstanding fighter pilot and leader.

Camel Troop of the Aden Protectorate Levies guards a debrief.

AIR CHIEF MARSHAL SIR ANDREW PULFORD

Following flying training on Jet Provosts (JPs) and Whirlwinds, Andy Pulford joined the RAF Support Helicopter Force as a Wessex pilot, initially with 72 Squadron then an exchange tour with the Royal Navy. He converted to the Chinook in 1982 and completed four tours on the type, including an exchange with the RAAF. His operational service included Northern Ireland, the Falkland Islands, the Balkans, Beirut, Afghanistan and Iraq. He commanded RAF Odiham and 2 Group and became the first helicopter pilot to command the RAF as CAS.

GOOD FORTUNE ON FORTUNA GLACIER

"Mayday! Mayday! Mayday!" Three short but distinctive words which leave no doubt in anyone's mind that someone is in serious trouble. As a second-tour Wessex pilot, with over 1,500 hours in my logbook, I was only too aware of the implications of that radio call. But it was not made by me; in fact, I wasn't even airborne at the time. The Mayday was broadcast by the leader of the two surviving Wessex aircraft from a flight of three which were engaged in a desperate mission to extract a small detachment of Special Forces (SF) from 2,000ft up a glacier on South Georgia, a small British protectorate in the South Atlantic. The radio transmission went on to report that the number two aircraft in the formation had crashed onto the glacier.

A second Mayday call was received only minutes later, reporting that the number three Wessex had also crashed onto the glacier. Things looked bleak, but what were the aircraft doing so far from the UK and what happened next? Furthermore, why did what happened that fateful day leave such an impression on me, an impression that would last for the remainder of my service life?

The events formed part of the opening actions in what became known as the Falklands War, following the illegal Argentine invasion of the Falkland

Sir Andrew Pulford.

Islands in early April 1982. I was then a young, enthusiastic exchange pilot on 845 Naval Air Squadron (NAS) at RNAS Yeovilton, thoroughly enjoying my time as the 'Tame Crab' on a 'Jungly' squadron – and the opportunity it brought to broaden my experience of the maritime environment and the rigours of operating the Wessex HU5 at, and from, the sea. Our normal squadron routine had been rudely interrupted by the invasion and in what seemed like only hours of the news coming through we were ready to deploy. For my flight, C Flight, this meant loading two aircraft onto an RAF Belfast transport aircraft and our personnel onto a C-130 Hercules and deploying to a small island in the middle of the South Atlantic, Ascension. Here we rebuilt and test-flew our aircraft in readiness for the arrival of a small Royal Navy Task Group of two warships, a frigate and a destroyer, supported by a Royal Fleet Auxiliary tanker, RFA *Tidespring*, which was to be our home and operating deck for the next couple of months. This task group brought additional helicopters, as the destroyer was equipped with a single-engined, anti-submarine Wessex HAS3, and the frigate had a Wasp HAS1. The land element of the Task Group was made up of a cadre of mountain and Arctic warfare specialists of the Royal Marines and a detachment of SF from the British Army.

Amid considerable secrecy, as the public narrative of an invasion force being sent to the Falklands was only just beginning in the UK, we set sail for the south and the prospect of an early victory. The intention was to deliver a demonstration of the political and military resolve of the British government through the liberation of South Georgia. This was the island where the Falklands conflict had begun, with the landing of 30 Argentine scrap metal merchants to plunder the old whaling station at Grytviken. This group had been reinforced as part of the Falklands invasion plan by a large Argentine army detachment.

The voyage south was used to cross-deck vital equipment and stores across the Task Group and to sharpen the flight's operational skills, including air-to-ground gunnery, two-inch rocket firing and night formation. This latter task proved the most demanding of all, as we had no night vision goggles (NVG) but utilised small Beta lights on the fuselage and rotor tips to provide visual cues on which to maintain close formation. Not for the faint-hearted! It was certainly some of the most demanding flying I ever experienced, particularly the airborne join-ups. As we only had one deck for two aircraft, the first aircraft would launch, allowing the second to be towed from the hangar, spread and started. The airborne aircraft would then fly a dummy approach to the deck, aiming to time his run to join up with the lead aircraft as it took off. It all sounds simple – but we had a lot of fun perfecting the art.

With the long transit to South Georgia finally over, thoughts turned to the military plan for the liberation of the island. Following much discussion within the senior command of the Task Group and with pressure from London to 'get on with it', it was agreed that a recce force would go ashore to assess the strength and deployment of the Argentine garrison thought to be located at Grytviken. To accomplish this, a small group of SF would be landed on the island by helicopter and would then move forward on foot to their target. While the plan was relatively simple in concept, it was also bold. The recce force and their equipment would require the lift capacity of all three Wessex; the drop-off point was 2,000ft up a glacier and ... Oh! The insert was required in the dark.

Following an assessment of the feasibility of the flying aspects of the plan, and some strong and wise advice from the senior aviators, it was eventually agreed that while an insertion onto Fortuna Glacier was feasible and within the capabilities of the Wessex aircrew, a night insertion was too high a risk. The compromise was a first light take-off, which would allow the aircraft to land in the hostile mountains with adequate light. In the meantime, another aspect of the operation began to make itself known: the weather – with an approaching Antarctic low increasing wind speeds and sea states. I am sure that in normal circumstances the weather on the morning of the assault would have caused a cancellation, but these were not normal times. So we briefed, started and launched. The radar-equipped anti-submarine warfare (ASW) Wessex from the destroyer led, with the two 'Jungly' Wessexes as numbers two and three. I piloted number three. The weather was extremely poor, with low cloud, barely acceptable visibility and very strong winds. A number of powerful squalls were passing through the area, which reduced both cloud base and visibility even further. As we approached the rugged shoreline of South Georgia at low level, the incredible scale of the island and its mountains became apparent; like the Alps in winter, the terrain rose almost vertically upwards from the sea, with each valley system playing host to huge glaciers.

As we entered one of the valley systems, the weather took a major turn for the worse as a large squall passed through, reducing the cloud base and visibility in driving snow, such that we could no longer see the mountains around us or, importantly, the start of the glacier we intended climbing to reach the drop-off point. With no alternative, we carefully retraced our steps back the way we had come, and in almost zero visibility returned to the Task Group. An indication of the severity of the conditions was provided when we finally reached *Tidespring*. The ASW Wessex landed on the destroyer, number two landed on the deck of the RFA and I sat off the ship's port quarter to wait for the maintainers to fold number two, push it into the hangar and make space on the deck for me. Any thought of flying circuits while waiting was quickly dismissed – I couldn't see the bow of the ship, let alone the surrounding area. We waited patiently in the hover, watching the whole propeller of the ship breaching the surface as the vessel pitched in the huge waves. The maintainers commented on the thick ice covering the aircraft when I landed. We had returned to the ship as a green Wessex but were landing as a white one. I distinctly remember seeing 70kts on the air speed indicator (ASI) once safely on the deck of *Tidespring*.

Following a rapid debrief, a nerve-calming coffee and a considered assessment of the situation, it was decided we would make a second attempt at the insertion later that morning. The launch and transit ashore were again without incident and whether the weather had abated or we were just lucky, I don't know, but we were able to climb up the glacier in excellent visibility with patches of blue sky above us. In another world it would have been champagne skiing conditions! The landings themselves went almost without incident, the lead Wessex having the most difficult task of settling on the ice sheet with virtually no visual references. This aircraft provided some visual assistance for number two and me, but even then number two found himself disoriented and had to overshoot and make a second attempt. It was ominous – a warning for what was to come later – that shortly after landing and disembarking our SF loads, fog enveloped all three helicopters, reducing visibility to zero. Eerily, just as we were contemplating a night on the glacier, the weather cleared and we quickly took off. We returned without incident to the Task Group. British Forces had returned to South Georgia.

Unfortunately, this early success was to prove a false dawn, as overnight the weather conditions deteriorated once again with storm force winds, blowing snow and freezing temperatures. The SF force ashore made it quite clear they would need to be evacuated from the glacier the following morning if they were to remain alive. This news came as no surprise to the aircrew, who had set up a search and rescue (SAR) standby from the moment we returned to the ships. Within hours of receiving the request for an extraction, a rescue mission was launched. It was a repeat of the operation the day before, with one exception: my cockpit was now occupied by one of my naval colleagues, whose turn it was on the standby roster. I assumed the unglamorous role of aviation adviser on the bridge of the *Tidespring*. It was from here that I would hear not one but two Mayday calls and have first-hand experience of a dramatic rescue mission going seriously wrong – but being recovered thanks to some highly skilled and courageous flying.

Despite minor challenges with both weather and terrain on the way to the pick-up, the three Wessex arrived with the SF detachment in good order and the troops were quickly embarked on the aircraft. Once loaded, the number two Wessex took off, not bothering to wait for the radar-equipped Mk 3. On doing so, it immediately encountered 'white-out' conditions, the crew losing all external visual references. Shortly afterwards the pilot observed the radar altimeter winding down below 50ft. Unable to prevent contact with the glacier, he cushioned the landing with power and almost pulled off a miraculous blind landing, but unluckily the aircraft turned over onto its left side. Once it settled, it became apparent that both passengers and crew had experienced a miraculous escape; there were no injuries.

Having witnessed the crash, the lead aircraft put out a Mayday call on behalf of the stricken Wessex and, together with the number three, hovered over to the crash site. Almost immediately the crews realised how fortunate everyone aboard had been, and with no time to lose, the troops and aircrew from number two were loaded onto the remaining two aircraft. By now the visibility had cleared once again and the two Wessex took off and joined up for the return to the Task Group. However, this was not going to be a good day. Shortly after they joined up, visibility once again reduced to zero. The pilot of number three attempted to maintain formation with his leader but, in a repeat of the first accident, saw his radar altimeter counting down and he too pulled in power and braced for impact with the glacier.

Astonishingly, this aircraft also hit at low speed and turned over onto its left side. Equally astonishing, once again there were no serious injuries to either troops or aircrew. For the second time that morning, the lead put out a Mayday call on behalf of one of his formation, this time informing the Task Group of the fate of number three. With an already overweight aircraft there was little the leader could do but recover to the Task Group to unload and assess the situation.

Despite the appalling weather conditions there was no doubt in the leader's mind as to what to do next; a further recovery flight was required. Without hesitation, the crew of the Wessex Mk 3 returned to the double accident site to rescue the remaining troops and aircrew from the glacier. Although testing the load capacity of the single-engined aircraft, and the flying skills of the whole crew, this was achieved without further drama. By the end of the day all personnel were safely recovered to the Task Group. The two Wessex HU5s, which represented the group's main helicopter lift capacity, were left on the glacier, where they remain to this day.

The successful recovery of personnel from Fortuna Glacier brought the first action of the Falklands War to a close. Disaster had been averted – just; but at the expense of two troop-carrying helicopters and with no military gain. Despite this, over the next few days South Georgia would be liberated, to cries of "Rejoice ... rejoice"[3] in London. And the scene would be set for eventual victory in a hard-fought and costly campaign many thousands of miles from the UK. For me, the events of those few days in April 1982 would have a lasting impact and affect how I approached flying, planning, risk and even life itself for the remainder of my military career.

It was my first exposure to the powerful influence of politics on military operations; it was clear that there is no such thing as 'leaving it to the military'. Politicians demand success, preferably quickly, at limited cost and with minimal loss of life. They will trust military commanders – but only so much and only so far. A successful relationship between the two parties requires understanding, patience and trust – qualities not always present.

I was also struck by the need for appropriate management of risk. Risk is a fundamental and unavoidable aspect of any military operation, but understanding the levels of acceptable risk is vital as a politician in London, as a senior commander in a headquarters or as a pilot in the cockpit of an aircraft. Interestingly, I believe the most difficult part of risk management is alignment of the levels of risk between parties: how does a group commander ensure an aircraft captain is not taking too much risk with his aircraft? Equally, how does a politician ensure a senior military commander is managing the job in hand?

The importance of appropriate training was a key feature of my experience, not just in South Georgia but the Falklands more generally. I was lucky to be operating with highly experienced colleagues in the air and on the ground. Little could have prepared us for the circumstances we found ourselves in, but the foundations of our training in the UK and overseas prepared us to make sensible decisions on behalf of our aircraft, our crews and our maintainers. Take away that training and the task becomes impossible, or the risk of failure unacceptably high.

---

3   After the Secretary of State for Defence, John Nott, announced the South Georgia news on the steps of 10 Downing Street on 25 April 1982, Prime Minister Margaret Thatcher said, "Just rejoice at that news ...". She repeated "Rejoice" as she re-entered No. 10.

The environmental aspects of the actions off South Georgia speak for themselves. We all thought we had flown in bad weather and demanding terrain until we witnessed the incredible power of the wind, snow and sea in the South Atlantic, and the unforgiving nature of the mountains and glaciers of South Georgia. In a flying career that was to last a further 21 years and thousands more flying hours, in locations as disparate as jungles, deserts and Arctic tundra, I never came close to anything quite so magnificent – the only word to describe the awe-inspiring conditions we faced that April morning. I never trust the weather now, rather I treat it with the utter respect it deserves.

Finally, I am in no doubt that my experiences in 1982 changed my approach to life. The events in South Georgia, and later operations in the Falklands themselves, served to emphasise to me the fragility of life, the importance of making the most of the time you are given and to respect the views, attitudes and opinions of those around you. This approach has not changed since, indeed, my many travels and experiences over the years have merely served to strengthen those views.

I must have learnt more than just about flying from that …

* * * *

AIR CHIEF MARSHAL SIR GLENN TORPY

After studying aeronautical engineering at Imperial College, Glenn Torpy joined the RAF in 1974. Sandwiched between a first tour on 41 Squadron at Coltishall flying Jaguars and his return as a flight commander was a Brawdy tour as a Hawk qualified weapons instructor (QWI). He converted to the Tornado, commanding 13 Squadron in the First Gulf War and, subsequently, RAF Brüggen. Staff appointments followed, notably in 2004 as Chief of Joint Operations; then in 2006 he became CAS. He retired in 2009 with some 4,300 hours of fast-jet flying.

EMPOWERMENT AND RISK: GETTING IT RIGHT

When asked to contribute to this book it took a while for me to decide what tack to take. It would be all too easy to pick some 'near-death' experience and use that as the theme for what 'I learnt about flying'. Like many who have been fortunate enough to fly in the RAF, I have had more than the odd moment where I thought … there but for the grace of God! … and locked the experience away to, hopefully, not repeat in the future. Encouraging people to share such experiences, so that others can avoid the same pitfalls, benefits everyone, not least because it contributes to a healthy, self-critical ethos.

Sir Glenn Torpy.

Besides the sense of enjoyment and professional satisfaction that I gained from flying in the RAF, I think my major lesson has been to do with risk management. This stretches from the tactical – the risk judgements you make every time you strap into an aircraft – to the operational and strategic, when as a commander you sometimes must make genuine life or death decisions affecting the people under your command. How we make those judgements is an interesting combination of education, training, experience, process and intuition.

Over recent years we have become increasingly focused on the management of risk, with the creation of the Military Aviation Authority bringing some much-needed discipline to the RAF's thinking. There is always a danger, however, that by trying to create greater clarity, we introduce an associated bureaucracy. People feel obliged to follow set procedures and are reluctant to deviate for fear of making a mistake and then being accused of 'not following the process'. This risks disempowering people, which is exactly the reverse of the behaviour the service should encourage.

The RAF needs an empowered workforce that, within the boundaries set, use their initiative and all the resources and skills at their disposal to deliver the best possible outcomes. There is, of course, a risk that if people are genuinely exploiting the full extent of the authorities they have been given, there will be occasions when things go wrong. When this happens, and it is the result of a genuine mistake rather than the wilful overstepping of a boundary, the organisation needs to support the individual(s) concerned and ensure that everyone learns from the experience. To do otherwise, which might be the natural reaction, risks creating an environment where people 'play it safe' and we end up with a risk averse culture that ultimately undermines operational capability.

This is not to say that processes should be ignored – far from it. They are there for good reasons, to guide thinking and ensure that in arriving at a decision all the issues that might have a bearing on a particular outcome have been correctly considered and factored into the decision-making process. There is a danger, however, that process can be viewed more as an algorithm which produces an answer once fed with the requisite facts, removing the requirement for personal input and initiative – thus minimising the danger of making a mistake. However, there must still be room for personal initiative and inspiration, otherwise a bland 'vanilla' solution emerges that whilst safe is simply not as good as it could be.

An operational parallel is the Combat Estimate, which is used extensively by militaries around the world to assist the planning of operations and provides a helpful template to ensure that all factors are considered in developing an appropriate course of action. But what wins battles is experience, imagination and initiative. So, whilst the estimate process is a valuable tool, it should be viewed as just that, and should not constrain commanders' thinking and willingness to explore 'out of the box' options.

In looking back over my RAF career, much of which was spent on the operational side of the house, there have been more than a few occasions when we embarked on a course of action that some might have considered risky, from both a reputational and operational perspective, but which at the end of the day delivered successful outcomes. Neither of the examples I will describe were underpinned by a formal analysis through the estimate process, but by dint of our collective experience, knowledge and, dare I say it, intuition, we undertook courses of action that delivered operational advantage.

The first occurred during my time in command of 13 Squadron at Honington. We were the last Tornado squadron to form and, with our sister unit, 2 Squadron, were one of only two squadrons dedicated to the tactical reconnaissance role. Equipped with the new Tornado infra-red reconnaissance system (TIRRS), the GR1A offered a significantly different output from the largely day visual capability of the Jaguar and its predecessors. Based on an advanced suite of three IR sensors, which provided horizon-to-horizon coverage, the system was designed to exploit the Tornado's night poor weather, low level capability. Data from the sensors was captured on digital recorders, which allowed imagery to both be replayed in the cockpit and data-linked back to purpose-built mobile ground exploitation facilities for further analysis. Given the advanced nature of all the equipment, our experience introducing the capability into service was not without its problems. When it worked, the system demonstrated considerable potential, especially in providing a much-needed night and poor weather capability, but there were some significant difficulties with system reliability.

Having re-formed the squadron in January 1990, we were gradually working through these equipment issues when Saddam Hussein invaded Kuwait just seven months later. Given the embryonic nature of our capability, there was initially little interest in considering our deployment as part of the UK contribution to the multi-national coalition.[4] Nevertheless, the squadron, working closely with the equipment manufacturers, started an intensive programme of work to improve functionality and reliability. At the same time, Group HQ gave approval for crews to start 100ft operational low flying (OLF) and night terrain-following radar (TFR) operations as a precursor to possible deployment.

As the situation in Kuwait unfolded during the latter part of the year, our marketing campaign began to gain traction, helped by a visit and briefing to the Coalition Air Component HQ in Riyadh. Although there were still concerns in some quarters about the robustness of the capability, a general lack of tactical reconnaissance assets, particularly those able to operate at night, convinced Strike Command (STC) that a small deployment of six GR1As was worth considering. Our eventual deployment came late in the day, just a week before air operations commenced on 17 January 1991, leaving little time for in-theatre preparation. Nevertheless, exceptional work by the whole detachment – a combined force of aircrew, engineers and imagery analysts drawn from both squadrons – meant that we just managed to pull things together for the start of the war. Over the course of the campaign the detachment undertook a range of tasks, notably being dubbed the 'Scud Hunters' by the media after the detachment discovered some of the elusive Scud missiles being launched against Israel.

Despite initial concerns about the risks of deploying a relatively immature capability, the use of the GR1A during Operation Granby was a success. It would have been easy not to use the capability. However, by adopting a forward-leaning approach to solving the various equipment issues, which stimulated greater focus and resources, we were able to field a valuable capability well ahead of when it would otherwise have been delivered. That is not to say there were not some very real risks, but these were carefully balanced against the potential benefits.

My second example takes us to the Second Gulf War, and my time as Air Officer Commanding (AOC) 1 Group and the Operation Telic[5] Air Contingent Commander. By 2002 the Tornado had been in service for 20 years and had matured into a capable platform, with the whole force very familiar with operations over Iraq

---

4   A US-led partnership of 42 nations.
5   More commonly known by its US codename, Operation Iraqi Freedom.

after flying missions for some 12 years patrolling the Iraq NFZs (no-fly zones). Lessons from the First Gulf War, Kosovo and the NFZs had given the Tornado GR4 a significant precision capability with GPS- and laser-guided weapons; testing was also underway to introduce Storm Shadow into service. It was no surprise, therefore, that the Operation Telic force structure included a large package of Tornados (31 aircraft) and that there was significant interest in accelerating the introduction of Storm Shadow to improve the coalition's capability against hardened C2 (command and control) targets, a particular focus for the opening part of the campaign. Although Storm Shadow testing was progressing satisfactorily, without a significant acceleration of the test programme there was little prospect of the system being available for potential operations in the Gulf. In addition, there was a considerable amount of work required on the mission planning software, and the training of aircrew and ground crew.

Despite these obstacles and the associated risks, it was clear from a 1 Group perspective that Storm Shadow would offer the coalition a valuable capability. Fortunately, HQ STC agreed with this assessment and, as a result, produced an urgent operational requirement (UOR) in October 2002 for the manufacture of 20 missiles by December and a further 30 by April 2003. This was the start of an intense period

No. 617 Squadron Tornado with Storm Shadow. (Geoffrey Lee)

of activity by 1 Group, HQ STC, MoD, BAE Systems, and the missile manufacturer, MBDA. By November, 617 Squadron – the nominated Storm Shadow unit – had trained 80% of its weapons engineers on the intricacies of loading and unloading the weapon, two aircraft had been modified with new software and by the end of that month three crews were declared limited combat ready (LCR). Preparations were also underway for service evaluation firings at China Lake in California, although these were delayed from December to early January 2003 due to poor weather.

In the end, after much hard work between the service and industry, 617 Squadron deployed to Ali Al Salem in Kuwait on 15 February 2003, and fired their first Storm Shadows against Iraqi C2 bunkers on 21 March – coincidently the squadron's 60th anniversary. Given the relative immaturity of the system, great care was taken in selecting the initial targets to reduce the risk of collateral damage in the event of something not working as hoped. We shouldn't have worried. Battle damage imagery showed that the missiles performed with uncanny accuracy, which gave us the confidence to select more demanding targets for subsequent missions. In all, 27 Storm Shadows were fired by 617 Squadron during Operation Telic. Fully integrated onto today's Typhoons, the weapon has gone on to prove one of the most successful in the RAF inventory – and very effective in the hands of the Ukrainian Air Force!

In many respects the Storm Shadow UOR was an exemplar, and demonstrated what can be achieved by cutting through the normal bureaucracy and taking a balanced but forward-leaning approach to the inevitable risks associated with accelerating a capability. In the case of Storm Shadow, we were fortunate that the MoD, RAF and industry had been working together as an integrated team for some two years and had developed a level of mutual trust and collaborative working that enabled the programme to be accelerated to meet the UOR timescale. In doing so, they had a clear understanding of the risks and how they could be most effectively mitigated. It also helped having 617 Squadron identified early as the lead squadron, which meant they could be involved from the start in development of the concept of operations (CONOPS) and planning procedures, which were inherently more complex than for most previous weapon systems.

In both these examples we see the MoD, RAF and industry responding positively to the imperative of operations, and in doing so delivering capability more quickly than would have been the case using normal procedures. In many respects it brings out the best in people: a willingness to push the boundaries, to challenge the status quo and take additional risk. This is just the sort of behaviour that I saw on operations, where personnel were frequently given more responsibility than at home; they enjoyed the challenge and rarely failed to impress. The relatively flat organisational structures we have on operations – to minimise the deployed footprint – acts as a helpful forcing function in this respect. Regrettably, when people return to their peacetime environment, with the straitjacket of bureaucratic process and layers of management, much of the job satisfaction and empowerment that they enjoyed on operations disappears.

Service life back at home will inevitably mean additional checks and balances. But if the RAF wants to get the best out of people – and make their jobs as satisfying and attractive as possible – it needs to draw on the positive aspects of how it does business on operations and embrace a more empowered culture, one where people feel they have the freedom to push the boundaries sensibly.

This returns me to my earlier theme of risk management, and the need to strike the right balance between what Hadden-Cave[6] termed a 'risk averse' culture and being 'risk sensible', with the latter being the ideal state. I sense that in recent years we have erred too much towards the 'risk averse' end of the spectrum, stifling initiative, inhibiting mission command and limiting empowerment of the individual – with all the consequences this has for the culture of the service and the way the RAF operates. Whilst the fallout from the Nimrod accident has brought some much-needed clarity to the identification and management of risk, the way this process has evolved potentially undermines the service's ability as a high performing, agile organisation that makes the most of its resources and is able to swiftly respond to the unexpected – a shortcoming that permeates every aspect of RAF organisation: from training, to procurement, to operations.

I was struck when I read a recent article about the challenges facing General Saltzman, Chief of Space Operations, US Space Force, and his desire to accelerate procurement and delivery of next-generation technologies. That desire, however, is tempered by a realisation that government bureaucracy will only allow him to 'go government fast, not SpaceX fast'. That might be a reality he is grappling with but it should not stop us all learning from how other organisations, including the civil sector, manage projects to reduce time and cost. Whilst there are aspects of the way that SpaceX operates that do not translate easily to government, there are others, including a culture that encourages the status quo to be continually challenged and

---

6   Charles Haddon-Cave QC (as he then was) conducted a review into the wider issues surrounding the loss of Nimrod XV230 in Afghanistan on 2 September 2006. The terms in quotes that follow are from his 2009 Report.

empowers the individual, that are readily applicable to the way we might wish to operate. Elon Musk believes that 'the only rules are the ones dictated by the laws of physics. Everything else is a recommendation.' That might be a bit too far for the RAF – it might even be too far for SpaceX. But it establishes a state of mind that permeates every part of the organisation and is driven from the top.

The two examples I have used here taught me a lot of positives about how the RAF, MoD and industry can work together to deliver quickly and efficiently, and how this benefits both individuals and the organisation. I could have chosen others. There are numerous examples from operations where, given the opportunity, people have proved capable of overcoming the toughest challenges. One of the most important things I have learnt over the years is that someone's chances of success, be it in the air or on the ground, are directly affected by the environment in which they operate. Helping create the right kind of environment – one where people feel able to utilise fully their training, experience and initiative – is everyone's responsibility, not just those in the RAF's upper echelons.

CHAPTER 3
THOUGHTS FROM THREE-STARS

AIR MARSHAL G.A. 'BLACK' ROBERTSON

Lucky to reach Cranwell in the first place – unbeknown to the college, he lacked the requisite academic qualifications – Black Robertson spent his entire operational career on fighters: Hunters first then Phantoms. His main command tours were as OC 92 Squadron and Station Commander RAF Wattisham. Late in a career where he flew all the RAF's fast jets, he also qualified as a helicopter pilot. He retired as Deputy Commander-in-Chief RAF Strike Command in 1998 after nearly 36 years' service with over 3,600 hours in his logbook.

YOU CAN'T THINK OF EVERYTHING

My father was the eldest of three brothers, each of whom served in the air force –

he and the youngest as pilots. To my eternal regret, it was nearly 20 years after he died before I was able to put together the full story of his wartime exploits. Like most of his generation, he spoke very little about the war. But the links were there to be seen: the odd photograph, a beautifully carved 72 Squadron shield and a wooden model Spitfire mounted on a plinth.

It was inevitable that I should eventually take an interest in the events of 1939–45.

'Black' Robertson.

Once I did, amongst the first books I read were *The Big Show*, by Pierre Clostermann, Larry Forrester's *Fly for Your Life*, the Bob Stanford Tuck story, and Guy Gibson's *Enemy Coast Ahead*. Much later, while I was waiting to take up a place at the RAF College, I came across a brief tale that was to influence my entire flying life. It appeared in Ernest K. Gann's *Fate is the Hunter*. An American who began flying airliners in the pre-war era, Gann recalls sitting at the controls during a lengthy transit, his mind wandering, his thoughts elsewhere. Scanning the cockpit instruments, he's dimly aware that for some time the altimeter has shown him to be 100ft or so off his assigned altitude. But the aircraft was trimmed out, and adjusting to the correct height would take him out of his reverie. So he continues to ignore this minor discrepancy. What prompts him, eventually, to break the spell he'll never know, but he finally makes an adjustment and levels at the correct altitude. No sooner has he done so than another aeroplane flashes by within a matter of feet – at the very level he'd been at just seconds before. Fate's intervention thus averted that would have been a catastrophic collision; no one on either aircraft could possibly have survived. While the details of this incident – I can't even recall whether it was day or night – are lost in the mists of time, the lessons I learnt remain crystal clear. Accuracy is important but, in the end, it all comes down to luck.

Once I began flying, the first and probably the most enduring lesson I learnt was that I was by no means a 'natural' – but then few are. As the son of a decorated Spitfire ace, I'd rather hoped that I might become quite good at this flying business. But early on it became clear that others were better. In the summer of 1966 I was disappointed not to be selected to represent A Squadron in the inter-squadron aerobatic competition that marked the conclusion of 89 Entry's three years at Cranwell – but I was up against stiff competition. That particular honour went to Senior Flight Cadet Russ Pengelley, who deservedly won the Hicks Memorial Trophy and went on to make a name for himself as a solo aerobatic pilot in the Lightning. Another from A Squadron, Under Officer Jerry Pook, was judged the best pilot on our course, winning the RM Groves Memorial Prize & Kinkead Trophy. He too subsequently enjoyed a distinguished flying career, both as a display pilot and during the Falklands War. To complete a remarkable treble, the flying prize on my Gnat course at Valley went to Flying Officer Peter Squire, another under officer from A Squadron, 89 Entry. A close friend, Peter also distinguished himself in the Falklands and later became CAS.

Clearly, if I was going to carve out a career flying aeroplanes, I'd have to do it the hard way. That said, no one was more surprised than me when I won the academic prize at Valley – top in the ground school exams. This unexpected and mildly embarrassing accolade (who wants to be labelled a swot?) owed everything to awareness that success in the cockpit would require every bit of concentration I could muster. I had to create enough spare capacity to allow me to concentrate fully on the flying task. The solution was 'compartmentalisation': ensuring that all the less glamorous aspects, the mundane issues, were dealt with, tucked away and demanded none of my immediate attention. Amongst other things, it meant becoming totally familiar with the Gnat and its complex systems, and committing all the associated checks and emergency procedures to memory. Only then would I be able to devote maximum effort to handling what was, after all, a demanding aircraft.

The importance of spare capacity was illustrated in an unexpected way during my final few weeks at Valley. The Red Arrows were there for few days' practice and some of us were fortunate enough to secure back-seat rides. In fact, I managed two on the same day. The first was with the leader, Squadron Leader Ray Hanna, and the second with Flight Lieutenant Frank Hoare, Red 5. As a demonstration of smooth precision, calm authority and anticipation, Ray Hanna's flying and leadership during those two sorties remains unequalled in my experience. If ever there was a lesson about the value of these qualities – spare capacity too, of course – it was delivered on 13 April 1967.

As background to the most embarrassing moment in my flying life, everything written thus far is germane to the development of a personal flying character that was arguably flawed. An obsession with accuracy and attention to detail meant it was difficult to accept any performance, my own or that of others, that was less than optimal. This perfectionist mindset was both a blessing and a curse: a blessing in that it drove a constant quest for improvement, a curse because it led to intolerance – hardly the ideal attribute for the instructor I was to become.

My initial experience of this new role came when I returned to 6 Squadron after completing the first Phantom QWI course. It was followed by a short spell on the Phantom Operational Conversion Unit (OCU) and then an exchange posting with the USAF in a similar role. This broadening of my aviation portfolio reinforced some of the limitations of which I was only too aware. To compensate, I prepared assiduously for every sortie and took a similarly comprehensive approach to debriefs. No more a natural instructor than I was a natural pilot, it was an approach aimed at leaving absolutely nothing to chance.

That was until the evening of 24 January 1972 at Decimomannu in Phantom XV394: a night ground-attack sortie with a close friend, Geoff Frankcom. Multi-talented, self-effacing and the nicest of men, Geoff's pre-RAF claim to fame was as a centre three-quarter with four England rugby caps. We were scheduled for a bombing and strafing dual sortie on Cape Frasca range – the only location where we could fire the gun at night. Parked in the back seat while the pilot in the front hurls himself at the ground with monotonous regularity for 40 minutes or so in the pitch-black was never my idea of fun – albeit an experience that added to my respect for F-4 back-seaters. When it was time to return to base I needed a break, so I asked Geoff if I could fly the recovery to Decimomannu, a simple round-the-houses instrument approach. He agreed, of course. It was a relief, a relaxation even, to get my hands on the controls for the first time that night. All went well until the final stages of the ground-controlled approach (GCA). As we neared the touchdown point, Geoff piped up from the front seat, "Do you want me to land it or will you?"

The recovery and landing back at Decimomannu was the one thing I hadn't covered, or even considered, in the detailed brief for a demanding sortie. Fatefully, I made a snap decision: "I'll do it." I hadn't landed from the back seat at night for some time and this was the perfect opportunity, or so I thought. Events would prove me wrong. Limited forward visibility because of the front-seat pilot's ejection seat, made back-seat landing from a straight-in GCA far more difficult than the norm, which was from a circuit in a curved approach.

Phantom overshoot.

We touched down with a bit of a thump – nothing unusual about that – and then I noticed something strange. Geoff had taken over control to pop the drag chute, keep us straight on the runway and apply the brakes. But what's this? I was seeing aspects of the airfield, of the runway, that were unfamiliar. And we seemed to turn off much earlier than usual. But I set these anomalies to one side as I read out the post-landing checks. After Geoff shut the aircraft down, we made our way to the line hut where I signed in the aircraft; it was serviceable – or so we thought. We then learnt that a small hole had been discovered in the trailing edge of the port flap. It later proved to be the result of impact with the last runway centreline approach light. Despite a reassuringly normal commentary from the Italian GCA controller, I had been slightly low on the glidepath and apparently landed short of the runway threshold, in the undershoot. What followed was the most difficult hour or so in my RAF life.

Geoff and I were ushered into the boss's office and made to stand facing his desk. Here I adopted the practice I'd used previously in similar circumstances: stare at a point just above the head of the man reading the riot act. This was essential if I were to withstand the broadside that would inevitably follow. A strong character and a good boss, Wing Commander John Nevill then set about delivering what was, by a considerable distance, the fiercest rocket I ever received. When, finally, he asked if I had anything to say for myself, other than an unequivocal admission of culpability, I simply suggested that since I was the captain and solely to blame, then perhaps Geoff might be excused. The boss agreed and, after a brief hiatus, launched into phase two of his demolition effort.

Once I'd effectively been hung, drawn, quartered and dismissed, there was nothing else for it: head for the combined officers' mess for a beer. I needed to drown my sorrows. Imagine my surprise at being joined there almost immediately by OC A Flight, Squadron Leader Ian Tite. Throughout the boss's tirade he had been leaning against the wall to one side, almost out of my line of sight. Now he was on a rescue mission.

Appreciating that he'd done a highly effective destruction job on his young QWI, the boss apparently thought he'd better have someone ride shotgun on me for the rest of the evening, lest I put a metaphorical gun to my head. After a couple of beers with the deputed OC A Flight, I went back to my room and wrote a pathetic letter to my wife, explaining that my career was over. It had been fun while it lasted but I'd just blown it completely.

That was last night. Next morning the sun rose over Sardinia as normal and life went on, largely as normal. I was on the programme for a day strafe and retard bombing sortie. Another lesson: 'sufficient unto the day ...'. Well, not exactly. While the boss seemed almost to have forgotten my transgression, the senior engineering officer (SEngO), Squadron Leader Les Parker, made sure I would remember the event for days, nay weeks thereafter. He refused to have the replacement flap, which soon arrived, painted to blend in with the rest of XV394's camouflage. For some time it remained a dull grey reminder of my stupidity. That said, the behaviour of both the boss and the SEngO thereafter – the way they treated the miscreant – was an object lesson in man management. Whilst my leg was pulled occasionally, neither individual dwelt on the matter. In fact, nothing more was ever said officially – or so I thought. That was until I read the published incident report, where the Station Commander Coningsby, Group Captain Chris Neville, concluded by saying I had been disciplined. I can only assume that the boss told him I'd suffered enough and learnt from the experience. Of that there is no doubt. But what was the nature of this particular lesson? I'm tempted to suggest that it was a classic example of the axiom that 'to err is human ...'. John Nevill was a hard man but a fair one. Despite tearing me to shreds at the time, he held no grudge whatsoever afterwards.

What really irked me about the event was less that I'd screwed up the landing, based on an impulsive decision; it was more that I'd failed to consider the implications of the return and landing back at base. While I'd certainly anticipated flying the instrument approach, I'd failed to mention it in the brief – something that might have triggered thoughts about the landing. In short, a man known for his attention to detail, missed a trick and paid the price. Lesson learnt!

A final thought, which takes us back to Gann's aptly titled book. The port flap took the impact because I landed a few feet right of the runway centreline – a natural result of peering to the left of the front ejection seat. But what if I'd been lined up perfectly? Chances are the nosewheel or, more likely, the SUU-23 gun pod we were carrying on the fuselage centre station, would have hit the light. And then what would have happened? I shudder to think.

* * * *

AIR MARSHAL ANDREW TURNER

Andrew Turner served in the RAF from 1985 to 2022, retiring as Deputy Commander. A helicopter pilot with 5,200 hours, 1,850 of which were flown on 19 operational tours, he commanded on operations at every rank and spent a year in the White House. Most of his flying was on Pumas and Chinooks and included command of 28 Squadron, the UK Chinook Force, RAF Odiham, the Puma Force (Kosovo), Merlin Force (Iraq), and the Joint Aviation Group (Afghanistan).

Andrew Turner.

NEARLY CAUGHT – THE FOURTH OF NINE LIVES

12 June 1999 was a hot, dry day in Skopje, Macedonia, but this wasn't really at the top of my mind. We were a kilometre short of the Kosovan border, hovering high in the mountains near the Black Mosque, and with all six of the Pumas I was leading fully laden with UK Parachute Regiment Pathfinders. Down in the valley, 2,000ft below, eight Chinooks were circling at 60kts, two with heavy six-tonne JCB diggers swinging wildly beneath as if trying to free themselves from the mighty 'wokka'.[7] We had been in country for only seven days, but all the frantic planning, full-scale rehearsals, and buckets of 'hurry up and wait', was now behind us.

Then the distant crackle of the tactical comms broke into the strained voice of the 5 Brigade Air Liaison Officer, Squadron Leader Chris Hunter. 'Chunter' was with the Commander KFOR (Kosovo Forces), General Sir Mike Jackson, affectionately 'Jacko', on the Blace border crossing point, attempting to secure safe passage from a Serb and Russian delegation. Then the words we had all been waiting for came through loud and clear, "Execute! Execute! Execute!"

---

7   A nickname for the Chinook.

But the tale I'm about to tell started well before this. In October 1997 I was posted into my dream job: OC AMF(L) Flight, 33 Squadron. The Allied Command Europe Mobile Force (Land) was NATO's highest readiness reaction force and I was in a privileged position: commanding all the force's helicopters on exercise and operations. In addition to four RAF Pumas, this included ten Belgium army A109 anti-tank helicopters, 12 German army UH-1Ds, three US Army UH-60Ls and six Czech Mi-17s. It was tremendous fun, but 35 helicopters at the extremes of climate and thousands of miles from the command chain was a lot of responsibility so early on. We deployed annually for three months to the high north – Bardufoss Air Station – to hone Arctic flying skills; if you can survive and fight there, you can do it anywhere in the world.

Back now to 1999 and Kosovo, where an ethnic conflict whose origins went back six centuries was coming to a head. In that spring, we had just returned from Arctic training in Norway, and were individually and collectively at the top of our game. With a sense that something might happen, and soon, I took A Flight on an SF escape and evasion exercise in Wales in late May, to sharpen our night tactical formation insertion and extraction skills in poor weather. Then on 3 June came a message from OC 33 Squadron, Wing Commander Colin Miller, "Get to Macedonia as fast as possible; you'll get the brief there." Next day we were en route to the unknown. It was all a bit mad.

We transited to the region as a four-ship of Pumas via Paris, Lyon, Florence (overnight) and Poggio Renatico, landing into the Macedonian training area at Prilep by nightfall on 6 June. Now part of what UK called Operation Agricola, on 7 June we moved the Pumas to a disused hardened aircraft shelter (HAS) area in the north-west corner of Skopje airport. Squadron Leader Steve Shell arrived that day with eight Chinooks from 27 Squadron at Odiham, and our Puma and Chinook flights were put under his boss, OC 27 Squadron, Wing Commander Karl Dixon. A frantic 72 hours followed, covering high-speed intelligence analysis, rapid correlation of anti-air and aviation forces that we might face, whilst tracking the advance of the Russian armoured deployment racing to beat us to Pristina airport.

We spent the next two days with 5 Brigade, 1 RGR (1st Battalion Royal Gurkha Rifles) and 1 PARA (1st Battalion The Parachute Regiment), trying to work out how to get 5,000 troops 100 miles up the road in three hours. Years of airborne and airmobile exercises had developed pilot-proof methods of shifting a lot, quickly and without comms, so the challenge was adaptation, not creation. In parallel, reconnaissance patrols were going out to find areas near Skopje where we could park eight Chinooks, six Pumas and six Apaches with a brigade of troops at high readiness. We conducted a number of integration trials with the Paras and Gurkhas to confirm what we could lift and how fast, tested plans, mitigated the risks and, finally, by 10 June we were ready. After the final 'O' Group[8] at HQ 5 Brigade's tactical headquarters, that evening I gave 33 Squadron our orders. Serbian and Russian activity, mines, random actors and excited, liberated Albanians with guns were all in the 'enemy forces' paragraph. Our mission was to get 5 Brigade on the ground safely and fast – speed was key because operational surprise had already been traded. Earlier that day the final full rehearsal had been conducted in front of the world's media as part of the strategic messaging to the Serbian president, Milošević, but more tactically to his forces in southern Kosovo, about what was going to happen. The message was clear: 'Get out of the way.'

Tomorrow, 11 June, was to be the big day. With Chinooks first and Pumas following (to avoid dangerous downwash), we flew the ten miles to HLS (helicopter landing site) Piper – a huge cornfield 5 Brigade had found. We married up and loaded our first troops, the brigade's Pathfinder Company, while the remainder of 1 RGR and 1 PARA waited impatiently on the edges of the field. The atmosphere was electric with throngs of RAF aircrew, Paras and Gurkhas all eager for action. It was baking hot, and the corn was bone dry, which all added to the tension and sense of 'the moment'. We were there for about six hours, waiting for the order to reposition to the border, and came to RS5 (first assault wave airborne in under five minutes) four times, only to be stood down each time. Then at around 1500 hours that afternoon, Jacko arrived in a Lynx to tell his ground commanders, "Not today". Weary and frustrated, we recovered the aircraft to Skopje.

The morning of the 12th was just like those before – hot at 0400 and getting hotter. We received the final 'Go' to reposition to HLS Piper at 0430 and all 20 helicopters were there by 0530. Finally, word cascaded down the line that we were off. APUs (auxiliary power units) fired up, more than 40 jet engines burst into life; rotors turning, troops loading, seconds later we lifted. The Apache screen departed to the border; I was followed by the rest of the Puma formation, the Chinooks were behind me and the Apache close escort was last. It was mentally massive, and visibly staggering. By 1000 we were all airborne fully loaded and on our way, waiting for Jacko's final clearance to cross the border.

We didn't have long to wait. With "Execute! Execute! Execute!" NATO's ground intervention was underway. We had crossed the border by 1030 and were into what

---

8   The Orders Group was the brigade commander's moment to gather and direct his COs.

was to be a long day. Our initial part in this combat ballet was to secure footholds with the Paras and Gurkhas who would screen the approaches and protect the ground link-up. 4 Brigade were driving up from Skopje, via the Blace border crossing point, inching through six miles of mountain gorges and road tunnels known as the Kaçanik Defile, and then on to Pristina. Even though we had identified drop zones (DZs) from map study, one of our biggest challenges was finding safe places to land. We knew that the Serbs had literally covered the ground with mines, there were dismembered horses, cows and sheep everywhere, so we had decided to land only on hard surfaces – car parks and roads.

We got the Pathfinders in and raced back towards Piper. We crossed back into Macedonia at Blace at around 50ft and 150kts, inadvertently directly over a massive refugee camp. Blace must have had more than 2,000 refugees and it seemed that every single one of them was outside on their feet, jumping up and down in exuberance and frantically waving their flags. There was an overwhelming air of jubilation that we quite simply had not expected. We had been so consumed by the enemy, mechanics and plan, that we had lost touch with what this all meant for the Kosovan Albanians who had been pushed out of their houses, farms, villages and country. It was quite a sight.

However, we inadvertently added to their sense of celebration when, just beyond the camp, our automatic missile detection system released a brief ripple of super-hot, short-duration flares. The system protected the aircraft from infra-red seeking air-to-air and surface-to-air missiles and was triggered primarily by man-made ultraviolet traces. It was usually set to 'automatic' because it is impossible to see above, below and around the aircraft all the time and no matter how good your lookout or how fast your reactions, you would never beat a Mach 2.5 missile fired at close range. The missile detector must have seen something in the camp that it liked and dutifully followed its algorithmic orders. Although the flares stoked emotional fires in the Albanians below, we were lucky not to have strafed the camp; I broke radio silence and ordered the formation's flares to 'manual' at the border.

With dignity intact, we took a quick suck of gas, and then were lifting 1 RGR into the screen position up the valley. Their objective was a particular vantage point that commanded the approaches to the defile and so we landed the whole formation directly onto the viaduct in the centre of the defile at Gjurgjedell. Immortalised in the press that day and paintings since, that frame – helicopters delivering troops onto a gently curving, yellow-railed bridge – became a defining image. Six waves later, 5 Brigade was complete on the ground in Kosovo and had linked up with 4 Brigade on the highway. We got back to Skopje with six hours on the clock, no casualties, minor gunshot battle damage requiring speed tape patching and no unserviceabilities. Our role now switched to casualty extraction and close-support tasks as the combined 4 and 5 Brigades manoeuvred up to Pristina.

But all of this – the intensity of combat – was simply background for what was about to happen. Support helicopter flying can be routine: lots of loops doing similar things over short distances. There is a tendency to set patterns – fly down the same valley, navigate via known points – which makes the aircraft and operation highly vulnerable to an alert enemy. So, our tactics were always to vary routes, DZs, heights and speeds wherever we could. It was not being shot at during the initial assault that took the fourth of my nine lives, but a return transit down a new and narrow valley.

Insertions went progressively deeper and deeper into Kosovo, and we contested the airfield at Pristina with the Russians. They had placed their base there and used to regularly shoot at us as we went into the city. It was particularly noticeable by night as the one-in-four tracer arcs lazily looped in front and behind our aircraft before burying themselves in the countryside. As their aim gradually improved, we shifted our ingress routes east, out of their range. One of these was the poppy-filled Bresalc-Labljane valley, which was an alternative mountain route from Pristina back to Skopje. The maps were poor, mostly massively out of date, and no one had operated in these regions yet, so we did not have any up-to-date data on how things had changed.

On an empty return loop to Skopje from Pristina, we came out of 'Film City' (where KFOR was based), turned east and then south down that valley. I recall we were flying at around 140kts and about 50ft above ground to give the least possible notice of our presence to potential assailants. By convention, we were about two-thirds of the way up the west side of the valley to allow a 3D manoeuvre away from hostile fire – guns, missiles, mortars – and/or the opportunity to do a 180 and exit the valley quickly if weather or some other reason demanded it. Flying down the centre of the valley offered no options if anything were to happen and was a fool's game.

And then I saw them, sky-lined and contrasting with the blue sky above – about 50 metres ahead of the aircraft, ranging from 30 degrees below my horizon to 30 degrees above – seven strands of high-tension cables. There was almost no time to react; the aircraft didn't have wire-cutters (they're standard now) and so I simultaneously snatched the cyclic back into my stomach and shouted to the crew to duck. Almost immediately I realised the futility of this instruction. Faced either with being decapitated or having the aircraft sawn in half and falling to one's death, in hindsight, I think I would rather see what's going on and it all end quickly. But it was a grim choice.

In the split-second between seeing the cables, reacting and the aircraft rotating, I got the nose to about 45 degrees nose-up. The Puma is a very graceful aircraft. You fly it gently, moving the cyclic about 2–3 inches from the centre point and never to the stops. It's nothing like a fast jet. I remember being shocked by how violently 'Noz' Norris flew the Harrier in the hover on a T4 sortie at Gütersloh in June 1988 during Exercise Bold Gauntlet. But to feel the control stops in a Puma seemed like an act of mechanical vandalism.

Back in the Kosovan valley, there was a brief moment when I thought that we might have got away with it. But then, all of a sudden, the aircraft snatched violently and there was the most dreadful metallic rasping sound and a very high-pitched vibration like a struck tuning fork. The sensation of being cut up seemed to go on forever. A combination of the wires and pitch-up slowed the aircraft dramatically to about 60kts. My navigator, Dave Warren, and I looked at each other and I noticed that over his lap, stretching down into the valley, was a trailing wire. My eyes traced it along its full length and up to a pylon on the far ridge, buried in 100-foot-high fir trees. There was no way we could have spotted it.

The rasping and graunching continued for what seemed like several spine-tingling seconds and then suddenly stopped. I glanced down and left to see behind Dave's knees the wire was falling away, twisting and flicking from side-to-side like a snake that had somehow broken free from its captor. Then the aircraft pitched forward of its own accord and it all went quiet.

We didn't speak for about ten seconds. We were still in the air. The Puma was still flying. The engines were still driving. The rotors were still turning. The crewman, Carl 'HR' Hamilton-Reed, was still in the cabin. We did not appear to be out of control. We were all breathing hard. For a moment, all three of us felt as if we had just been subjected to a very loud bang or brilliant flash of light.

So, back to basics. Fly the aircraft, deal with the emergency, seek help – a good set of priorities then and now. HR said that the broken wire was on the road beneath. At that time in Kosovo there was little traffic and if there was something driving it was generally heavily armoured and had a very big gun. So we were not bothered about having caused any civilian hazards.

Given the violence of the impact, and the sawing nature of the metal-to-metal contact, I could not be sure the tail rotor was working properly or that the flying controls were intact. So I decided to use the minimum possible control inputs to avoid causing a subsequent catastrophic failure of a crucial component. I asked HR if he could see any damage to the aircraft. All we knew was that we were flying. Every second seemed like a massive bonus, every minute an unlikely gift.

For now, the aircraft appeared to be responding enough to maybe get it on the ground safely, but where? Everywhere was mined and we had seen enough of them to convince all three of us that just landing wasn't an option. Gingerly I got the aircraft turned round (ten degrees of bank, one kilometre turning radius) and we tracked back towards where we knew KFOR were on the ground, but that was ten miles away. We couldn't possibly go that far without some form of inspection. We had to find somewhere we could land, obviously on a road, and for long enough to give the aircraft a good once-over, but without shutting down.

Curiously, time was moving fast – things were happening quickly – but at the same time everything seemed slowed down. I had a lot of considerations on my mind and began to juggle a huge range of options open to us, but my concentration kept being interrupted by the possibility of a lot of very bad things that might happen. I felt that if we landed at the T-junction in the middle of Mukate, it would be sod's law that the Serbian police would be holed up there. Even if we could land safely, they would rake the aircraft and us with 7.62mm fire from the hotel; that would not be a great outcome! I also felt that, whilst I was the aircraft captain, the decision on what to do was not mine alone – Dave and HR both had equity in the outcome. I decided that we should hold the first of a series of XW218 (the aircraft registration) committee meetings. We had a great deal to talk about, we needed to make some choices, but we were only looking at deeply unappetising options. At its most simple, we needed to pick the choice that would give us the maximum chance of enjoying dinner.

Luckily, we were of a single mind – probably a bit in shock – and we agreed to try to land on the road – but further back, up the valley towards Pristina. As we descended, we discussed a 'crash on the road if control were lost' option – not terribly appealing either. We thought that, probably, at least two of us would be able to walk, one of us would need cutting out of the aircraft, and then we'd be straight into escape and evasion – cruelly ironic given where we were in Wales only a few weeks earlier.

I manoeuvred the aircraft with great care, picked a spot on a bend to land and began a very gentle flaring stop. Dave was heads-in the cockpit checking for any signs of failure – engines, rotors, surrogate systems – and HR had his head out of the doors scanning the road and surroundings for telephone wires (surely we couldn't hit two sets of wires in ten minutes), land mines, other obstructions, and for cars travelling in either direction. Minimising power changes, I used a decelerative flare to slow and descend the aircraft, and ground effect, high-pressure air under the rotor disc, to cushion our descent and landing onto the road, whilst limiting myself to the slightest of cyclic movements. More than anything else, at that moment I feared the need to overshoot, which would demand high power and manoeuvre and surely destroy the aircraft.

I need not have worried. The Puma settled gently onto the road, straddling the centreline. I kept the power on and asked HR to quickly check the aircraft for visible damage. Dave and I looked at each other nervously. More to keep us busy than anything else, I asked him to look down the road to the south-east to warn of approaching cars while I would look north-west; that way we would have at least 15 seconds before a car or truck impacted us. Humorously, I reflected on what a driver might say to their insurance company in describing how their vehicle had been written off. It is more than probable that any response would have been met with laughter, ridicule, derision, and then possibly an accusation of inebriation by rakija (the local 80% proof home brew). It's odd how humour comes so quickly to mind in moments of adversity.

HR broke comms, hopped outside, and was gone for what seemed like an interminable period, but was probably only 60 seconds – again time was moving both quickly and slowly to tease and test us. Eventually he plugged back in and said, "I've looked as thoroughly as I can, but can't see anything. The tail rotor appears all there. Everything seems OK." But that can't be true. We had sawn through a high-tension cable – a sound that will never leave us. So I asked him to check again, paying particular attention to the rear of the aircraft and the leading edge of any protuberances. Again, HR was gone forever, but this time it was about two minutes. He hopped back inside and said, "There is damage to the rear radar warning receiver housing, and I can see some witness marks on the left undercarriage sponson." Bizarrely, this was good news. At least we had found a reason for the noise; it would have been far worse to have found nothing.

In the space of ten minutes, we convened the second XW218 committee meeting. As chair, I said that the aircraft seemed fully functional. There were no signs of any damage to the flying surfaces (all the control mechanisms are at the root and hub of the main and tail rotor blades) and the engine housings were intact with no signs of damage to either. We were unanimous – this was extremely reassuring. I suggested two options: shut down and take our chances or take our chances and then shut down – both a bit grim. There were a few more moments of dark humour as we discussed who would last longest before spilling the beans under interrogation; none of us fancied an evening with a car battery in the hands of some sadistic individual. We also reflected on the stress positions we might find ourselves in if we opted to shut down and call for help. Whilst we might get dinner, it wouldn't be what we were used to, or on our terms. It was also probable that the aircraft would become a trophy for Belgrade to parade (like the F-117A shot down three months earlier) before parts went on to adorn mantlepieces all across the Balkans. We agreed to take our chances and then shut down.

We plotted the shortest path to the nearest KFOR unit, about ten miles away. It would take us back the way we had come: alongside the Liqeni I Badovcit reservoir, left out of the valley south of Pristina, and then south to the nearest safe location (behind security wire, out of direct line-of-sight and surrounded by a form of quick reaction force) at Dobratinë. We agreed that we would fly at minimum power, away from turbulence and in the straightest possible line – brevity of flight was the highest priority. We also discussed the possibility of crashing on the way – the need constantly to identify places to land, steering clear of woods and water, and remaining aware of low-lying power cables. All this meant that a transit at 70kts would need about ten minutes of luck to get us safely back on the ground. Given the alternatives, it seemed like a reasonable bet, especially as we felt confident about how we had cut the wire. We were also convinced that we were invincible.

Eyes on stalks, full of tension, and with some trepidation, I gradually lifted off from the road. It seemed like we had been there an eternity, and we knew we must have attracted attention, so to get away from there was very positive. Just as with traffic jams on roads, there is some psychological benefit from simply moving. Leaving seemed wholly positive. Throughout our time on the ground in the narrow valley we could not raise any KFOR unit on VHF comms or the NATO airborne warning and control system (AWACS) aircraft on UHF and the HF was poor, so we couldn't even relay a message to RAF Benson to say that we were, for the moment, safe and well. But as soon as we were airborne we connected to AWACS and, once out of the valley, had good comms with KFOR on the Clansman radio – thank goodness for VHF! After what seemed like a second eternity – two in a day – we landed safely at Dobratinë. The Puma engineers were gathered on the HLS awaiting our return and, rather like Yasser Arafat arriving back to Gaza in April 2000, the aircraft was swamped by onlookers almost before the rotors stopped.

I leapt out to see what I could of the damage. Remarkably, it all appeared to be superficial. It seems in that split-second I had got most of the aircraft out of the way of the wires. We had cleared the main power lines but snagged the upper earthing wire. Initially this was on the sponsons, where there was damage to both. Luckily, this was tertiary structure and they were surface blemishes only. The main damage was to the rear radar warning receiver fairing, which had cut through the earthing wire. Its leading edge was flattened and the glass-reinforced plastic cover was trashed. The former was secondary structure, locally load-bearing only, while the latter was tertiary. The engineers immediately set to, attempting to find any other damage, but they could find nothing. The aircraft was put through a rigorous flight test in the vicinity of Dobratinë and, remarkably, was declared serviceable the next day.

Rightly, an operational incident enquiry was convened by my boss, OC 33 Squadron. All the data was captured, interviews were conducted the next day, map analysis was completed and, rather bravely, another aircraft went back to the valley with the boss on board to see the circumstances for himself; thankfully, they left the remaining wires in place. Of course, there were lots of observations and things that we then did differently after the incident. But gratefully, the enquiry concluded that we had followed our tactics fully, reasonably and rightly had used that valley; and the wires were invisible until sky-lined at the point we saw them. The incident was put down to one of the many operational risks we faced.

The banter from colleagues, Steve Shell in particular, was merciless. 'Wires Turner' became my handle before I got back to Skopje; there were hijinks in the HAS and sticky notes dotted around gently carping at my inadequacies – it all goes with the turf. But for Dave, IIR and me, we were just glad to have had dinner together that night, and on our terms. Rather poetically, three days later, Steve himself flew through another set of unmarked wires – again in a valley, again with pylons hidden in the trees and again it was put down as an operational risk. Touché!

Looking back on a near life-changing moment in that valley, I still think it remarkable that we got away with it completely. The most significant damage was to our pride, and in my experience that's never a bad thing.

CHAPTER 4
ADVICE FROM AIR VICE-MARSHALS

AIR VICE-MARSHAL CLIVE BAIRSTO

Navigator Clive Bairsto's first operational tour was in the Phantom air defence role. Then in 1984 he was sent to fly the F-4S with the US Marine Corps at Yuma, Arizona, before returning to the UK with the F-4Js destined for 74 Squadron at Wattisham. In 1988 he converted to the Tornado F3 and rejoined 111 Squadron, this time as QWI leader. He later commanded both the Tornado F3 Operational Evaluation Unit (OEU) at Coningsby and RAF Leuchars. With some 3,000 hours on 38 different types, notably, as Air Officer Scotland, he was also combat ready (CR) on the Tornado F3.

Clive Bairsto.

THE STORY OF A TAILSLIDE

I arrived on 111 Squadron at Leuchars in March 1981, fresh out of the Phantom OCU as a newly minted navigator. Unusually, I was a pilot officer – in those days holding between courses was quite rare – and I had been lucky to sail through almost all my flying courses at Finningley, Brawdy and Coningsby without too much stress. I was pretty confident – which all seemed to be part of the drill then anyway.

By the end of June 1981, I was CR and crewed with a former Vulcan pilot with whom I flew almost daily, sometimes two or three times. We knew we were pretty good. We were probably pretty cocky as a pair. Let's return to that.

An innocuous entry appears in my logbook for 25 May 1982: XT 870, Navigator, Supersonics, 1 hr 05 min. In fact, once out in the 'play area', 50–100nm east of Leuchars, our number two (the target) had gone unserviceable. We were left with a bunch of gas, a pretty clean aircraft and a completely blue sky. What could possibly go wrong?

Well, there had been a profile we had been looking at in the F-4 simulator – an evading 'high-flyer' target. Normally, to intercept an aircraft at 45,000ft you would offset laterally by 12–15nm, accelerate supersonic and then do a climbing decelerating turn to overtake the target (usually a Canberra cruising at Mach 0.7 or so) a few hundred yards away, declaring it friendly or hostile in the passing VID (visual identification) mode. The only issue with this was that if the 'bandit' turned away, you would never catch up and get into the weapons envelope, let alone see the thing to make a visual identification.

The profile we had devised was to keep the bandit right on the nose. With the target 40 degrees up and you 15,000ft below and supersonic, simply pitch up into a loop and do a 'roll-off-the-top' hi-flyer intercept. Easy. Went pretty well in the F-4 full-motion simulator. From Mach 1.2 at 30,000ft in full afterburner (AB) you can roll out 2–300 yards behind the bandit, upside down. Roll right way up and declare the ID. No snags. Worked fine ... in the simulator ...

On this bright, blue-sky day, it seemed a perfect opportunity to give this a go in the air. Everything went as planned. Buchan cleared us supersonic, a bit of bunting and we were up to Mach 1.2, full AB and pitching into the vertical. Horizon disappears below, easily through 45 degrees nose-up ... 50, 60 ... no problems here ... 70, 80 degrees ... and then the rate of pitch starts to slow really quite dramatically and indicated airspeed drops off a bit too ... 85 ... and just as we touch 90 degrees, the airspeed needle thumps off the bottom of the clock and disappears below the minimum reading. And there we are, for about two seconds – 39,000ft, zero knots, full AB and pure vertical – oh yes, and lovely weather. It wasn't supposed to be quite like this. Worse still, with me squawking "Don't touch anything!" (you just don't retard the throttles too much in this part of the flight envelope as the engines will flame out, and tempting as it is, you don't want to make any significant flight control inputs as the aircraft might spin), the aircraft cabin altitude suddenly switches our oxygen regulators into full and unpleasant pressure breathing.

At this stage the aircraft, majestic and *Titanic*-like, slips silently backwards at increasing velocity, tail-first towards the lovely crest-free ocean waves below – pushing us forward, weightless in our straps. Accelerating downwards and backwards under gravity – wow, this is new! The engines don't seem to mind – I guess there's not too much air up here anyway. We are going backwards for what seems like an age – probably only four or five seconds. Of course, you cannot really tell it's going backwards – no clouds, no reference – but the earlier weightlessness suggests that it must be.

And then, blessedly and infinitesimally slowly, the nose of the aircraft gently tilts towards the nearest horizon. It then comes slashing down alarmingly to pure vertical-down – and carries on through to 60 degrees down, inverted. With airspeed now building, we recover to straight-and-level at about 24,000ft. Looking up, there is the most extraordinary corkscrew contrail tracing our path, up and then down again. "Shall we go home now?" "Yeah, why not?" Chastened, we flew back to Leuchars in silence.

What did I learn from that? The simulator performance was nothing like the same as the aircraft. May seem obvious to say it, but we did not know that. And simulator staff never suggested it was a bad idea. We had not discussed the profile with anybody else in the crewroom before trying it at full-blood – and frankly, we could have done some oblique, non-pure vertical rolls-off-the-top to check performance. And to repeat, we were a bit cocky, were flying 30 hours a month, were familiar with the aircraft and thought we could do almost anything with it.

We never tried the profile again, didn't debrief it, and never discussed it. But we certainly learnt about flying backwards that day.

* * * *

AIR VICE-MARSHAL STU BUTLER

Stuart 'Stu' Butler was commissioned in 1974. He spent much of his career on the Nimrod, initially with 206 Squadron at Kinloss, a unit he went on to command before becoming station commander at the same base. Including his time as a JP QFI, and as crew captain during the Falklands War, he amassed over 6,000 flying hours. Stu left the RAF to join BAE Systems in 2008 and finally retired in 2023.

EVERY DAY IS A SCHOOL DAY

Looking back to what I learnt about flying, four events stick in my mind. The first shows what can happen when you push the envelope, the second still makes me laugh,

Stu Butler.

the third is a tribute to experience, while the fourth was the result of several improbable coincidences.

Despite spending most of my career on the mighty Nimrod, the first two incidents involved the JP T5, as a Cranwell flying instructor. I was lucky enough to do nearly five years on JPs, having been promoted to squadron leader around halfway through my tour. I confess that towards the end of my time as a squadron commander and deputy chief flying instructor, if flying didn't involve close formation or low level it generally ended up on somebody else's schedule. But my last sortie on the jet turned out to be slightly more memorable than I would have liked.

I had planned my last trip as a solo staff continuation training (SCT) event, with a little formation at the start followed by some low level and a return to Cranwell for a final run-and-break. All went well and I returned to the circuit in wonderful weather and positioned for a break. To set a good example to my students, and to keep me out of the station commander's office, I was generally very observant of the rules but, on this occasion, I thought I had earned a low-level break that stretched the limits of the minimum break height. I had also decided that whatever speed I could get on entry to the break was good enough and that nobody was looking or even cared about what that speed was. The consequence of these thoughts was that I was on the limits of speed and the ground seemed much closer than normal.

As I passed over the threshold, pulled the throttle fully back and flicked the airbrakes out for a left-hand break, I got a bit of a surprise. Rather than roll smoothly to the left, the jet rolled violently to the right, my helmet smashed against the side of the cockpit and the ground started to get even closer. Instinctively, the airbrakes were flicked back in and the roll stopped – followed very quickly by a controlled roll back to the left and a pull to get clear of the ground. I can't say for sure at what height I bottomed out but you could certainly measure it in tens rather than hundreds of feet! My heart was beating very quickly at this stage, and I had probably sent some of the higher-level circuit traffic into avoidance mode. But then training kicked in – a visual look around the aircraft showed that nothing appeared amiss, so I set up for a low-speed handling check. Given that the incident seemed to be airbrake-related, I left them in and configured the aircraft for an approach. But on lowering flap, despite no obvious external signs, another rapid roll ensued. However, in a flapless configuration all appeared well all the way down to landing speed and, given I was now quite short of fuel, I opted for a straight-in approach to an uneventful landing.

As I taxied in, all became clear. Looking outside the aircraft, the port flap was hanging loose. On further investigation, the eye bolt fastening holding it to the flap control rod had sheared off, leaving the flap to do its own thing. As the airbrake was selected out, the airflow must have pulled the flap down on one side, making it like a very large aileron – hence the rapid roll rate. Similarly, when selecting flap, only one side operated, producing a similar effect. Morale of the story: if you do fly at the limits of the envelope, things can happen that you are totally unable to anticipate – and if you are close to the ground at the time, you have significantly less time to recover.

My second incident happened around a year earlier and was during a regular Central Flying School (CFS) instructor check. I will not name names, but my Standards examiner was a delight to fly with so I was very relaxed. As an experienced instructor, I felt that my A2[9] category was safe. On the day, after a ground school test, he asked me to teach spinning and, at the appointed time, we started the climb to 30,000ft for the first spin entry, with me doing my normal spinning 'patter'. The first entry was my demo and, feeling confident, I slowed the jet down and applied full pro-spin controls. Almost immediately there was an almighty bang and the cockpit filled with a thick mist. I duly recovered from the start of a full spin and levelled the aircraft at around 20,000ft while starting a slow descent just in case we had any resultant oxygen issues. Rather than take control, my Standards examiner offered useful advice and we commenced a visual inspection to see if we could spot the problem. With the mist now clear, a distinct whistling sound indicated a problem with my side of the cockpit and, on closer inspection, it was clear that the cockpit rail had come adrift from the airframe, leaving a quarter-inch gap. Keeping the aircraft at low speed to avoid further damage, we did a low-speed handling check and, subsequently, made an uneventful approach and landing.

It was soon after we started to taxi in that I realised why I was a run-of-the-mill instructor and my fellow instructor was on the station's Standards Flight (in addition

---

9 CFS instructors are graded A1, A2, B1 and B2, the last named on graduation as an instructor.

to the fact that he had that god-of-gods A1 rating!). As we taxied in, I tried to motor back the canopy but, due to the twist in the cockpit rail it would not budge. We then disengaged the electrics and attempted to slide it back manually, still to no avail. At this stage air traffic control asked if there was anything we needed (the crash crews had lost interest at this stage). As I was about to say negative, quick as a flash, my fellow pilot keyed the mike and said, "Can you ask catering to make us some very thin sandwiches?" On arriving at our stand, slight pressure on the canopy from the outside enabled us to pull the canopy back sufficiently to exit the aircraft ... and I hung on to my A2 with an additional comment on an emergency well handled. For me, it showed that training is critical and, over time, much of what you learn becomes instinctive – but it's individuals who make our flying careers so memorable.

Now to the mighty Nimrod. Fairly early in my career I had the distinct pleasure of flying with 206 Squadron's Canadian exchange officer. As was typical of both the Australian and Canadian exchange officers of the time, he was a delightful man with, in his case, lots of experience on the Canadian maritime patrol aircraft (MPA), the Argus. It was a Tapestry[10] fishery protection sortie and, as was quite common in the Nimrod fleet, I was a qualified first pilot (normally with a navigator aircraft captain) but, on this occasion, was flying as a co-pilot. All went well during the sortie but the weather deteriorated quickly and, on recovery from low level, we were hit by lightning. Ordinarily, this was not a major issue. Despite a strong smell of burning, a full visual inspection and low-speed handling check revealed nothing amiss. Returning to the Kinloss overhead, we descended into the circuit in almost perfect weather.

At this stage I was flying the aircraft from the right-hand seat in order to meet a mandatory training requirement. About halfway round finals all looked tidy (cross-cockpit visibility was not great in a left-hand finals turn from the right seat so it was a matter of hitting suitable 'gates' until the final line-up), although I had that uneasy feeling that all was not quite right. Watching the airspeed start to drop slightly I pushed on a little power, at which stage I heard a powerful shout of "Speed" from the left seat. My immediate thought was that my fellow pilot was being a little pedantic as I was only a couple of knots below the ideal speed for that stage of the turn; however, to placate him I gave the throttles a quick nudge forward and continued to scan for the appearing runway ... at which stage the shout was repeated and the stick-shakers, indicating we were approaching the stall, went off. The first pilot then shouted, "I have control" and, to my complete surprise, pulled the power back and raised the nose.

---

10 As part of Operation Tapestry, Nimrods patrolled the UK's EEZ (Exclusive Economic Zone), locating and identifying vessels inside the zone.

The view from a Nimrod flight deck. (Derek Bower)

A quick check across the cockpit dials showed that while the right-hand seat ASI was decreasing, the opposite was happening in the left-hand seat – but which one was correct? With all his experience, the first pilot then did what we are all taught from commencement of flying training: 'fly the aircraft'. He simply put the aircraft into straight-and-level flight, a known configuration and power setting, before saying, "Now, let's find out what the hell is going on". A check with the electronically based, but very accurate, navigation kit showed that neither ASI was reading correctly but, surprise, surprise, we were within a few knots of what you would expect in the configuration he had chosen. After that, while we had no idea what was happening to the system, we completed a quick low-speed handling check, followed by an uneventful approach using the navigator's airspeed data. Later rectification showed that the lightning strike had been quite extensive and, over a short period, had caused a major leak in the pitot static system – which only became evident when we recovered to base. The incident taught me a couple of valuable lessons: when things don't feel quite right, they probably aren't. And there's no substitute for experience and training.

Unlike the fast-jet world, you get to fly large aircraft once or twice a week (if you're lucky). However, the final incident relates to my time as a station commander when, much like the earlier JP example, I could largely pick and choose my trips – some of which I flew as captain and some as co-pilot, depending on the task and how much preparation time was available within my working day. This particular day was very different. The station was tasked to fly about 30 ASC (Advanced Staff College) students on demo sorties and, as we were short of aircraft and crews, the plan was to fly them in blocks of about ten on a single aircraft, with intermediate landings to swap passengers over. I was to be co-pilot for the first sortie and captain the aircraft for the second and third events.

We launched on the last of the three sorties with the intent of doing a broad-spectrum capability demo in the danger area just to the north of Kinloss. As was normal at the time, we were carrying a simple SAR fit in the bomb bay, comprising a life raft and two tethered survival containers. Given we were at light weight, once we were established in the danger area we shut down the outboard engines to conserve fuel and commenced the demo. Again, in accordance with standard operating procedures (SOPs), we were listening to the Lossiemouth approach frequency – and it was here that we heard the call that would change the plan. As we ran in to conduct a simulated weapons drop, we heard: "Mayday! Mayday! Mayday! Jaguar aircraft preparing to eject."

At this stage we had no idea of the emergency aircraft's location or the nature of the problem but, given we had a SAR load we offered our assistance if required. The response from Lossiemouth confirmed the aircraft was local and that a SAR helicopter was being readied – hence our help was not required. We therefore continued our demo and all returned to normal. However, after a very short pause, Lossiemouth came back with information that the helicopter had a short-term problem and it would be really useful if we could make the ejection datum ready for easy location and a later pick-up by the helo. At this stage we were still unaware of the Jaguar's location but, in anticipation of a climb and transit we restarted both the shutdown engines and did a quick fuel calculation to ensure we could reach the stricken aircraft's location. At the same time, Kinloss was informed and the reserve-ready SAR crew was brought to cockpit readiness in anticipation of a scramble. At some stage during this preparation an ejection call was heard from the Jaguar pilot.

Lossiemouth then passed us the datum and asked if we could mark the position for the follow-on helicopter. The word 'datum' was quite important in this conversation. The navigators quickly plotted the position and we ran in at speed (for a Nimrod at least!) towards it. All lookout positions were manned and as many eyes as possible scanned the sea surface for signs of a dinghy – and anyone who has done this will know that dinghies are not that easy to see, even down at 200ft. The first pass over the datum was completed with nothing seen and, after a quick wingover at the far end, we returned from a slightly different direction. It was at this stage that one of the beam lookouts shouted: "Mark! Mark! He's 200ft above us!"

As normal, the lookout's call also initiated release of a flare to mark the position – which hit the water well before the pilot splashed down. By this stage the helo was serviceable and approaching the area, so we were able to exit the position to allow the recovery to commence. The helicopter soon spotted our flare and the Jaguar pilot in his dinghy; he was quickly recovered back to Lossiemouth with only minor injuries from the ejection.

By pure coincidence, the Jaguar pilot was the station commander at Lossiemouth which, given I was in command at Kinloss, kicked off an interesting local media report. While we played only a small part in the rescue, the Staff College students thought it was an amazing demo and went away thinking our coordination was second to none. I don't recall OC Lossiemouth's exact words, but he did make the point that all was going well during his ejection until he was almost run down by a Nimrod! The bottom line: 'datum' can mean lots of things so, in common with many things aircrew hear over the radio, don't jump to conclusions; and make sure you have assessed the situation as fully as possible in the time allowed before rushing in to help. As it happened, all ended well and the cooperation between our two stations was impeccable – with a valuable and respected pilot rescued from a very broken Jaguar.

These four incidents show exactly why in the flying business 'every day is a school day'. While incidents in large aircraft tend to unfold over an extended period, with such long sorties it is rare not to find something that contributes to the data bank of knowledge – something, indeed, that may have much wider applicability. That said, for a maritime patrol crew operating a long way from home, having time to think about the potential outcome of a series of 'happenings' is not always a good thing.

CHAPTER 5
AIR COMMODORES' COMMENTS

AIR COMMODORE RICK PEACOCK-EDWARDS

Rick Peacock-Edwards joined the RAF in 1965. Offered helicopters after basic flying training, he was adamant that it was only the fast-jet route to fighters that interested him. His persistence paid off. He retired in 2000 with some 7,000 flying hours in his logbook, mainly in fighter-type aircraft, including over 1,500 on the Lightning and more than 1,000 each on the Gnat, Phantom and Tornado F2/3. Unusually, Rick filled flying appointments in every rank from pilot officer to air commodore, latterly as the RAF's Inspector of Flight Safety.

Flying was in my blood. My father was a Battle of Britain pilot and flew in many different theatres during the Second World War. He and his wartime colleagues were my heroes as a youngster, and indeed throughout the 35 years I spent in the RAF – most of them in the cockpit. In all that time I never stopped learning, as this story bears out.

EARLY LEARNING – AND THE FIRST FEW MISTAKES
I grew up in South Africa and joined the RAF through the British Defence Liaison Staff (BDLS) in Pretoria after attending the University of the Witwatersrand in Johannesburg. I completed my aptitude tests at the university, carried out my medical tests through the South African Air Force and underwent my final interviews with the BDLS.

It was during my medical tests that I learnt my first lesson. Together with a young Indian candidate, I was tested in an altitude chamber. We were taken up to around 36,000ft and then the pressure in the chamber was quickly brought back to ground

Rick Peacock-Edwards.

level. We had been briefed beforehand on what to expect, and what to do if the pressure built up in our ears, and we were being supervised. Like an idiot, I looked at this venture as a competition and I wasn't going to be beaten. The pressure did build up in my ears but I didn't blow my nose as briefed. I wasn't going to be the first. On climbing out of the chamber, the doctor asked how my ears were. I could just about hear him through my deafness and indicated that they were fine. He said, "I'll just have a look" and immediately saw that I wasn't being honest.

I failed the test but luckily I was asked to come back and do it again two weeks later. My future career depended on the result. Fortunately, I had learnt from my first rather immature effort and did not make the same mistake again. I passed the test. To say that I was relieved is an understatement.

After initial officer training at South Cerney, basic flying training on the JP at Acklington brought a couple of 'I learnt about flying from that' moments. On my first solo sortie out of the circuit I suddenly found myself above cloud. With little flying experience and no instrument flying training, this was indeed a worrying moment. Luckily I managed to find one of only a very few gaps and was able to get below the cover

– much to my relief. The second uncomfortable experience was with my instructor, exploring the characteristics of high-level flight. It was winter; it was a horrible day and the thick cloud that we seemed to be in permanently was very dark. Then we experienced some serious airframe icing. As the ice created drag we could no longer maintain either speed or rate of climb. A rapid descent into warmer air eventually saw the ice disappear, but not before we had a few worrying moments. We even made a Pan[11] call.

Flying the Gnat at Valley was a very special experience. I loved the aircraft from my first flight. It was ideal for advanced fast-jet training, although if mishandled it did have certain characteristics which could easily kill you. I learnt almost as much about people as I did about flying the Gnat. Some of my fellow course members would return to the crewroom (we were separated from the instructors) from training sorties and talk about how good their performance had been. I used to think to myself, 'these guys are much better than me'. I rarely considered my own flying performance to be as good as they described, but I tended to keep my thoughts to myself. So you can imagine my surprise at the end of the course when I won the flying trophy. It meant I was posted to my dream aircraft, the Lightning.

LEARNING THE LIGHTNING

I did my pre-Lightning training on the Hunter at Chivenor. The course was intensive and very enjoyable but it provided a sobering dose of reality. Sadly, a good friend was killed in a flying accident, while another pilot had to eject when his engine failed. Next, it was the Lightning OCU at Coltishall, where the pace progressively increased as we learnt how to employ the aircraft in an operational environment. The Lightning used fuel fast, especially in reheat. You never had much left at the end of a sortie. It was vitally important that you managed your flying to ensure that you recovered to base with the right amount of fuel at the end of a sortie. I certainly learnt about flying – about airmanship – in this respect.

I joined my first squadron, the famous 92 Squadron, at Gütersloh in Germany, three years to the day after disembarking from the *Capetown Castle* mail ship in Southampton. During those three years I will never forget, a few incidents stand out.

Whilst the runway at Gütersloh was being re-surfaced we boltholed (deployed) for four months, first to Brüggen and then Wildenrath. Once the runway was re-opened we arrived back at Gütersloh as a nine-ship formation. I was number five or six, I can't recall exactly, but I do recall bursting both tyres on touchdown. It felt like

---

11 A repeated VHF radio call, short for 'possible assistance needed'. It alerts air traffic control to an urgent, but not an emergency situation.

landing on sandpaper. I was just receiving my initial admonishment from the boss when the SEngO reported that every tyre in the formation was shredded. The wrong coefficient of friction had been used for the resurfacing of the runway.

Against the backdrop of a Cold War that was very real, amongst the lessons from my time on 92 Squadron were, first, the importance of the bond of trust that develops between squadron pilots who fly together all the time. At a more mundane level, when testing the guns over the North Sea I came to anticipate radio and instrument failures – caused by the vibration of two integral guns positioned very close to the cockpit. Then there were the silly things.

During practice diversions to Hannover (a commercial airport used regularly as our weather diversion), to impress the air hostesses who we assumed would be watching, full of youthful exuberance we would sometimes clean up the aircraft in the latter stages of an instrument approach, plug in the burners and accelerate like a rocket. On one such occasion, I learnt just how easy it is to overstress a Lightning at 600kts. Enough said!

Hannover was the scene of another minor incident. Leading a pair, I experienced a main instrument failure in cloud – no great problem because we had standby instruments. But as we broke cloud at about 6,000ft, warning captions again attracted my attention. I now had a 'Hyd 1' failure. Again, no great problem because the aircraft had two hydraulic systems. However, there were certain systems that would not work with a Hyd 1 failure, plus the possibility that the tail chute would not deploy. We diverted to Hannover where I landed without difficulty but with a little more fuel than normal. My tail chute did not deploy but, as I was already carrying out a precautionary landing (I was not going round again if I had a problem on the runway), I stayed on the runway and relied on my brakes. Hannover has no barrier so is not an ideal diversion for an aircraft with a Hyd 1 failure, but there was no alternative. I managed to stop before the end of the runway, but I admit that I had my moments bringing the aircraft to a halt.

Another great lesson resulted from when the boss and I were doing a flypast with a Victor tanker for, I think, the Wildenrath air show. Most air-to-air refuelling is done at high level where the air is smooth. The opposite is the case in the lower levels, especially over land on a windy day, or in cumulus clouds. We were both plugged in as we overflew Wildenrath but I had never seen so much up-and-down movement of the deployed refuelling hoses.

Finally, I learnt the dangers of rough aircraft handling. I was in trail on one of the more experienced pilots as he completed a VID on the target aircraft. As he broke off from the identification, he was rather ham-fisted on the controls and departed (i.e. lost control of the aircraft). Fortunately, the departure did not develop beyond the incipient spin stage, but I watched him lose a lot of height very quickly. Over a beer in the bar that evening, he said that he had rather surprised himself. Me too!

My second Lightning tour was as an instructor on 65 Squadron at the Lightning OCU at Coltishall. I have always regarded this tour as the one that taught me most about my own performance as an RAF pilot, and a tour during which I had always to perform as close to perfection as possible, simply to establish and maintain my own credibility – I was one of the youngest instructors.

We had a secondary operational role as one of the Lightning squadrons declared to NATO. As such, we were also involved in many of the various types of exercise. One I particularly recall had been called at around midday. During the afternoon I was scrambled and landed at Binbrook. Late that evening, I was brought to cockpit readiness, where I remained for several hours. I was eventually scrambled, taxied to the runway and commenced my take-off run. I quickly realised that there was some unusual vibration and then noticed the illuminated canopy lights – it wasn't locked – so I immediately aborted take-off. I was lucky; another few seconds and the canopy would have departed the aircraft. Why did that happen? Fatigue. I should not have been kept in the cockpit for as long as I was. But I also should have realised myself that I was fatigued, and hence prone to error.

Before I finally said my goodbyes to the Lightning, an aircraft, or should I say a manned rocket, that I loved flying, I had one more pulse-quickening experience – again at night and again during an exercise. I had been scrambled on an intercept mission over the North Sea. On commencing my recovery to base, my radar (which I could have used to highlight the coast) failed; my TACAN (which indicated range from selected locations) was not working, and my radio was being jammed, it seemed on all frequencies. I was unsure of my position and beginning to run short of fuel. With the adrenalin count rising considerably, I breathed a huge sigh of relief when I managed, eventually, to make radio contact with one of the controlling authorities and recover safely. There was clearly something about night exercise scrambles!

A DIFFERENT KIND OF INSTRUCTING

A change from the front line – becoming a Gnat QFI – taught me just how useful had been my two Lightning tours in climbing the learning curve. On commencing this tour at Valley, I was determined that all my students would be the best on their course. Well, I very quickly realised that was never going to happen; there were such differences in natural abilities, both in flying coordination and mental capacity. You simply did your very best to help your students graduate, and the great majority of my own students did graduate. But it was a non-instructional sortie that brought my most difficult moment.

I was one of four aircraft tasked to carry out a photoshoot for a national newspaper, using Snowdon as a backdrop. During the sortie I was aware that one of my 'slipper' tanks (fuel tanks below the wing) had failed to feed; no great problem if you recover to base and land before the overall fuel weight drops below a certain figure. I cut it very fine on meeting that fuel landing limit; the result was that on the final approach I needed increasing amounts of aileron and was running out of lateral control. Put another way, I was barely able to keep the wings level. If ever I needed a demonstration of why limits are set, then that was the occasion. I landed the aircraft without incident but, obviously, very heavy in one wing. As I taxied the aircraft back to dispersal, the senior air traffic control officer (SATCO) observed that my Gnat looked very lop-sided.

IT TAKES TWO

I somehow managed a fourth flying tour in a row, converting to the Phantom and learning to fly with navigators, or 'fightergators' as I preferred to call them. It took a while to settle into the new two-seat environment. Briefings were longer, sorties were longer, there was greater use of training aids and, most importantly in capability terms, the Phantom was a quantum leap forward compared with the Lightning. The aircraft was a real war machine.

My time on 111 Squadron at Leuchars was immensely enjoyable, although it was not a tour without accident or incident. Three aircraft were lost and two crews killed in one awful three-month period. These accidents had a profound effect on the squadron spirit. Over the next two years, one further aircraft was lost when the radome came open in flight. Another landed short at Sola in Norway and the lip of the runway pushed the undercarriage up into the wings, and that is saying something for an aircraft built as strongly as the Phantom. It took 18 months to recover the aircraft back to Leuchars.

These issues apart, there were a few other incidents that exercised me. We used to alternate between weeks of day flying and night flying. I was on a night-flying week and leading a pair of Phantoms on an intercept sortie which included air-to-air refuelling. I was flying in a three-tank fit, or put another way, I was carrying the maximum amount of fuel possible. We had just filled the tanks to full on the tanker and the time was around 2300. Then my number two had a problem and had to return to Leuchars. My navigator and I first decided to go on a heavyweight practice diversion to Lossiemouth. I was too heavy to do a touch-and-go and so we planned to do an overshoot from just over the runway. All went smoothly until I commenced the overshoot, whereupon there was an almighty bang and flash. I could see that my right engine had seized, and air traffic control were calling out that I was on fire. I also knew that the aircraft was not going to fly very far until the reheat on the good engine lit. I put out an immediate Mayday call and at the same time I pushed the good throttle forward to maximum reheat. Fortunately, the reheat lit and I knew that I now had an aircraft that I could fly out of trouble. At that stage, from the back seat suddenly came, "What the hell (or similar words) is going on?" We sorted the aircraft out, dumped fuel down to landing weight and landed as soon as possible and, after dealing with the immediate aftermath, we retired to the 'scruff' bar in the officers' mess. Meanwhile, air traffic picked up one-and-a-half bags of compressor blades from the runway. The engine had well and truly exploded and was a complete mess. It was not an event that I would like to experience often.

On another occasion I was doing an air test, part of which involved selecting the autopilot and checking that it de-selected in a turn. The procedure required you to check that the autopilot did not disconnect until you had pulled 4g. However, I overdid the pull and the aircraft flicked. Recovery was almost immediate, but not before I had lost 4,000ft in seconds. If that was a surprise, witnessing another Phantom depart on withdrawing its probe from the refuelling hose was an even bigger one!

Then there was a mildly concerning communication problem. I was on a four-ship sortie in a low-level exercise against Harriers and Jaguars. We successfully engaged our targets and the resulting melee went on for several minutes. On completion, I said to my navigator, "That was a great exercise" but got no response. In fact, he did not answer my questions for what seemed a very long time; he was, initially, out cold in the back. I declared an emergency and recovered immediately to Leuchars, where the medical team met the aircraft on landing. Fortunately, the navigator's problem was nothing serious: low blood sugar. He had not eaten properly before the sortie. There is a lesson there.

A CHANGE IS AS GOOD AS A REST

A short ground tour in London followed by staff college and then I was back in the cockpit again, for my fifth flying tour. It was a challenge that I had long wanted: introducing the new Tornado fighter into RAF service. I was to form the OCU at

Coningsby and command what was also to be the first squadron, 65 Squadron. It would be a challenge.

Together with my back-seater, Nobby Clark, I began my Tornado conversion in January 1985. We had less than two years to train crews to fly and instruct on the aircraft, and get everyone CR for our declaration to NATO on 31 December 1986. Suffice to say that, despite several problems, especially with the aircraft's radar, we were ready for NATO declaration on time. We had converted and trained over 60 instructors, the squadron now had over 300 engineers and a total of 22 aircraft; we had successfully proved the missile- and gun-firing capabilities, and we had carried out myriad additional tasks. I will always look back on this achievement with great satisfaction and pride; it was a real team effort. And talking about the additional tasks, these included leading the Queen's 60th birthday flypast and the flypast for the opening of the Commonwealth Games in Edinburgh, a deployment to Oman and a sales tour of the Middle East on behalf of the British government. All we achieved in two uniquely testing years came down simply to having the right team – a team that, like me, never stopped learning throughout.

AND THE NEXT ...

More time on the ground – a couple of jobs in London – after which I was off again for yet another flying tour. I loved the challenges of commanding a front-line operational base. As the station commander at Leeming I had under my command three Tornado F3 squadrons, an RAF Regiment squadron, a university air squadron (UAS), an air experience flight (AEF) and a mountain rescue team (MRT).

My official allocation was ten flying hours per month, a total that I usually met or exceeded. I used to fly with all the Tornado units, alternating between the squadrons from Monday to Thursday. On Friday afternoon, when the station was probably at its quietest, I flew the Bulldogs belonging to the UAS/AEF. But things suddenly changed with the outbreak of the First Gulf War. With one hour's notice, I was deployed to Saudi Arabia as the first RAF commander in theatre. That alone was a very rewarding and immensely satisfying experience. It also provided invaluable insights for when I returned from the Gulf to resume command of Leeming whilst some station personnel remained in theatre.

After another brilliant tour came what turned out to be a very short one in Washington DC, as one of the air attachés in the British Embassy. I thought my flying was at an end, but I was wrong. I was soon back in the cockpit as the RAF's Inspector of Flight Safety, an appointment which carried with it a requirement to remain current on several types, one of which was required to be a front-line aircraft. This was another job I had long hoped that I might one day have the privilege to do. I was current on four different types: Tornado, Tucano, Hercules and Bulldog, and I flew almost all aircraft in the RAF inventory. I completed a helicopter course and flew all the RAF's helicopters too. Then there was the bonus of flying aircraft in other countries, notably the Viggen in Sweden and CF-5 in Canada.

I spent nearly four years as Inspector of Flight Safety and learnt so much – learning that has continued to serve me well in the years since I handed over to my successor. For nearly three decades I have remained closely connected with aviation safety matters, carrying with me many of the lessons I took from a job that was an eye-opening experience. As a fighter pilot, I had not appreciated just how demanding was some of the other flying in the RAF – notably for Hercules SF crews, helicopter operators in Northern Ireland and those conducting night low-level operations over the sea in a Nimrod.

From a personal perspective, I regarded landing a Puma in a field in Northern Ireland on a dark, dirty night, using night vision goggles, as a special achievement – one that taught me a huge lesson about trust. Being brought into the confidence of those involved in flying operations at all RAF bases was a similar experience: I learnt to understand their problems, problems which they sometimes had difficulty transmitting to the upper levels of the RAF. Being able to help in this respect brought its own reward.

I was concerned when I took over as inspector at the apparent blame culture that existed around the RAF, a culture which was leading to problems not being properly reported. That all changed during my tour. After a review of accident Board of Inquiry procedures, the subject of blame was removed from the process. This alone was a major success.

I will conclude with a special memory that arguably says more about the learning process that any of the incidents previously described. When his service was suffering a lot of accidents, very bravely I thought, the Chief of the RAAF approached CAS to ask if I could conduct a review of their aviation safety. I spent almost a month in Australia and completed a report which I presented to the Deputy Chief of Air Force; it made over 200 recommendations. The deputy accepted my report without amendment and the recommendations were implemented. That the accident rate plummeted, and remained low in the years that followed, is a tribute to all I learnt about flying over the years. This Australian experience was proof too that you never stop learning about flying.

* * * *

AIR COMMODORE GRAHAM PITCHFORK

Graham Pitchfork entered the RAF College Cranwell in 1958 as a navigator. After a first operational tour on Canberras in Germany, he spent three years on Buccaneers with the Fleet Air Arm, including a year at sea on HMS *Eagle*. He later commanded a Buccaneer squadron and then the RAF's largest flying training base at Finningley. One of the last Commandants at the Officer and Aircrew Selection Centre (OASC), Biggin Hill, after a final appointment in MoD he retired in 1994.

BECOMING A BUCCANEER BOSS – LESSONS ALONG THE WAY

By the mid-1950s, my passion for Biggles and Rockfist Rogan[12] had begun to wane as a number of books about wartime heroes began to hit the market. *The Dam Busters, Reach for the Sky* and *Wing Leader* soon adorned my bookshelf. A visit to my uncle's farm at the head of the Derwent reservoirs to watch Lancasters roar over the Ladybower Dam as film crews captured the images for the iconic film that followed, was sufficient to convince me that I wanted to be an RAF pilot.

The Air Training Corps was soon added to my activities and a 20-minute flight (my first) in a Chipmunk during a summer camp at RAF Driffield was a dream come true. Shortly afterwards, at a routine training evening at the squadron headquarters in Sheffield, we were inspected and formed up for 'an important visitor' who would present proficiency certificates to those who had recently passed their exams, which included me. The door opened and in stomped a man we instantly recognised, Douglas Bader no less. He was on a visit to his wartime Auxiliary Air Force squadron and was to spend a brief period with us. His strong, positive and enthusiastic personality lived long in my memory.

As I joined the sixth form at school, I became aware of a scheme the RAF had introduced allowing those with aspirations to fly to be 'tested in advance'. Success would ensure entry within two years; failure allowed other careers to be explored. I was summoned to RAF Hornchurch aged 17, completed the test and was very happy to a receive a letter offering me a Direct Commission 'B' (DCB) as a pilot when I completed my studies.

I was thrilled but allowed the excitement to take my eye off the ball and, in due course, I flunked my A levels. My father, quite rightly, insisted I stay an extra year, get

---

12 Flight Lieutenant 'Rockfist' Rogan was a fighter pilot and boxer who appeared in *The Champion*, a boys' story paper from 1922–55.

Graham Pitchfork, Cranwell cadet.

my head down and complete my studies, which I did. I had alerted the RAF to my enforced delay and, when the time came, I was invited back to Hornchurch to confirm my medical status.

After the test, I went before the selection board to be told that the offer of a commission was still available, but due to a small eyesight defect, it was for navigator training. A kindly squadron leader could see that I was shell-shocked, and he took me to one side. It was then that I noticed he was wearing a navigator's brevet above a row of ribbons that included the DFC.

He outlined the opportunities open to navigators and finished his chat by offering me the chance to travel with some of the other candidates to the RAF College Cranwell to be tested for suitability for a cadetship. This had not figured on my agenda but, recognising the unexpected chance for a few more days off school, I agreed. I was one of 16 young men who completed the tests and a few weeks later was offered a navigator cadetship at the college in lieu of heading for Officer Cadet Training Unit (OCTU) to start my DCB.

Three years at Cranwell represented a huge learning curve. The environment was very different from that of my grammar school, and it took me time to settle. Initially, the most fascinating aspect was the people. Wartime heroes filled the senior ranks, most instructors were aircrew, and I soon learnt that the real power was in the hands of the college warrant officer, his senior non-commissioned officer (SNCO) drill instructors and the senior cadets.

There were seven navigators in my entry – a small minority surrounded by 50 pilot colleagues. We soon began our training but facing backwards in a lumbering Valetta and Varsity was not my idea of the thrills I was seeking. However, the way forward was clear, and I decided that I must be the best navigator possible. I had two outstanding instructors; one had flown in Mosquitos and the other had recently completed a tour on Canberra bombers. I liked and admired them both.

At the time, navigators who displayed high potential were being sent to the new V-Force as navigator/radar operators. That did not feature in my plans. During the final year at Cranwell each cadet had to undertake a project: write a thesis and submit it for a prize. Thanks to my instructors, we devised a plan that my project should reflect the role I wanted to follow – photographic reconnaissance (PR). The director of studies tried to dissuade me, since 'navigators do not go to the PR world on their first tour'. I refused to be deterred by this possibility and, with the help of my two instructors, I paid visits to 58 Squadron at Wyton, operating the new Canberra PR.9, to the Joint Air Reconnaissance Intelligence Centre (JARIC) and to Hunting Aerosurveys.

Throughout my navigator training, and subsequently, I never got the hang of drawing neat lines on maps, 'shooting' stars and spending hours over the North Sea on a creeping line ahead search. But that was the task, so I did my best. Being a navigator took on a new meaning when the course headed to RAF Thorney Island for a three-week jet familiarisation course flying in converted Meteor NF14s. It was a revelation; one could see out and work with the pilot who introduced us to the two-man crew concept. I was so enthused, I even accepted extra sorties with the instructors during their night continuation training exercises flying in a Meteor T7.

I hoped that the results of my thesis, and my enthusiasm and performance at Thorney Island, would persuade the hierarchy that my future was not facing backwards in a white 'flatiron'.[13] The arrival of a new assistant commandant, who wanted to see me, undoubtedly helped; my perseverance, and a lot of help and support worked too, and I left Cranwell to join 101 (PR) Course on Canberras at Bassingbourn.

Cranwell taught me a great deal. I remember some inspiring people on the staff and amongst my colleagues. There was great pride in doing things well, not just as an individual, but more importantly as a team. Self-discipline, particularly when the way ahead seemed tough, was paramount and I discovered the need to balance the work hard/play hard attitude, and the importance of both. Above all, there was an opportunity to learn from others how, and how not to manage situations and people. For me, I grew up at Cranwell and its influence has remained with me for the rest of my life.

After completing the PR course at Bassingbourn, where I learnt to avoid disgruntled, passed-over flight lieutenants, I joined 31 Squadron at Laarbruch in April 1962 with my pilot, Terry Close, who had escaped from the V-Force. As a 21-year-old pilot officer amongst a formidable group of older, highly experienced PR

---

13 The Avro Vulcan bomber (early versions were painted white).

men, I soon discovered the delights of running the coffee bar and being responsible for the issue of British Forces Germany (BFG) petrol coupons.

During the early days, the best tactic was to keep my head down, my eyes and ears open and watch how the other navs prepared for a sortie. The highly experienced senior flight commander and his navigator kept an eye on me, and their unfussy support and encouragement set me off on the right road. There was much to enjoy for a young officer overseas in the 1960s. A super job, a great social life, and an open road to Europe. All that plus good pay and allowances and a bachelor way of life in a mess full of attractive young ladies. This gave plenty of opportunity for the 'play hard' aspect of my creed.

However, it was the day job that mattered. Within a year, Terry Close and I were selected to be one of the five crews entered for the annual Sassoon Trophy for the best PR squadron in RAF Germany. It was here where the flight commander took a hand and guided and encouraged us through the long work-up period. Come the day, there were plenty of nerves as we were to be the third to go. After the frantic 30-minute plan, and a leap through the briefing room window to the jet a few yards away, the boss, who had been alerted that Sortie 3 was the most difficult, put his hand on my shoulder: "Just do what you did throughout the training, and you will be fine." With those words of encouragement, we were off.

It was a difficult sortie, particularly the final target in the Ardennes, but the training and the planning kicked in and we managed. Within days, it was announced that the squadron had won the competition. Elation! We felt that we now truly belonged on the squadron. A year later, it was the squadron's turn to take the night slot for the NATO Royal Flush reconnaissance competition. We had just started the training phase when Terry Close suffered a medical problem; he was grounded and, sadly, never flew again. OC B Flight's navigator was struggling with map reading at night and I replaced him.

Our training officer was brilliant. Highly experienced, he devised a night programme that saw us airborne three or four times a week for the best part of two months (goodbye social life). He and his pilot visited almost every weapons range withing our radius of action and we got to know the surrounding areas, likely initial points (IPs), and approaches to targets. I found this impressive. Equally impressive was the reaction of the other 12 crews on the squadron. Their support was magnificent, and they gave up a lot of flying and their time to support the three competing crews. Leadership from the top was the key, so how could we let them down?

Come the competition week, when we flew our three sorties the value of our training kicked in. Crew cooperation was essential, and we understood each other perfectly.

We were familiar with the nine target areas and, lying in the nose to release the photo flashes, I was able to confirm we had hit all the targets. We were up against a USAF RB-66[14] squadron with radar-equipped aircraft and a crew of four whose sole role was night reconnaissance. We came second by a handful of marks but were awarded the best crew award. It was disappointing for the squadron, but to be expected.

The competition embodied many facets for me. Train and prepare hard and realistically, support each other, develop sound crew cooperation, and compete as hard as possible. The prior loss of Terry Close also opened a new chapter for me. The boss, the charismatic, cool Wing Commander Peter Scott, wanted to lead the squadron from the front but his navigator was struggling and soon to depart. I was summoned to his office and given two choices: return to the UK early or stay an extra year and become his navigator. He told me to think about it. I closed the door, immediately knocked, and told him I had thought about it. I would stay. In the event, it was a life-changing decision.

Over the next 12 months, I had a very fulfilling time in the air and on the ground. The boss had a unique way of leading from the front. He took the difficult exercise sorties, flew in marginal weather, came back with some of the best photographs but did so with apparent consummate ease. As I discovered, he achieved this by doing his homework in the privacy of his office, and we planned our sorties meticulously. I had a marvellous relationship with him. He was always the wing commander but, once we closed the aircraft hatch, we were a close-knit crew with a very relaxed style, and we mixed our professional approach to the task with a lot of banter and fun. Open the hatch after landing, and he was the wing commander again.

With my tour coming to an end and no posting in sight, the boss asked me what I fancied. "An exchange tour" was my immediate reply. Not only was he a superb leader and pilot, he was also extremely well connected and said he would investigate. Weeks passed by and then he called me to his office. "An exchange posting has come through for you," he said. Immediately the sunlit beaches of California or Australia and the Rockies in Canada flashed through my mind. "You are off to Lossiemouth in north Scotland." Long pause, then a sheepish, "Thanks, boss." The Royal Navy had offered an exchange for a pilot and nav for their new Buccaneer. So, a fantastic tour with some great people came to an end after three years and almost 1,000 hours of flying.

On arrival at Lossiemouth in April 1965, I met up with the pilot half of the first RAF Buccaneer crew, Graham Smart. The Buccaneer was a revelation to me.

---

14 A reconnaissance version of the Douglas B-66 Destroyer light bomber.

Big, ugly but very purposeful looking. The navigator's position gave superb all-round visibility and, with the slightly offset seat, an excellent view forward over the pilot's shoulder to see the standard warning panel and the stand-by flight instruments – a godsend during carrier landings as I was to discover. And the smooth ride at low level was a revelation.

After a short conversion course, we headed for 800 NAS and six weeks later embarked in HMS *Eagle*. It would be 12 months before I returned to the UK. Flying with the Fleet Air Arm was different: fascinating, exciting and frequently interrupted by some very worrying moments. I admired the flexibility and 'can do' spirit, often with the minimum of fuss. In the space of a few weeks we were flying over the Radfan and then off the coast of Indonesia, soon followed by 71 numbingly boring days on patrol in the Mozambique Channel implementing UN sanctions against oil tankers trying to enter Beira to offload oil for Southern Rhodesia. This was all interspersed with night flying from the deck, night tanking from a Scimitar off China Rock, and night rocket firing against a 'splash' target towed by an RAF air-sea rescue launch off Aden. It all came at a cost – we lost three aircraft but, thankfully, no crews.

Living in a large noisy metal box for a year gives plenty of time to observe one's shipmates. I found the squadron command structure odd. The squadron commander always flew with the senior observer, irrespective of talent, and this limited the CO's opportunities to lead from the front. Indeed, he rarely did. Graham Smart and I were split up and paired with weaker members of the squadron, thus reducing our effectiveness. Similar combinations were a feature of the squadron. With two notable exceptions, most crews were of modest quality, notwithstanding that individually there were some excellent pilots and observers.

We were commanded by a former single-seat ground-attack pilot who treated the back-seater as a talking checklist. His cold, awkward personality did not endear him to us. In stark contrast, the senior pilot, Lieutenant Commander David Howard, was quite brilliant in every regard. A former Sea Hawk and Scimitar pilot, he immediately recognised the added value of an observer and the greatly increased operational capability stemming from good crew cooperation. He was the true leader of the squadron. He was an outstanding carrier pilot, tactician, and airborne leader. And at well over six feet, he had a presence which, allied to his calm demeanour, gave him authority and attracted our unquestioned loyalty. When not flying, he would be found on the hangar deck discussing issues with the squadron's maintenance team.

At the end of *Eagle*'s commission, I joined the staff of the Buccaneer training squadron. Two months later, Dave Howard arrived as the CO and I was to spend the next 18 months flying with him, watching his style and effectiveness at close quarters. In addition to being a great pilot, the best of the very many I flew with, he constantly sought to develop the capabilities of the Buccaneer. In particular, he experimented with night-attack tactics, something alien to the Fleet Air Arm at the time. I spent numerous hours in the back seat as we headed off for the Cape Wrath area to practise attacks under some dodgy parachute flares before turning to dive under the illumination to fire rockets. His meticulous planning and detailed debriefs were a lesson to any aircrew – something I never forgot and tried to copy.

This attention to detail was never more in evidence than when we bombed the stricken oil tanker, *Torrey Canyon*, off the Scilly Isles in 1967. Faced with a plethora of media interest, and under the critical eyes of the RAF, Howard realised that this was an unexpected showpiece for the Fleet Air Arm, which had to be got right. I listened intently to his briefing and left with a clear understanding of what my role was. It worked ... and was exciting too.

When my three years came to an end, I realised that I had learnt a great deal about maritime attack. Amongst the many challenging sorties, and numerous frights, I had seen an ineffective leader in command and was able to contrast this with the leadership style of a man I had the greatest respect for, and whose watchword was 'professionalism'.

The Labour government's decision in the late-1960s to cancel the next generation of aircraft carriers led to the RAF inheriting Phantoms and Buccaneers from the Fleet Air Arm. In early 1969 I was sent to RAF Honington, which had been on 'care and maintenance' for three years, to help re-open the base and establish the operations support function pending the arrival of the first Buccaneer unit, 12 Squadron, later in the year. What should have been a standard two-and-a-half-year ground tour became one that lasted four years. But I managed plenty of flying.

During that time, we had two station commanders. They could hardly have been more different. The first was a charming man who had a word for everyone. Steeped in V-Force mentality, he struggled to adjust to the professional and social thrust of a lively, and often irreverent, bunch of young aircrew. He was more comfortable with the necessary need to re-establish good relationships with the local community. In two years, I never once saw him in a flying suit. His replacement, a well-established and accomplished fighter pilot, adopted a totally different approach. First, he moved his office from station headquarters to the operations block, a few doors from my office, and he was rarely out of a flying suit. He was a good pilot, and he became competent in all the maritime-attack tactics. I recall being in the back on a very dark night one November north of the Shetland Isles when we tossed Lepus flares against HMS *Lincoln,* before pulling round to deliver a rocket attack against the splash target. He was good.

Honington and its maritime wing developed an excellent and justified reputation, but it came at a cost in human terms. To put it crudely, the station commander ruled by fear. He had no respect for his wing commanders, some inherited from his predecessor, and he created a small cabal of six or seven squadron leaders who he always turned to for advice, cutting out the wing commanders. This created a tense and uncomfortable atmosphere for everyone. My second OC Operations Wing boss, a former V-Force navigator on his first tour as a wing commander, was a decent, hardworking man, but he struggled under the constant barrage of criticism (some public). It presented me with split loyalties. I had a job to do but I was always aware of the difficulties my boss had and offered help whenever I could.

After attending Staff College, I returned to Honington, this time as the senior flight commander of the newly formed 208 Squadron, tasked in the overland role in support of Allied Forces Northern Europe (AFNORTH). The squadron commander, Wing Commander Pete Rogers, a former Canberra pilot, was older than his contemporaries and had been out of the cockpit for several years. He very wisely chose a young navigator with Fleet Air Arm and RAFG Buccaneer experience to be his back-seater. He knew his limitations and flew accordingly; he recognised the skill levels of his crews and employed them wisely and enjoyed the lively atmosphere of the crewroom. Apart from being a delightful boss to work for, his greatest strength was his ability to delegate. He knew he had a strong team, some very experienced Buccaneer operators and excellent ground support. He passed on his orders and then left us to get on with the task and was happy to receive occasional progress reports. Sucking on his pipe, he was a comforting, almost fatherly figure in the crewroom and we all liked and admired him. We were a happy squadron under his command.

In the summer of 1978, I was approaching the end of a tour in MoD and eagerly awaiting a telephone call from the Air Secretary's department with news of my next appointment. I was expecting a command tour; however, I had one major worry. Since 1965, all my flying time had been on the 'last all-British bomber' and no navigator had ever been appointed to command an RAF strike/attack squadron. I did not fancy the likely alternative of a posting to the V-Force, so a summons to see the Air Secretary at the end of 1978 generated a few nerves. That was until I discovered that he was an air marshal and a navigator, the most senior one in the RAF. He was sympathetic to my case, then proceeded to announce: "I am sending you to command 208 Squadron.

Don't screw it up or else every fast-jet nav in the RAF will be after you for ruining their career prospects." The message was clear, but I took comfort from the knowledge that the Fleet Air Arm had already set a precedent for back-seat bosses, and with 1,500 hours on the Buccaneer I knew the aircraft and the people well.

I took over 208 at Honington in July 1979. I had spent the previous few months on the base completing a refresher course. With eyes and ears open, I got a good feel for the mood of the station and the squadron. Despite being a navigator, I was determined to lead the squadron from the front, so it was essential to have a top pilot who also had credibility as a leader of formations of eight aircraft. After scouring the list of pilots due for postings, I spotted the name of Eddie Wyer, who was leaving XV Squadron in Germany and about to do the prestigious QWI course. He was just the man for me, and so it proved over the next two-and-a-half years. A brilliant pilot, and great fun to fly and be with, he made my last flying tour the most fulfilling and professionally rewarding one. I was also blessed with outstanding flight commanders who came from the Hunter and Phantom worlds.

During the handover period with my predecessor, he gave me a run-down on all the aircrew, most of whom I already knew. He singled out one as, 'the man who is most likely to get you fired'. I took note of the name, Stan. Within a week of my arrival, the squadron headed for the Royal Danish Air Force base at Aalborg in the north of Jutland. It was an excellent opportunity to assess the crews and our support. Eddie Wyer was completing his QWI course, so I took the opportunity to fly with all the other pilots, particularly Stan. He was a very interesting character. Small, wiry, lively, irreverent, he had been a Sea Vixen observer before becoming a pilot and flying the Lightning. In his late thirties, he was older than most of his flight lieutenant contemporaries. By the end of the Aalborg detachment, I had seen enough to realise that he was a good pilot, but the squadron was not using him to best effect.

A few months later, in a routine review of squadron duties, I discussed Stan with my flight commanders. We needed a new instrument rating examiner and I decided to give the job to Stan. There were a few raised eyebrows, but I had understood that what he needed was a recognition of his experience and status as one of the senior pilots. He completed the course at the OCU and immersed himself in organising instrument flying training and the routine testing of the squadron's pilots. I made him an authoriser, the only flight lieutenant at the time, and his responsible approach was a revelation. It taught me a good lesson. Identify someone's talent and then use it. They will respond, and Stan did; he became a stalwart on the squadron without losing his effervescent and irascible character.

In February 1980, we headed for Nellis AFB near Las Vegas in Nevada to take part in Exercise Red Flag and meet up with our chums from Germany who were coming to the end of their two-week exercise. We were to take over their aircraft and participate in the next exercise. On their penultimate day, my senior flight commander and I called in to the Red Flag facility to say 'hello', but were met with the tragic news that an aircraft and crew had been lost an hour earlier. The Buccaneer concerned had suffered a wing failure due to fatigue.

The Germany crews returned home, and we were left to take care of the situation. The Buccaneer fleet was grounded. We waited (in the event for two weeks) for instructions and it was decided to leave the aircraft at Nellis until further fatigue tests had been carried out by the British Aerospace engineers at Brough.

The next few months proved to be the most testing of my time in command. There was great uncertainty about the future of the fleet. It was possible that the aircraft would be scrapped. Alternatively, some might be recoverable; if so, how many, and what effect would this have on the squadrons? With their strike quick reaction alert (QRA) commitment, it had already been decided that the two RAF Germany squadrons would have to be safeguarded, as would 12 Squadron, the only maritime strike squadron in the RAF inventory. This left the future of 208 in the balance. In the event, just enough were recovered to re-equip the squadron with ten aircraft.

In the meantime, to keep the squadron operational, some of the two-seat Hunters used by 237 OCU were allocated to 12 and 208 and several single-seat F6s were obtained. So 208, a former Hunter squadron, once again had Hunters, but this time with a navigator boss! For four months we kept our hands in, and this proved hugely beneficial when the Buccaneer was once again cleared to fly in August. Not only had the aircrew benefitted enormously from flying the Hunters, it had also been a great fillip for the ground crew to have a meaningful and important task maintaining them. When I saw that they had re-designed the squadron badge to wear on their overalls, I realised we had a great and loyal team.

With our Buccaneers back, we hit the training hard and were soon heading for Norway, Scotland and all the weapons ranges we could reach. Also, our Phantom chums had another opportunity at trying to get on our tail. Some hope! I was tremendously impressed and very proud of the air and ground crews when 208 Squadron was declared operational again within a few weeks.

After an epic visit to CAF Cold Lake to take part in Exercise Maple Flag, we returned in May 1981 to find that we had been tasked to take part in the Strike

Command Tactical Bombing Competition. I selected four crews, and we headed north. The flying was exhilarating but I will focus on just one sortie.

On the fifth and final day, it was time to put the Rapier teams in their place, so we devised a new tactic for our attack on Otterburn Range. We elected to carry out an unconventional attack from the south, over a ridge and across the main valley at 540kts in finger-four formation, 25 metres apart. Eddie and I were number four at the back, and I can admit it was a hell of a lot closer than that. We delivered a cluster-bomb attack on a convoy ranged on the south-facing slopes on the northern side of the range. Inbound to the target we tracked the edge of a distinctive forest, skimmed

No. 208 Squadron at Maple Flag. Graham Pitchfork (front centre) flanked by Rob Wright (left) and Geoff Frankcom (right).

over the ridge as one unit, dropped down rapidly to bombing height, spotted the target, and then all bombed on the leader's call; immediately off-target we each selected a depression that we flew down to escape. The most amazing ten minutes I think I ever had in an aircraft.

Hardly a word had been spoken. All our tactics against the fighters revolved around our knowledge of the opposition's own tactics and capabilities, and of what each member of our team would do, dropping a wing to indicate a move, staying low, covering each other, widening when needed and, if necessary, taking separate valleys and re-joining on the timeline. Again, a huge feeling of satisfaction – a job well done and a sortie that no-one in that formation ever forgot. What made it so memorable? Training, planning, execution and teamwork.

By December my tour in command was over. My final sortie was to lead an eight-ship with my outstanding deputy, Rob Wright, in the front seat. After a nostalgic trip to all our old haunts, the weather closed in. With no hope of a final airfield attack over the base that had been my home for so many years, we had to send the other seven ahead to make singleton approaches before we joined the GCA pattern to land with a 200-foot cloud base. It was not the way to fly the last of my 2,000 hours in the Buccaneer, but any disappointment was softened when we taxied into dispersal to be met by all the squadron aircrew and ground crew. My flying career on the Buccaneer was over – surrounded by the men I admired the most.

EPILOGUE

Many years later, as Commandant at Biggin Hill, assessing over 12,000 potential candidates provided a fascinating opportunity to study human nature: the aspirations and disappointments of some outstanding young people. Perhaps the most rewarding moments were interviews with young officers who returned to OASC to have their future in the RAF reviewed after failing successfully to complete their professional training. Some were released, others were offered service in a different branch. Each required a different approach, but before seeing them, I spent a few moments thinking of my own reactions and disappointment at Hornchurch 30 years earlier. Having proved that setbacks can be conquered, it was my duty to encourage these talented youngsters to take a different route in their own RAF careers. After retiring, it gave me great pleasure to meet some of them again – and to learn how successful they had been.

CHAPTER 6

GRUMBLES FROM GROUPIES

GROUP CAPTAIN JIM BELDON

After completing his degree at the Royal Military College of Science, Jim entered Cranwell in 1994 as a navigator; by the end of 1997 he was CR on the E-3D Sentry. His tours on the type that defined his flying career were timed with commendable precision: NATO operations over the Balkans, including the Kosovo conflict of 1999, Afghanistan in 2002 and Iraq in 2003. A flight commander on 23 Squadron, in 2012 he took over as OC 8 Squadron. Jim retired in 2023 as the RAF's ISTAR Force Deputy Commander but remains a part-time reservist.

CREWS CONTROL

For a number of reasons – not least what were then mysteriously described as 'the vagaries of the service' – I found myself arriving at RAF Waddington on the evening of Sunday 2 February 1997 as the first true ab initio navigator trainee to be posted to

the then still relatively new E-3D Sentry. Within the AWACS community it was known simply as 'the D' or, to the Fighter Control sub-group, 'the Jet' – the only flying opportunity available to that normally subterranean cadre of bunker-dwellers. The RAF's fleet of seven aircraft and their 8 Squadron crews had already established themselves in Balkan skies as probably the most credible AWACS force in the world.

Jim Beldon.

Acquired with great urgency following the Nimrod AEW (airborne early warning) debacle of 1986, the Sentry was a rare (and, it has to be admitted, probably accidental) triumph of UK MoD procurement. It was unique at that time among its NATO, US and French stablemates through being equipped with electronic support measures (ESM) and, like the French E-3F Sentries which were manufactured alongside the UK jets, had the ability to refuel from both USAF flying boom and RAF probe-and-drogue tankers. Together with the increased range and endurance yielded by its new and highly efficient CFM-56 turbofan engines, this provided enormous operational flexibility.

Whilst former Shackleton aircrew and ground crew were still very much in evidence on the Sentry force that I joined, it had become a very much broader kirk by that point, with one of its major strengths the diversity of skills, knowledge and experience it embodied. Former VC10 and Lightning pilots, flight engineers from all types of large aircraft, Phantom and Canberra navigators, ground avionics experts and fighter allocators, all brought the best of their worlds to the aircraft, giving it arguably the most knowledgeable cadre of operators together in a single aircraft type. Little wonder they were good – indeed excellent – at what they did. With all the objectivity I can muster, I *do* think the fleet and its people were at their very best in my first three-year stint on the Sentry. They benefited from extraordinarily high flying rates, depth of knowledge of their principal theatre of operations (the aforementioned Balkans) and an enviable serviceability record that kept skills sharp and morale high. We were blessed with fine and plentiful engineers who invariably could provide a 'spare' when the prime jet was unserviceable. These rare occasions led to an E-3D crew's greatest complaint about life in that era: the 'bag drag', when compelled to move from one aircraft to another.

Such happy circumstances were maintained for a while, but my later incarnations on the force were characterised by limited aircraft availability, low experience levels and generally sub-optimal morale. Events had taken their cumulative toll. Operations over Afghanistan in 2001–03 and Iraq in 2003, coupled with the failure to secure the 'Eagle' upgrade,[15] were followed by a budgetary measure that resulted in a reduction in front-line engineer establishment by a third and the simultaneous removal of access to the RAF Waddington 'Alpha' hangar in favour of its use for depth engineering, which effectively put it beyond front-line use. Maintenance normally conducted in

---

15 Amongst other upgrades, Project Eagle would have included an enhanced mission computer and modern ESM equipment. It would have resulted in greater mission crew capacity and likely have maintained Sentry's relevance for another decade.

An 8 Squadron E-3D Sentry over Iraq.

the hangar either took place outside (when wind conditions allowed) or, more often than not, was delayed.

The operational contributions made by the Sentry were as profound as they were largely unsung, but in that era when aviators around the world met – whether at Red Flag at Nellis AFB or at the Royal International Air Tattoo in the Cotswolds – it was far from uncommon to receive genuine plaudits. It might be a friendly slap on the back from a bear-like USAF B-1 pilot, or meeting a tiny, smiling Italian F-104 Starfighter pilot whose day might have been considerably worse had it not been for a calm British voice using the 'Magic' callsign. On one memorable occasion, one of the RAF Sentry's most revered tactical directors (TDs) – an ex-NCO flight lieutenant fighter controller – was sent a stars and stripes flag from an F-117A Nighthawk pilot, who had been shot down over Serbia and whose rescue this TD had coordinated. If the incidents recounted below are less dramatic, they represent significant steps in my professional education as an airman.

By the time the Kosovo conflict kicked off in March 1999, I had been on 8 Squadron for just over 18 months. I knew the aircraft well, and according to my contemporaneous F5000[16] was assessed as 'above average' and 'one of the best navigators on the squadron'. Looking back on this a quarter of a century later, such

16 Individual Record of Service – Flying Personnel.

a grading was probably more a reflection of potential rather than actual performance and was arguably premature. Notwithstanding, I was meticulous (the charts and logs I kept bear testimony to that at least), I knew the operating area well and had learnt when to pass advice and when to shut up. I liked my crewmates, and I had been accepted into the clan.

So much for the background. My first tale revolves around an RV with a KC-135R tanker over the Adriatic shortly after the onset of hostilities with Serbia in March 1999. The tanking part of what was a night sortie proved uneventful; it was the pressure to execute the aerial ballet to hook up with our mate in the first place that caused the problem. The flight deck crew of an E-3D comprised the pilot captain, co-pilot, flight engineer and navigator. On this particular crew, the ages of the team were split down the centreline, with the young captain and navigator on the port side, and the considerably older co-pilot and flight engineer on the starboard. All were flight lieutenants except for the flight engineer, who was a very experienced, highly revered and, it has to be said, somewhat feared, master aircrew – effectively a senior flying warrant officer. A giant of a man, the worst things that could ever occur to this particular leviathan were either to have to crawl into the claustrophobic aft lower lobe of the jet to close an uncooperative auxiliary power unit door, or, even worse, for someone to get between him and his steak on the barbecue. He was, in short, no shrinking violet. The captain, in his late 20s, had established himself as a fine handling pilot and crew captain, and was rightly proud that he been appointed as captain on the RAF's most valuable aircraft when he was a flying officer. He was, however, given to the odd tempestuous outburst.

The sortie itself was flown from our forward operating base in Aviano in northern Italy, right in the middle of Operation Allied Force – the NATO air campaign aimed at preventing genocide in Kosovo. The chain of events before and during the sortie pressed all the pilot's grumpy buttons. First of all, the jet snagged on crew-in because the overhead air refuelling light bulbs were unserviceable and needed changing – a matter the captain, with some justification, believed should have been checked, spotted and dealt with by the ground crew. The delay immediately put pressure on our RV time with the tanker. Then, having overcome that issue, an over-taxed air traffic controller issued taxi instructions that led us down the northern taxiway, only for us to come to a grinding halt because it was blocked by an ordnance lorry unloading its cargo of precision bombs to the Nighthawk detachment. It took forever, with every estimate for completion being superseded by further delay. The captain was, for want of a better expression, 'doing his nut' on the radio.

All the while fuel and time burned, and we were no longer just in jeopardy of losing our RV with the endurance-giving tanker, but also of being late on station for our mission, potentially leaving a gap in the vital radar cover and coordination service AWACS existed to provide. By the time the ordnance truck scuttled off the taxiway, the captain had reached such a height of fury that he was, by any objective measure, unsafe to fly. But this was war, and we had to go, so I held my own reservations, as I suppose the others did. The transit to the tanker racetrack over the Adriatic was conducted with the barest essential chat on the flight deck; in any case, the Mach warning bell's incessantly repeating 'ding-a-ling' made conversation difficult as we raced south and then east. We nevertheless met the tanker, took the fuel and, as we set course for the orbit area, the flight engineer and I made our calculations and conferred off-headset to agree a 'Bingo' time – the latest time at which we would be able to leave our mission orbit area to arrive safely back at base on minimum fuel (enough to conduct an approach with sufficient reserves to divert to another airfield and land on vapours there if necessary). Just as the flight engineer and I concluded our conference, the captain declared a Bingo time to the TD, who duly relayed it to the Combined Air Operations Centre, whose plan for our relief would be refined on the basis of the information passed.

Normal operating procedure dictated that the Bingo calculated by the navigator and flight engineer would be passed to the captain, who would perhaps adjust the calculated time to avoid over-promising; but normally the supporting cast's recommendation would be scrutinised and agreed without issue. On this occasion, the captain's decision not to consult his aides elicited a thunderous off-headset explosion from the flight engineer: "Nav, did he ask you what the Bingo was?" When I replied in the negative, all hell broke loose on the intercom between the captain and the flight engineer. It turned out that the captain had declared an unsolicited Bingo because on the previous sortie the flight engineer had passed the Bingo time directly to the TD on request – something that hadn't caused any wrath at the time nor was discussed as a debrief point. Anyhow, for whatever reason, the captain had been brooding on this apparent act of insubordination and had taken his first chance to put the flight engineer back in his box. Not wishing to spend the next nine hours in a confined space in a toxic and potentially dangerous environment, I attempted to pour oil on troubled waters and declared I would make a round of teas and coffees in the galley at the rear of the jet. "Good idea, Nav," the flight engineer dolefully remarked just before I unplugged my headset. It was clear battle was likely to recommence in my absence. Nonetheless, applying the theory that 'everything is better after a cup of tea', I set forth to create the leaf-based elixir, wondering why the co-pilot had done absolutely nothing to help moderate the situation. I was puzzled.

The co-pilot – around 50 years of age – was no tyro. He had been on type for six months longer than I had, but unlike me, had thousands of hours' experience behind him; he had captained Shackletons and Nimrods and served as a QFI. He was, in my view, ideally placed to steady the proverbial ship and coax us back to equilibrium. Instead, he did nothing – absolutely nothing. Except, one supposes, monitor the autopilot, because by the time the last drop of milk had been poured into the fourth cup of tea the puce-faced captain had arrived in the galley area and delivered a soliloquy of somewhat un-Shakespearian content. Enraged and wagging a pointed finger as he goose-stepped back and forth between the galley and the folded bunks, he disgorged a hitherto unrevealed (and most probably erroneous) canon of knowledge of Air Force Law and Queen's Regulations – mighty volumes which, I was being persuaded, had apparently been created with the sole objective of ejecting a certain master aircrew air engineer from Aviano to Waddington (although the solution to the problem of replacing the engineer was not revealed). I was, to say the least, a little disappointed that the captain's temper had found yet another afterburner setting. Things did not look good. However, as the jabbing hand reached its apex, I thrust the paper teacup into his grip and made him drink it. We chatted about the sortie – the accumulation of pressures that had been brought to bear and how, really, all things were now well. He calmed down a bit, or at least for the flight to continue in a tersely borderline professional manner.

The stress on the young pilot was tremendous. I hadn't been in his position of authority, and nor had the flight engineer – so we were insulated to a degree from the ultimate responsibility held by the captain. The co-pilot, in my view, should have been able to identify with the captain's situation and exert a calming influence. He failed in this respect, and so it came as no surprise that a few months later when he was upgraded to captaincy, he lasted no time at all before being surreptitiously posted back to the training world. There he was clearly happier, although I pitied his students. I learnt about character that night, and how strength of character needs to be carefully exercised in a team environment. It was, by some margin, the worst crew experience of my career.

We were a safe unit when we landed, but we had been a reckless ship at the start of the night. In the end, the crew remained intact, and an uneasy truce remained in place for the remainder of the deployment. Both the captain and the engineer confided in me privately on the ground, with one memorable silver lining from the notoriously critical flight engineer: "I know I'm a good engineer, and I *suppose* you think you're a good navigator." It was probably the greatest professional compliment I ever received. What else did I learn? Well, I suppose, the adage 'one team, one fight' was apposite. On a flight shortly afterwards, a bona fide Serbian air force plan to shoot down an AWACS was reported by intelligence. Thankfully, by that time, our focus had returned to fighting the enemy rather than ourselves.

My second significant recollection concerns the RC-135S 'Cobra Ball' – an aircraft optimised for detecting and locating ballistic missile launches – and occurred in March 2003 during Operation Telic. Until very shortly before the conflict, we thought we would be based in Turkey in support of a northern offensive, but geopolitics put paid to that idea. Instead we deployed to the gargantuan Prince Sultan Air Base in Saudi Arabia, otherwise known as Al Kharj and, to those deployed, referred to either as 'P-Sab' or 'Al's Garage'. Flying-wise, the airspace on the Saudi–Iraq border was congested, with multiple ISR (intelligence, surveillance and reconnaissance) operating areas being tightly packed and de-conflicted by altitude. Naturally enough, aircraft needed to climb to reach their assigned operating altitudes, and it was the 'elevator' between transit and operating heights that posed fratricidal risk. No worries for the mighty AWACS, however; we had seemingly perfect situational understanding in the form of the battle-proven AN/APY-2 rotating 'Eye of Providence' sitting atop the fuselage. Nonetheless, in order to complicate Iraqi surface-to-air missile shooters' targeting solutions, all coalition aircraft were forbidden from transmitting their altitude data (a Mode C function), but it also meant that our IFF (identification, friend or foe) system was incapable of interrogating the altitude of friendly aircraft.

As we flew towards our operating area in the pitch black of the Al Jowf province of Saudi Arabia, we turned north to the western desert of Iraq, where our role was to coordinate time-sensitive targeting: in essence, to orchestrate the rapid application of kinetic force against pop-up Scud ballistic missiles. Suffice to say, although crude, they were weapons of strategic effect – as had been demonstrated by Saddam Hussein in 1991 when such weapons were targeted at Israel with the aim of inviting Israeli retaliation and fracturing the multi-national coalition. Our role, and that of the Cobra Ball, was clearly important in that sideshow of the war, and so it came to be that our operating areas would be closely juxtaposed. The Cobra Ball was a rare beast – there are only three on the USAF's books these days – so it wasn't airborne 24/7 as was the UK's AWACS. Their sorties were at night when the Scuds, cloaked by darkness, were more likely to scuttle out of their hidey-holes and launch at their (assumed-to-be) Israeli targets.

As we climbed towards our orbit area, our mission crew colleagues were busy exchanging handover information with the off-going RAF AWACS. It was always an extremely busy time, with datalinks being harmonised, details of legions of tankers' fuel states being exchanged and fighter-bombers being vectored to react to potential threats and avoid collision. The airspace was congested, and our onboard fighter controllers fought through Clausewitzian fog to build their as yet incomplete situational awareness. One member of the mission crew was always assigned the role of 'AWACS monitor' – essentially ensuring that the moving 'pineapple' icon representing the AWACS on their control screens avoided airspace transgressions or mid-air collisions. On that particular night our AWACS monitor was a very experienced operator – in fact, he was the TD in my Kosovo tale above – and had been drafted back to the E-3D from a staff tour as an emergency wartime measure to boost crew complements.

At the front of the jet, I was monitoring the returns from my small Bendix weather radar – unsophisticated, short range, and able to detect 'cloud and clunk (ground)'. It also had a semi-decent ability to detect other aircraft, and one such return travelling down my radar scope on a constant bearing caught my attention. As it maintained its interception course, I asked the AWACS monitor for a radar height on the contact. Distracted by the handover and the need to bring fighter formations under his control 100 miles away, our monitor hadn't spotted the convergence. All was well, however: the radar height of the contact was only 17,000ft and we were at 29,000ft and climbing. "Stop climb," I demanded. A few moments later, a black shape cruised a little above our flight deck windows! Our Cobra Ball companion was similarly climbing to its operating altitude, a little above ours, but we would very probably have 'kissed' on our way up in the elevator.

The reason for our potential mishap? Well, first of all, the airspace coordination order defining the operating altitudes and geographical coordinates of all of the tanker tracks, defensive counter air patrol areas, AWACS and ISR tracks, had only been issued very late in the day, owing to the change in the operational plan caused by Turkey's decision not to host coalition forces. This meant that some planning information was not as robust as it might have been. Incomplete situational awareness, heavy tasking, mission tunnel vision and the information overload created by the handover period were the immediate problems that allowed the situation to develop and go unnoticed. The absence of Mode C – an operational necessity, but one clearly not without risk – made the accurate assessment of height a real challenge. And, it turned out, raw radar assessment of altitude using the AWACS' mission radar was far from reliable.

What saved us? Funnily enough, it had simply been through attending a multi-national coalition briefing – held separately from our UK-only crew brief – that alerted me to the fact that an RC-135V/W Rivet Joint and the RC-135S Cobra Ball were likely to be operating near us that night, and I noted their altitudes and operating areas. I knew the Cobra Ball wouldn't be at 17,000ft, so I effectively called 'bullshit' on our multi-million dollar mission radar, and trusted only the facts I knew, and what my bargain-basement little radar made by a company best known for making washing machines was alerting me to. My captain that night listened, trusted, levelled the jet and flew us under the nose of our unwitting nemesis. What did I learn that night? Scepticism is healthy.

In the light of this second experience, I can't resist a footnote related to the comments on fate in the introduction to the book. Having arranged to meet a collocated US Air National Guard KC-135R crew one stormy night over the Caribbean at a precise point and time, when we joined at the RV we turned out to be 1,000ft separated and 180 degrees out! During the aerial waltz that ensued in radio silence against a backdrop of electromagnetic fireworks, I pondered yet again on the role that luck plays in this flying game of ours.

* * * *

GROUP CAPTAIN ALI McKAY

Ali McKay was one of those talented youngsters good enough to earn a first operational tour on the Lightning after graduating from the RAF College Cranwell. He went on to command 56 Squadron, flying Phantoms at Wattisham. Later, as station commander at RAF Wildenrath in Germany, in March 1989 he was the last to 'solo' on 60 Squadron's aged Pembroke communications aircraft.

FOR TWO PINS

Looking back on a career that started in the Royal Air Force and continued with the John Lewis Partnership, I feel very lucky to have had so much pleasure in spending my working life with two outstanding organisations. Each offered unique challenges and opportunities. One special difference – the RAF let me fly the Lightning. Excitement, a lot of fun, some fear and the occasional moment of pure stupidity emerged. Certainly my experiences on my first Lightning tour provided a rate of maturity through learning that mirrored the exceptional climb rate and overall performance of that most wonderful aircraft.

Ali McKay.

My first tour, towards the end of the sixties, was at Binbrook. Our salubrious married quarter near the cement works at Immingham, 15 miles from base, did nothing to diminish my jealousy of the lads who had postings to Cyprus, Germany and Singapore – despite the incontestable advantage of being able to get ten minutes' instrument meteorological conditions (IMC) whilst driving away from our quarter through the pollution.

On 5 Squadron tension was high. Aircraft serviceability was poor and there was doubt about our ability to deploy all the aircraft to Singapore in a few months' time. The unease grew as I worked my way through the CR programme. Then, a few short months after my arrival, the squadron saw considerable change: a new interim boss posted in, several heads rolling and the threat of more of the same. Feeling vulnerable just doesn't describe it. And I was just about to peak on the stupidity graph.

The boss proved to be a man concerned with results rather than popularity. He was an exceptional and extremely experienced Lightning pilot who did not suffer fools gladly. We were all out to impress where we could – so, no pressure.

Although the serviceability rate had improved, with several aircraft away on missile practice camp, we were down to just three Mk 6 jets. Not being CR, I was back at Binbrook when a short-notice task arrived. Because Saudi Arabia had decided to procure the Lightning and Kuwait was also involved, there was some interest from a South American country as well. So Binbrook Ops got notice that a posse of their air force generals were coming to watch the aircraft in operation.

I was paired up with the boss to fly a performance demo. The brief was very straightforward: "We'll hold off the coast until air traffic control (ATC) tell us the visitors are in place on the runway operational readiness platform (ORP). We'll run in at high speed in fighting wing and after passing over the ORP I'll pull up for a wingover and you'll join in echelon. We'll then proceed to wire the ORP until you call Bingo 2,[17] whereupon we'll go out and position for a very fast run-in and break, followed by overshoots and reheat rotations down to 800lbs per side." I had no questions.

It was a surprisingly warm day, so by the time I got strapped in whilst wearing an immersion suit I'd worked up a good sweat. Then my jet wouldn't start and the sweat was pouring off me as I ran past the boss, who was engines running and impatiently drumming his fingers on the front canopy. Apparently ATC had informed him that the generals were at the entrance to the station. Having slithered into that second cockpit and started up with minimum checks, the boss called for taxi and the chase was on. As I lined up in echelon I had a quick last-minute check around the cockpit. My heart more than missed a beat when I did the pin check and discovered to my horror that the main gun sear (servicing) pin wasn't stowed. Had it been dropped or was it still in place? If still in place then there was no way of me ejecting from the aircraft in an emergency. And the Lightning was prone to emergencies that necessitated ejection. What should I do? Well, it was obvious. I would have to declare my predicament and taxi back. What would the repercussions of that be? Everything seemed to slow down as I fought with my inner self. So what did I do? Suffice to say the next thing I remember was raising the gear and trying to stay as close to the boss as I could. The sweat intensified as the stupidity of my actions sunk in.

The boss really did wind things up over the airfield. I hung onto his wing like glue, hoping that his inevitable survivability would translate into mine. When I was on the outside of the turns looking down through him at the ground I just couldn't believe how low and fast we were. When I was on the inside of the turns I could only imagine how close my wingtip was to the ground. I stuck very close to the boss! At one stage I took some solace from my assessment that even were I able to eject I wouldn't survive given the height we were winging past our visiting generals. On the odd occasion I had a chance to carry out a quick visual sweep of the cockpit essentials, the only thing that came into focus, through the dripping sweat, was that small black hole where the main gun sear should have been stowed.

I was wise to fake an early Bingo call to try and shorten the sortie, but after the break I not so wisely carried out one reheat rotation. More stupidity. I shouldn't have risked any – the boss did three. The relief when I landed and decelerated through 90kts still lingers and is impossible to describe. After shutdown I very quickly unstrapped, stood up and removed the pin and stowed it. Even the ground crew were

---

17 A relatively low advisory fuel state (lower than Bingo 1), briefed to take account of specific sortie conditions, e.g. weather and diversions.

A 5 Squadron Lightning with refuelling probe and overwing tanks. (Ian Black)

not going to have any hint about what had occurred.

The debrief was reasonably short and sweet with the boss complimenting me on hanging on in there. But I did get a bollocking for using up my fuel so quickly. I just went 'ziplip' on the whole thing but stowed the experience firmly in my 'I learnt about flying – and about myself – from that' locker.

And to this day I feel ashamed that I didn't have the courage to do the right thing and abort the sortie. I demonstrated weakness – got my priorities wrong – on that occasion, but thereafter I progressed through life with a markedly different attitude when facing up to pressure. Furthermore, I'm pleased to be still around to tell the tale.

A sobering thought is that in the 12 months following that formation sortie, the RAF lost 13 Lightnings; four of the pilots were killed. One of these was the USAF exchange pilot serving on the same squadron, more of which below. Ironically, I was number 13 on that list. My ejection was successful – the main gun sear pin had been stowed.

UNAUTHORISED TOUCH-AND-GO

It was always hard work on the squadron, but averaging around 30 hours a month in such a fantastic aircraft was utter joy and I would regularly pinch myself to confirm that I really was there in that cockpit enjoying such an amazing privilege. However, the task – driven by the perceived threat – often saw us flying this demanding aircraft in challenging conditions where the margins for error were minimal. As a measure of this, and to update the previous statistics, in the two-and-a-half years I spent at Binbrook, the Lightning force lost more than 20 aircraft and, sadly, several pilots too.

Throughout the late 1960s and early 1970s the nature of the Soviet threat saw us tackling more and more complex target profiles, particularly at low level. Using the radar at night to close to 300 yards on a low-level, high-speed target was not easy, particularly when the target had its navigation lights turned off. Furthermore, the altimeter error on the Lightning, which would see it winding down towards zero as you accelerated to high speed closing with the target, could be a trifle distracting. That said, the training regime was thorough and as long as you applied a disciplined approach to your task and understood your aircraft and its weapon systems you could operate in the most marginal of conditions. By the time I was about halfway through my first tour I was pretty confident in my ability to take on most target profiles. But one night that confidence took a bit of a battering.

I was carrying out interceptions against a Canberra target from 85 Squadron, also based at Binbrook. The moment I heard the distinct Irish lilt of the Canberra pilot I realised the target was being flown by my next-door neighbour, Rory Colhoun. For the first couple of intercepts his lights were on but I requested 'lights out' for my final run. Once I stabilised 300 yards behind I could just make out the rough shape of the Canberra and decided to close in a bit further and achieved quite a good visual at around 200 yards.

It was a reasonably clear night with a calm sea and I was aware of a line of lights along the coast from Hornsea up to Bridlington and Flamborough Head. Anyway, time to give my neighbour a wake-up call. So I pushed the throttles forward and selected reheat. As I closed the last few yards I could see the glow from the Canberra cockpit and rattled past on his starboard side; looking over my left shoulder, I could feel my aircraft accelerating away rapidly. To compensate for the impression that I was climbing, I was conscious of pushing the stick forward – but at the same time my peripheral vision picked up a change in perspective of the coastal lights. This all happened in seconds but my immediate and instinctive reaction was to pull on the stick and pull hard. As I did so, there was a dull thud – I wasn't sure what it was but I certainly heard something. I confess to being pretty shaken up from that point right through to my recovery into Binbrook.

I became convinced I had done a quick touch-and-go on the North Sea. When I finally climbed out of the cockpit I rather sheepishly took my torch and carried out a close inspection of the ventral (belly) tank, particularly the vanes at the rear. I could see no physical damage, but was that salt spray streaking on the ventral? No need for any forensic testing – the lesson learnt was a severe one. Later in the night-flying bar, I had the opportunity to talk to Rory. The truth is he took me aside to explain that he was a very unhappy bunny – his starboard engine had nearly snuffed it as I went past. I was too embarrassed to explain that I had nearly snuffed it myself.

This incident occurred in April 1970. I learnt just a few weeks later that a close colleague and fellow Scot[18] had been killed in Singapore when his Lightning hit the sea carrying out low-level interceptions. Then in September came the incident mentioned above: our popular USAF exchange officer, Bill Schaffner, was killed in similar fashion. Sobering thoughts indeed.

RUNNING ON FUMES

Every Lightning pilot, bar none, has a story about coming up short on the fuel stakes. Several times I was forced to make difficult decisions due to low fuel where the worst outcome was ending up at a base rather than Binbrook. However, on one occasion, despite landing back at Binbrook, I faced a scenario that was well out of my comfort zone.

The squadron was working up for the Allied Forces Central Europe (AFCENT) air defence competition and I was chosen as one of the team of six. Our competition was mainly Belgian F-104s and USAF F-4s, and the most difficult of the four profiles was the supersonic event. In the work-up we agreed that we would liaise with the Belgian squadron on practice profiles, in particular the identification task, which involved getting alongside the target pretty much in close formation to read off some key letters on the tailplane. The judges at the various radar units would not clear the 'killing' fighter in for a head-on shot unless the correct letters were read out. There was only limited time allowed from when the target crossed the competition start line and the aim was simply to achieve the fastest possible 'ident' and kill. Sounds straightforward – but not when the target is travelling at Mach 1.4 at 40,000ft plus.

On this particular day we agreed to provide two individual Lightning targets for two F-104s from Beauvechain. The first Belgian aircraft was late taking off so I had to hang around a bit, but eventually completed my target run at Mach 1.3 at 42,000ft. The F-104 messed up his intercept geometry, ending up with very little overtake about two miles astern. He then ran out of time. It was about then that

18 Flying Officer John Webster was killed on 26 May 1970.

we were informed that the second Lightning was unserviceable and would not be available as a target. However, the second F-104 was already airborne. I was then asked if I could provide another target run. My fuel gauges were already hinting that it would be foolish to agree, but I thought I could manage one further run at around Mach 1.1. So we set that up and the F-104 carried out a successful ident. I watched him 'contrailing' all the way in when I should have been paying attention to the fuel gauges.

When I did finally glance at my fuel level, along with realising I was way out over the North Sea and still heading east, it caused my heart to miss more than a few beats. Next came mild panic. However, I managed to control my emotions and take immediate actions: shut down number two engine, transfer fuel to the port side, turn back towards Binbrook and use excess energy to climb. A call to Patrington, the controlling radar unit, but I'm out of luck: no tankers available.

At this stage I did not declare an emergency, although I did mention to Patrington that I might have to declare fuel priority when I was handed over to Binbrook radar. Unfortunately, my initial calculations indicated that I would probably run out of fuel around Spurn Point. My spirits lifted a bit when Patrington informed me that the weather at Binbrook had improved slightly and the mandatory radar approach restriction had been lifted; even better, the runway in use had changed in my favour. So I concentrated on smooth and accurate flying, maximising range, and discovered again what an amazing aircraft my Lightning was. She just slipped through the air gently, losing altitude, but using little fuel. I had considered diverting but there was little choice in terms of either location or weather – and I certainly didn't want to get involved in a complex TACAN approach procedure at one of the USAF bases. Fortunately, my fear of flaming out around Spurn Point diminished as my steed floated past the headland at a decent height, but the fuel state dictated that I continue to apply the absolute minimum of control inputs lest I upset the aircraft's balance. I had read somewhere in Pilots' Notes that you should avoid sideslip at low fuel states as it can result in an increase in unusable fuel.

A little earlier on the recovery I had watched two Lightnings turn in towards me. I ignored them and continued to float towards Binbrook; I was now visual with the field and, fortunately, beautifully lined-up with the runway in use. At this stage all I had declared was 'fuel priority'. I decided to leave it at that because when I went to the tower frequency it was obvious that there was no other circuit traffic. I informed the local controller that I would be delaying putting my wheels down and I have to say that both he and the caravan controller remained pretty cool as my 'three greens' failed to appear until just moments before touchdown. The rumble of those wheels on the tarmac was sweet music indeed. After clearing the runway onto the ORP, I remember making some lame and untruthful comment about having a fluctuating services pressure gauge and would therefore shut down and be towed in. The truth was that I didn't have enough fuel to taxi back.

Sometime later, as I sat in the crewroom feeling ashamed but deeply relieved, my flight commander burst in through the door and demanded to know who was in the single Lightning recovering to Binbrook around 1030. I confessed it was me and he bellowed, "Call yourself a fighter pilot? Didn't you see us turning in on you?" I tamely replied that I had seen them. "Then why didn't you react?" he bawled. I had no choice but to confess that I didn't have enough fuel to react. "Then why didn't you waggle your bloody wings to acknowledge you had seen us?" he said. "I didn't have enough fuel to waggle!" I replied. I was concerned that if I made the slightest control movement I might lodge a few pounds of that precious juice where it might prove irrecoverable. At this stage my flight commander suggested a quiet and private chat. Before that, I visited the line hut and explained to the chief technician running the line that my aircraft did not have a hydraulic services problem. "Thank you, Sir," he replied, adding with a wink, "Just filled her up with fuel. Didn't realise these beauties ran on fumes!"

By way of a footnote, around two months later we actually won the air defence competition.

* * * *

GROUP CAPTAIN DICK NORTHCOTE

A Cranwell graduate, Dick Northcote began his operational career as a DFGA (day fighter/ground attack) pilot on 208 Squadron in Bahrain. Next came the Phantom: 54 Squadron at Coningsby initially and then an exchange tour with the USAF. Conversion to the air defence role followed, first as a flight commander on 111 Squadron at Leuchars, and later as the first CO of the re-formed 74 Squadron, flying the F-4J(UK). He retired from the RAF in 1991 to join British Aerospace.

EXPECT THE UNEXPECTED

Both these brief tales stem from my time with the USAF as a squadron leader in the early 1970s. I was with the 13th Tactical Fighter Squadron, an extremely professional outfit with just the right amount of aggression, confidence and humour. But as many

Dick Northcote.

of us know, flying fighters can have its moments.

In late November 1975 at MacDill AFB in Florida I was serving as an instructor pilot on the Phantom F-4E. I was scheduled for a 1-v-1 dissimilar air-combat sortie with a T-38 Talon from one of the USAF Aggressor squadrons simulating a Russian fighter. In those days the Aggressor units consisted of specially selected pilots who were trained in Russian fighter tactics.

I was leading the sortie from the back seat of the Phantom with a student in the front and briefed how the training mission would take place. The basic idea was that we would start together line abreast and on the call of "Outwards turn for combat, go," both aircraft would turn away from each other and continue in opposite directions, maintaining height and speed until about 20 miles apart. The call would then be "Inwards turn for combat, go," whereupon we would turn back towards each other and the fight would be on. During the brief, the Aggressor pilot highlighted the type of tactics that could be expected from a MiG-type fighter and explained that on this occasion he would use just one of those tactics to see how we coped, as it was the student's first dissimilar combat sortie. I was impressed by his professionalism and knowledge and looked forward

USAF F-4 with an F-5 Aggressor.

to learning more about air combat, particularly as at the time we didn't have a similar set-up in the RAF.

The format of this sortie, however, was one I had flown many times before, Phantom v Phantom, and the set-up was simple and safe. Or so I thought. My student was flying the sortie and the Aggressor pilot was making the calls. I was thinking ahead to the exciting part of the fight when I heard the call, "Outwards turn for combat, go." Suddenly I saw the T-38 start to turn towards us! I grabbed the controls – fortunately, I had a stick in the back – and pushed hard downwards while watching the T-38 flash over the top of us, perilously close, a matter of just a few feet. There then followed an exchange of expletives and I asked the Aggressor if he had a problem. He replied in the affirmative and said he would see us back on the ground.

During the debrief, I was amazed to find that the problem was the Aggressor pilot himself. He could not explain exactly why he had become confused and turned the wrong way and apologised profusely. He said he would explain to his CO what had happened and consider whether to file an airmiss[19] or not. As a fairly new exchange officer, I felt I would have to leave that to him and his CO, so I did. As I heard nothing further, I guessed that it was considered an exigency of air combat by the Aggressor team and no more was ever said.

I'm not sure if I learnt a great deal from that sortie other than to expect the unexpected, regardless of who you're flying with. Certainly the incident strongly reinforced the principle of 'look before you turn'.

Talking of the unexpected, it was on that same tour that the unexpected happened again. I was tasked with doing an air test on one of the squadron's aircraft. The sortie was to take place on a Sunday when air activity over the Gulf of Mexico was minimal, allowing us to take the jet up to Mach 2 out over the sea. This part of the air test was the last to be done with the WSO (weapon systems operator, or navigator in RAF-speak) having run through a checklist of all the other items required on the test. I pointed the aircraft away from base, selected full reheat on the throttles and started the run. I'd never before gone much over Mach 1.6, so was quite excited about hitting Mach 2.

Out over the sea at around 40,000ft with not a cloud in the sky (it was Florida after all) there was no visual awareness of speed, but just looking at the dial hitting Mach 2 was thrilling enough. The thrill suddenly became mild panic when I saw a fire warning light come on. Experience had taught me to check carefully which

---

19 A formal report of a potential collision risk.

engine had the problem as the warning lights for both engines were on the right side of the control panel. It was the right engine and I warned the WSO, declared a Mayday, gingerly came out of reheat on both engines and then slowly started a turn back towards base while throttling the right engine further back to idle. At that point, the fire warning light went out and all other indications were normal (which was rather encouraging), but at high Mach numbers the turning circle is huge and my nerves were somewhat on edge as we slowly got back onto a heading for base. With no further indications of any problem I decided to leave the engine at idle and get back on the ground ASAP.

We soon landed at MacDill, fortunately our nearest airfield, and as we taxied in we were met with the usual gaggle of fire engines and safety trucks. We climbed out of the aircraft and were driven back to the engineering section to complete an incident report. There I was met by a large USAF sergeant and explained what had happened. "Oh," he drawled, "didn't we warn you? That often happens on the Mach 2 run on this aircraft." I signed the report silently thinking, 'Hmm – thanks a lot. I hadn't expected that'.

The first incident here bears an uncanny resemblance to one involving another exchange officer, one of Dick's erstwhile colleagues, flying F-4Cs at Luke AFB at the same time. Told during his arrival interview: "Beware the turkey in the front seat. He's out to kill you and given half a chance he will," the advice proved prophetic. Later in his tour, during a 2-v-1 Aggressor sortie involving two Phantoms and a single T-38, one of his squadron's aircraft collided with the Aggressor, resulting in four fatalities. The cause, however, was never established. [Ed.]

CHAPTER 7
WING COMMANDERS' WISDOM

WING COMMANDER IAN GAWN

After earning his wings as a Cranwell cadet, Ian Gawn's flying career came to a premature end in 1969 when he was grounded medically. After a decade or so as a civilian and Territorial Army officer, working first in the aerospace industry and then local government, in 1980 he rejoined the RAF as a secretarial officer. After a final tour at Wyton, Wing Commander Gawn returned once again to civilian life, finally retiring to France after ten years as secretary of the Royal Lymington Yacht Club.

A NARROW ESCAPE

I had always expected that my flying ability, such as it was, would send me to transport or the dreaded V-Force, so I was surprised at the end of my Cranwell course in December 1965 to be streamed fast jet and sent to 4 FTS (Flying Training School) at RAF Valley for 22 Gnat Course. At the time the Red Arrows, led by Squadron Leader Ray Hanna, were flying the diminutive Gnat, the team having increased to nine aircraft from the seven with which his predecessor, Squadron Leader Lee Jones, had begun. So there we were, a bunch of young hopefuls, most of us from Cranwell but with a number of guys who had trained at the other flying training schools, to fly what the RAF's aerobatic team flew: cool. However, one of the first things we learnt was that we had not necessarily escaped the V-Force. It would prove the destiny for a number of us. Sadly, one of these would die as the co-pilot of a Victor tanker that collided with a Canberra over Norfolk in 1968.

Ian Gawn in a Chipmunk.

After the training regime at Cranwell, Valley saw us treated differently – more like we might end up as adults. We had a taste of 'station duties', but the whole thrust of the place was to get us to a standard of flying to fit us for whichever OCU we would eventually go to. For most of us, first choice was the Lightning or Hunter, followed by the Canberra, especially the PR.9. Bottom of the list were the Vulcan and Victor.

After ground school and a number of simulator sorties it was time to fly the aeroplane. For a reason I cannot recall, I flew Ex 1, 'Famil' (Exercise 1 was 'Familiarisation'), with an instructor other than my primary QFI. It was basically an instructor's benefit: low level around Wales, I think the A5 and Llyn Ogwen figured somewhere, ending going up Snowdon at 250ft, rolling, pulling down the other side before returning for a run-and-break back at Valley. Ex 1 was fun and exciting – until the run-and-break converted to a downwind leg at 1,000ft and, "You have control". My brain, still operating at JP speed, caught up with the aeroplane passing Holyhead, but we ended up with a passable circuit and landing. Twenty-something years later I repeated the sortie, this time in a Hawk with the same instructor, by then the station commander, whilst I was supposed to be carrying out the command accountant's inspection.

The Gnat was a challenging aircraft, especially in the event of hydraulic failure and loss of powered flying controls. Our trainee fighter pilot then became a one-armed paper hanger, with a need for more hands than evolution provided. Engine failure was an exponential leap from hydraulic failure, to the extent that after a couple of fatal accidents a flying order was issued that in the event of engine failure a solo student was to eject; an instructor was to use his discretion, then eject.

Most of my flying was with a Rhodesian instructor. This was just after Rhodesia declared independence and the UK imposed an oil embargo. My instructor was not best pleased, especially as it meant his elderly mum was forced to ride around on a moped. On this particular day the sortie was a low-level navigation exercise followed by a run-and-break to land. I guess we were about mid-course, so self-confidence was unjustifiably high, indeed it could have been labelled overconfidence. I reckoned I had the Gnat hacked. Well, this time the aeroplane reckoned it had me hacked, and nearly the instructor too.

We hit the 'target' almost to the second, and set up for the recovery. I was cleared for the run-and-break. I obviously had not listened too hard for the wind; in our absence it had swung to a crosswind and strengthened a bit. Across the airfield at 250ft and I guess 300kts, the procedure was to close the throttle and pull up and round, half-undercarriage for the airbrake function, and downwind checks. A bit closer than planned but we have this under control – no worries. 'Finals' call, throttle adjusted ... Aah, we're going through the centreline. Just pull a bit harder to tighten the turn ... Ooh heck! What's happening? We're going down like a lift and I'm fresh out of ideas. Then from the back: "I have control." I wasn't sure at the time what action my QFI took. Unload, I guess, level the wings and fly away breathing hard. The debrief in the air was to the point. "If you'd been on your own you would be (expletive deleted) dead." Not a lot was said in the debriefing room, other than a brief explanation of what aerodynamics had nearly done to us – or rather what I had nearly let it do to us.

I completed the course, but later realised I was cheated out of the last five hours of a 70-hour course. One Tuesday, after a long weekend, I was greeted at breakfast by my South African flight commander with a brief, "Are you packed?" My quizzical response was greeted by: "You're on the evening train from Holyhead, and you had best look at the programme." It revealed a busy day: dual, simulator, solo and FHT (final handling test). Only after that would I learn where the train would take me. Some nine hours later I was told I had passed my FHT and that I was posted to the Canberra strike role. Oh, and my course started yesterday. So I missed all the end of course festivities, and I never made it to the 'strike' part of the course either. I was posted to Signals Command in an entirely different role – more of which below.

Some 50 years later my QFI and I found ourselves on the same aviation website. A few days later I got a message. He said it was the apology he should have made 50 years previously. He had been pretty happy with how I handled the aircraft, and had nor foreseen me getting us into that sort of difficulty landing in a crosswind. He'd suddenly latched onto there being a problem because my breathing rate had gone up exponentially. He was sorry he had let it happen. What a gentleman!

My five months at Valley in 1966, flying Petter's[20] 'pocket rocket', still remains one of the highlights of a varied career, in and out – and sometimes on the fringes – of the aviation world. But the flying lesson I learnt – beware tightening the finals turn in a crosswind, especially in a swept-wing aeroplane – is one that's stayed with me forever.

WHAT IS YOUR BREAK-OFF HEIGHT?

I arrived at 231 OCU at Bassingbourn two days after the start of my Canberra long strike course. I had never expected to fly Lightnings or Hunters, but in those days the Canberra was still a pretty hot ship, so after the relative sophistication of the Gnat I cheerfully began relearning the use of flying instruments of yesteryear.

Destined for Cyprus or the Far East, I was crewed with a first-tourist nav plotter and a former master nav (his daughter was older than me!) as nav/bomb aimer. The Canberra was pleasant though challenging to fly well, but the cockpit showed its age – an ergonomic slum. Its Achilles heel was asymmetric flight. Practice engine failures killed crews in my first and last tours, and a few in between as well. Before going 'solo' I was re-crewed with an ex-V-Force navigator, destined for Germany and the B(I)8. We did the 'dual-to-solo' exercises together. The trainee pilot was first sent off solo in the T4 with a vacant instructor's seat. Next the instructor flew a demonstration sortie in the B2 with the student pilot on the (non-ejection) Rumbold seat; the instructor then got out and the student pilot flew his first 'solo' in the B2. Needless to say, navigators had to endure these somewhat challenging sorties with their usual stoicism.

Just as I was about to start learning to operate the aeroplane as a weapon of war, delivering a nuclear weapon, I was told that the plan had changed. I was to fly my FHT 'now', and after that learn my posting. Where had I heard this before? So, late in the afternoon, test passed, I was informed that I was due 'yesterday' at RAF Watton. I had no idea where it was: in darkest Norfolk, I learnt. Long since closed, it was home to the RAF's signals and electronic assets, including 98 and 115 Squadrons, who

---

20 E.W. 'Teddy' Petter, the Gnat's designer.

flight-checked ground navigation and approach aids, and 97 Squadron, who were 'quiet' targets; in other words they had only basic or no electronic kit to rough up the fighter's radar. There was also a lonely Hastings that flew the Inspectorate of Radio Services, who went round the world listening to RAF radio conversations, checking for correct procedure, security, etc. No. 51 Squadron, who at the time no one talked about, had three Comets and a number of non-standard-looking Canberras, and whom we now know flew close to Eastern Bloc borders as electronic intelligence gatherers, a hazardous occupation at the best of times.

The newest arrival at Watton was 360 Squadron, formed from parts of 97 Squadron and 831 NAS, a Fleet Air Arm ECM (electronic countermeasures) trials unit, to provide ECM training for all three services. Having begun to form only weeks before, it was short of aircraft. The unit was due to receive the Canberra T17, but for the time being flew a motley collection of T4 and B2 aircraft, one of which, WD935, was the sixth Canberra built and still in the old black and grey colour scheme.

I was the only first tourist, not only on the squadron but in the whole of Signals Command. Additionally, a quarter of both aircrew and ground crew were Fleet Air Arm, whose customs and practices were different from those I learnt during my RAF training. I was also the only pilot on the squadron, indeed in the command, with a 'white' instrument rating, which required the addition of 500ft to the decision height for any landing aid. This was to have a significant bearing on a later incident.

We began by providing 'quiet', i.e. without an ECM capability, targets for ground radar stations and the RAF's fighters, and occasionally for RN warships. Most of the squadron were third and fourth tourists, so lots of experience for a tyro like me to draw on. Soon, the long awaited T17s, the Canberra reminiscent of a warthog, began to arrive. Looking new and shiny, they were actually reworked B2s, with the bomb doors welded closed, and with slightly less power. This was because the substantial electrical power for the jammers was provided by an engine air bleed to turbo generators, and there was still no engine anti-icing, which complicated the let-down in icing condition as there were now no bomb doors to open to increase drag. Over the next few months we developed our tactics to give the best possible training to Lightnings and Phantoms, RN ships and shore training establishments, AEW Gannets, and occasionally army gunnery radars.

On the day of the aforementioned incident, I was in one of six T17s that took off from Ballykelly in Northern Ireland to play with several AEW Gannets in the Western Approaches, then land at St Mawgan. The forecast was good so off we went into the wide blue yonder. We were in a fan-shaped formation several miles apart approaching the Gannets' barrier. The air electronics officers (AEOs) in the back of each Canberra were twiddling knobs to cause maximum disruption to the Gannets' radar (equipment that later ended up under the noses of the 8 Squadron Shackletons). One of the AEOs had got bored and was listening out on HF radio and picked up a change in the weather: fog forming rapidly over the whole of the UK with Shackletons from St Mawgan being diverted, at least one to Gibraltar. There were no diversions available for us. I never did find out what the Gannets did, but the leader of our formation called us together for recovery into St Mawgan, which was when my day started to deteriorate. As number six in the formation, I was at the top of the stack and I suspected the boss had forgotten my white card – or maybe not. Perhaps he was thinking to get the other five down before the boy screwed things up and blocked the runway.

By now a few things were playing on my young mind. Oddly, the first was that one of the rear crew had just become a father and I had better not deprive the child of its dad. It was also clear that my instrument flying, fortunately one of the better arrows in my quiver despite my white card status, was about to get a serious workout. The guys in front of me were all seeing the runway at several hundred feet below my limit, but there was nowhere else to go. Whilst I was captain, my crew were vastly more experienced, so we discussed the options and decided to make one approach not below 125ft on the radalt (radar altimeter), an instrument that gave a read-out of actual height above the terrain. This was way before CRM (crew/cockpit resource management) came into vogue, of course. If we couldn't land, we'd carry out a missed approach, fly over the airfield at 2,000ft, the rear crew would leave courtesy of Messrs Martin-Baker's explosive seats, and I would take the aircraft out over the sea and do likewise.

With five aircraft at last safely on the ground, my rear crew with straps tight and gear stowed, I set the aircraft up for a radar-monitored instrument landing system (ILS) approach. The AEO could crane his head a bit to see the radalt and the view ahead while the nav had an ASI and altimeter, so they could both monitor the approach. Down through the gloom we went, the ILS needles neatly crossed on the little centre circle. With the nav calling heights and speeds, the AEO called the sudden reduction in radalt height as we crossed the cliffs just before the runway. Then 200ft ... 150ft ... 125ft – at that moment the AEO and I called the lights in the same breath and we were down, following what I could see of the centreline.

A 'follow me' truck was waiting at the end of the runway and led me to the pan where five aircraft and 15 aircrew waited. By this time I had stopped shaking and was wondering what sort of reception I would get. After all, I had broken all the rules – but I had saved the crew and a £2 million aircraft. The engines wound down and the door opened. The boss stuck his head in and said sternly, "Consider yourself severely told off," or something similar. Then, with a warm grin, "I think I owe you a beer". Oddly, the incident was never mentioned again, but we did have a convivial evening in the bar – and I didn't buy a single beer. Next day we set off back to Watton; my white card got us fogged out and we spent the weekend at Manston.

What did I learn about flying from that? Well, some days the cards are stacked in your favour, even though it might not seem like that to start with. Oh, and instrument flying really does matter – almost as much as teamwork!

* * * *

WING COMMANDER JOHN GROGAN

John Grogan joined the RAF in 1964 and flew a variety of fighter aircraft: Hunters with 8 Squadron, Harriers with both 1 and 3 Squadron and Jaguars on 226 OCU. After attending the Indian Staff College in 1981–82 he commanded 27 Squadron, a Tornado GR1 unit. He retired from the RAF in 1987 and flew commercially for several years.

Looking back on a number of experiences I was lucky to survive, there's a common thread: supervision – or rather, lack of it. In some ways the stories recounted here reflect failures in leadership too. I certainly learnt from them.

WHAT ABOUT THE WEATHER?

It all started when I was a student pilot on the JP at Leeming. I was sitting in the crewroom minding my own business when an instructor asked if I would like to do a formation flight to make up a three-ship with a Jordanian student who was just finishing the course. I had already completed my formation phase but happily agreed. There was some discussion about the weather but the final decision was a 'go'. I was to fly as number three of three.

We got to height and I was cleared to do a break-away and rejoin. So I broke away left but, when I reversed the turn I couldn't see the other two aircraft, and this despite rolling almost inverted. I decided I shouldn't fly towards them when I couldn't see them and turned left, away from their last position, looking right across the cockpit from the left seat, to see if I could pick them up. Then two things

John Grogan.

happened simultaneously: I went into thick cloud and, not paying attention to my attitude, found myself almost inverted with the altimeter unwinding at a rapid rate.

After the initial panic, I remembered what my instructor said about entering cloud: go immediately onto instruments, roll the wings level, pull to the horizon, apply power and climb to a safe altitude. It took me a moment to realise which way was up; then I rolled the wings level and pulled as hard as I could to arrest the rate of descent. Once I was finally going up I started to think what was next and decided to look at my speed. Zero! Although this might seem a very bad situation, actually I was relieved because, at last, I knew where I was in space – going vertically up. So I pushed the control column to lower the nose. The aircraft hammer-headed down, the speed built up and I slowly pulled out of the dive and got back to level flight. Just at that point, mercifully, I came out of cloud and had enough brain cells to call the instructor to explain what had happened. After calming me down he said he had no idea where I was and told me to make my way home.

I returned to Leeming in very poor weather and taxied in, expecting a telling-off when I got back. The reverse was true. I hadn't realised how bad the weather was. It was on or below my limits, so the instructors were really relieved when I got in and congratulated me. In retrospect, the 'go' decision was clearly wrong. The reason I lost the other pair was because they had gone under a layer of cloud.

The moral: the instructors should never have allowed a student with only some 40 hours total to fly such a sortie when there were doubts about the weather.

MAN IS NOT LOST

I was a student at Valley on the Gnat course. Another crewroom and another question from an instructor: "Have you done Exercise 33?" I said that I hadn't, to which he replied, "A jet has just become serviceable. Get your skates on and off you go." Well, in those days most of us had our sortie maps pre-prepared and in pristine condition, but I had loaned mine to someone else, not expecting to fly that day. When I explained this to him, the instructor took a grubby map out of his pocket and gave it to me. So I hurriedly put a line on a map and set off. The route was high level to Chivenor, low level up through Wales to Wrexham, then high level back to Valley.

The weather was bad at Chivenor, which necessitated a GCA to get down to low level. Once I joined the low-level route the weather was poor all the way, but I did find Wrexham and climbed for home. At this point I was 200lbs down on fuel but I wasn't concerned because the weather at base was Blue,[21] CAVOK (ceiling and visibility OK). I arrived at Valley where from the overhead I could see the airfield clearly, and in a moment of *joie de vivre* rolled over and pulled through, heading for the run-in point for joining. Then I lost sight of the airfield, which was odd as I had seen it only moments before. I really shouldn't be barrelling into the airfield when I didn't know where it was, I thought, so I pulled well away. What I didn't realise until then was that there was a strong inversion and the visibility at lower levels was very poor. I could see the ground, but forward visibility was almost non-existent.

By now fuel was a real problem and I was getting very concerned that I had no idea where the airfield was and couldn't orientate myself with any features on the ground. In the end I decided to call the tower for a true bearing. Repeated calls received no answer so I got onto guard[22] on the standby radio. Still no answer. I was now very short of fuel, to the point that I tightened my straps ready for the ejection. In desperation I called Valley on 243.8 on the standby radio (it was used as a taxiing frequency). The duty pilot answered and I explained my situation, probably in a not very confident voice. I'm not sure what he could have done, but he was at least aware that a student was airborne and was likely to eject after running out of fuel. At that point I suddenly recognised the causeway to Holy Island, which was pretty much on

21 Three-eighths or less cloud at 2,500ft and visibility over eight km.
22 The emergency radio frequency: 243.0MHz.

the centreline, so I told the duty pilot that I was landing from my present position. I landed with the gauges reading zero, but managed to taxi back in.

It turned out that I had a main radio failure. The standby radio was working but the controllers on guard could only hear a garbled message and I couldn't hear them. Afterwards one of the instructors took me aside and asked me what happened, which was the last I heard about it. As a 19-year-old student I was pleased not to be in trouble. It was only much later that I realised the incident represented a very serious lapse in supervision: minimal briefing, limited preparation and the weather factor once again. But I guess it was all hushed up.

A TESTING BRIEF

Once I joined 8 Squadron in Aden, my first Hunter sortie after dual checks on arrival was a familiarisation recce of the local area. The brief, given by my flight commander, included going to the Lodar Plain, an area to the north-northwest of Aden, at 10,000ft; there I was to roll over and pull through, reporting back to him how much height I had lost. To an experienced Hunter pilot alarm bells would have rung immediately.

On the way up to the Lodar Plain I realised that it was 2,000ft above sea level; at 10,000ft that would put me only 8,000ft above the ground. That didn't sound good to me. So I climbed to 20,000ft, slowed down to get a better radius of turn, rolled over and pulled through. Perhaps I wasn't pulling hard enough because I bottomed out at 12,000ft. Even so I realised that I wasn't going to try the 10,000ft option.

When I got back the flight commander asked how it went. I admitted that I hadn't attempted the 10,000ft option because I didn't think there was enough height and could easily hit the ground. "Well done," he said, "glad you worked that out" and went off on his merry way. He had a reputation as a very good pilot; but I never trusted him after that.

ALL THINGS TAKEN INTO CONSIDERATION

By 1970 I was with 1 Squadron and we were due to take part in the Paris Air Show with five Harriers. We were short of serviceable aircraft and the boss, the inimitable Ken Hayr, decided to do a practice run with two aircraft from 1 Squadron and one borrowed from the OCU. The lead would be taken by Ken's deputy; I was number two and the number three would be Louis Distelsweig, the USAF exchange officer, who was the five-ship spare. We lined up for a formation take-off from the grass in echelon starboard. About two seconds after take-off my aircraft rolled rapidly to the

John Grogan's Harrier (far left) about to experience problems.

right. I had no idea what was happening but it was obvious that a crash was inevitable. I went eject but realised that Louis was directly above me about five feet away.

The aircraft then hit the ground with a loud bang and bounced left. At this point it was clear to me that the left wing would hit the ground and either cartwheel or bounce right over to the right – I knew that I would not survive – but it did neither. It did bounce right, but only far enough to stabilise the aircraft. So now it was steady on the ground but some 40 or 50 degrees off the original heading, speed unknown, nozzles still at 60 degrees down. It was only then that I realised I might survive this ordeal – about five seconds from beginning the take-off. I applied full power and pushed the nozzles forward (up) and tried to get as much speed as possible. I was approaching the taxiway, with a building ahead of me, so I pulled the nozzles back to the 60-degree stop and took off, missing the OCU building by feet.

I called the leader and explained that I had a problem on take-off and had damaged my undercarriage, and could he come back and tell me what I had left? He reported that all appeared to be fine, except for a tyre burst on the right outrigger. So I reduced the fuel as much as I could and did a very careful vertical landing, without incident.

In true Ken Hayr fashion, he asked if I was OK. When I said that I was, he said I should take one of the aircraft and go to the range and fire off a few rockets – on the basis that you get back on a horse after a fall. The scores were fine.

It turned out that the number three's aircraft was clean and hence much lighter than the other two, which was the cause of the problem. The difference in weight made it inevitable that the number three would move higher and forward of the other two on take-off. My rapid roll to the right was caused by the downward thrust from the number three on my starboard wing. The implications of different aircraft fits during the echelon take-off simply weren't considered during the briefing: another break-down in supervision that could so easily have proved fatal.

TRAVEL SICKNESS

While instructing on the Jaguar at 226 OCU, RAF Lossiemouth, I was scheduled for an instrument sortie – in the back with the front-seat student head-down behind screens. It meant that I was responsible for the taxiing and take-off. On the taxi out I did the pre-take-off checks aloud so the student would know that I'd done them. I got to 'flaps' and then realised I couldn't remember what came next. So I tried it again with the same result. I felt perfectly fine so gave it one final go. At that point I had no idea what it was, but something was clearly wrong. So I decided to taxi back to dispersal and requested the doctor – still feeling perfectly OK.

Fairly quickly the reason became apparent. It was raining quite heavily when we were strapping in, with water entering the cockpit and onto a panel (the radio I think). It turned out that water had got into the circuit board under the panel and shorted out some of the wiring. This wiring was covered with acetate (?) and the burning produced ether, which was filling the rear cockpit with invisible fumes. As a result I was in the early stages of anaesthesia, which produces just the symptoms I'd demonstrated. Had I continued with the sortie and attempted a take-off the result would almost certainly have been fatal for both of us.

The front-seat student told me later that he was very relieved when I made the decision to taxi in. All the more reason to do the checks aloud. Had we continued, I wonder whether he'd have been prepared to question the strange behaviour of the man in the back. On his part it would have been a clear case of 'Don't assume – check!'

* * * *

WING COMMANDER TIM JONES

Commissioned into the RAF Regiment direct from school at 18, Tim Jones spent much of his career overseas: in the Maldives, Aden, Singapore and Borneo on airfield protection duties and in Oman on loan service. He commanded 34 (Field) Squadron RAF Regiment in Cyprus and retired in 1985 to work for Rolls-Royce.

CLOSE AIR SUPPORT, OMAN – TRAINING COMES IN HANDY

In the 1970s, as a flight lieutenant, I was one of a number of RAF Regiment officers who volunteered to serve on loan as infantry commanders with the SAF (Sultan's Armed Forces) in Oman. We were deployed alongside others from the Royal Marines and the British Army on counter-insurgency operations during the Dhofar campaign. Our enemy, known as 'adoo' (the Arabic word for enemy), were well-trained, well-armed rebels supported by China and Russia from neighbouring South Yemen – Aden that was. Previous service both there and in Borneo and, more to the point, training as a forward air controller (FAC), were to prove invaluable during an episode in 1973.

Operation Simba had been launched a year earlier to cut the rebels' supply lines into Oman where they were channelled by vertical cliffs into a narrow, broken coastal strip. But first the high ground had to be taken and held. In accomplishing this, the SAF faced stiff opposition and were halted. Besieged and surrounded on high clifftops miles from other units, they depended entirely on SOAF helicopters and a few transport aircraft for resupply and to stock up for the imminent monsoon. And things were about to get worse.

My company took over four platoon positions along a dominant ridge known as 'Yardarm' – part of a large, isolated battalion position right on the border with South Yemen. Shortly after we arrived our elderly Caribou resupply aircraft was hit on the ground by an RCL (recoilless weapon) and destroyed. With no fixed-wing

support and few helicopters, in severe heat we were reduced to a litre of water per man per day. There was no question of withdrawal; it was politically unacceptable. In the end we were saved when Iran (!) provided more helicopters. A few days later, one of our three loan service company commanders was killed in a ferocious ambush. Shortly afterwards, I was wounded by mortar shrapnel and briefly evacuated to Salalah. With the operation clearly in trouble, it was the Strikemaster that regularly saved the day.

Tim Jones.

An armed derivative of the JP trainer, the aircraft didn't look much like a modern war fighter – 'a tadpole with wings' – but for SOAF, the dumpy little jets delivered a huge improvement in capability when they arrived in 1969. Rugged and easy to maintain, they were much faster than previous support aircraft and there were more of them. Strikemasters could support ground troops quicker and packed a bigger punch. Although not much by today's standards, various combinations of up to four

SOAF Strikemasters.

540lb bombs and up to 32 x 80mm SURA rockets could be carried on hardpoints under the wings. This was in addition to two 7.62mm GPMGs (general purpose machine guns) with 500 rounds (30 seconds' fire) each. We certainly appreciated the way SOAF flew them – to the limits! And we learnt from surrendered adoo that they really feared the jets.

Although Simba hadn't completely cut the rebel supply routes as planned, it was certainly a major thorn in their side and they made determined attempts to dislodge us. Our positions were hit most days by 75mm RCLs and 82mm mortars fired from hidden positions in dead ground. Sometimes 12.7mm HMGs (heavy machine guns) shattered our thick stone sangars with accurate bursts of fire from deep within caves. Night attacks were especially threatening, with automatic AK-47s supported by RPG-7s[23] used as short-range, airburst artillery to keep our heads down. Patrolling was always risky across barren forward slopes, steep ridges and deep wadis. Adoo snipers and mines made it more so and it was exhausting in the heat, especially when water was reduced. RCL and mortar engagements could last a few minutes or a few hours. If it looked like we were in for a long session, we called for the jets. But the adoo were smart and would take cover as SOAF arrived, hiding until they returned to base for fuel.

Although we were saved when Iran sent helicopters to resupply Simba, we needed to sharpen our response to the adoo stand-off attacks. A brainstorming session with SOAF pilots resulted in a proposal for a pre-planned attack on a much-favoured firing position and suspected storage cave area to the west, in Spider Wadi. Since I had patrolled out to Spider, was familiar with the ground and had also recently flown in a Strikemaster, they suggested I should fly in the lead aircraft to pinpoint the target so the pilot could concentrate on flying and aiming (a bit like the fast FACs in Vietnam – but slower and not so intense). I should use my army radio callsign rather than a SOAF one to mislead any listening rebels so that the first they would know of the jets would be us pulling up and tipping in for the attack. We all felt it was worth a try and details were agreed.

A few days later, the Simba troops were briefed and I was back at Salalah, refreshed on cockpit and ejection seat procedures and strapped into a Strikemaster alongside Sean Creak (formerly an RAF Hunter pilot and now a seasoned SOAF 'Strikie'). A second aircraft took off right behind us and en route to Simba we heard that Yardarm was under mortar attack from near Spider Wadi. For once, this was good news – we

---

23 A shoulder-launched, anti-tank, rocket-propelled grenade launcher.

had a real target. Some quick map reading and cockpit maths, then I gave the Simba artillery an 'On command' fire control order to mark the target. Once they'd done this we set off for the pull-up point. With 30 seconds to go at 300kts and fingers firmly crossed I was on the R/T again. Aware that the target was now marked, but unable to identify it yet, I called "Guns tight". We really didn't want to get hit by an artillery round.

Then we were pulling up and searching right two o'clock for a puff of artillery smoke. I recognised the high ridge at the neck of Spider Wadi and then saw a plume of smoke appear not too far away. Just below the crest was a long line of shadow and what were obviously caves. Sean focused on getting us lined up but there were more, smaller caves below and some movement in their shadows. There were no innocent goatherders out here in the wilderness – it must be adoo. Never mind the smoke; this was the target. As Sean began a 20-degree dive, the hillside in front of us suddenly sparkled with muzzle flashes. We must be onto something. A rocket leapt forward off our rail, leaving a trail of smoke towards a small cave; then I was pinned back into the ejection seat as Sean hauled the jet into a tight, climbing turn. Upside down now, I saw through the canopy roof the second Strikemaster fire a salvo of rockets and my soldiers on Yardarm told us excitedly we were getting 'waggid rami' (lots of bullets). Then it was another hard turn into a second attack, this time a bomb delivery accompanied by machine-gun fire: good for keeping heads down.

Our number two told us our bomb had dislodged a huge slab of rock; rubble had blocked the cave entrance and we stopped getting ground fire. As we climbed away I zeroed the Simba artillery onto the huge cloud of dust in a 'fire for effect' bombardment. Then it was back to Salalah. Sean made a pass along Yardarm and, with a quick wave to my soldiers, things were left to the artillery. We learnt later that an RCL and its crew had been destroyed.

It was a good day at the office – thanks mainly to all that prior FAC training. I went on to fly several more sorties with SOAF, but none was as exciting or professionally rewarding as that day with Sean. And I still treasure those memories of serving with a true 'band of brothers' in SAF and SOAF.[24]

* * * *

---

24 One of whom was Flight Lieutenant Jock Stirrup, later MRAF The Lord Stirrup (see also Chapter 1).

WING COMMANDER D.G. 'SAM' LUCAS

A 'Cold War warrior' in the air and on the ground, display pilot Sam Lucas served on two Hunter and three Lightning squadrons, clocking up some 1,500 hours on the former and over 2,000 on the latter type. On exchange with the USAF he flew the T-33, F-101, F-102, F-106 and C-54. As OC Operations at Leuchars he later flew the Phantom, Wessex and Bulldog. After leaving the RAF in 1987 he joined Flight Refuelling Aviation (FRA), flying the Hunter and Falcon. He finally hung up his helmet at the Cornwall Flying Club at Bodmin where he was an instructor, examiner and chairman.

DISPLAY FLYING – LEARNING THE LOW-LEVEL AEROBATICS TRADE

From the age of about 12 I had wanted to be a fighter pilot in the Royal Air Force. I achieved this by going from my Cornish grammar school to the RAF College Cranwell, and being posted to 66 Squadron, flying the Hunter. As a green, wide-eyed rookie I watched the squadron's aerobatic pilot practising his low-level aerobatic display. I thought that it looked a little dangerous – and demanded a lot of skill too.

Sam Lucas in a Hunter.

My second squadron was 111, of 'Black Arrows' fame, flying first the Hunter then the Lightning, and in the interim both. When I was given the chance to be the squadron's solo aerobatic pilot, initially on the Hunter and then on the Lightning, I found that with forethought, practice, supervision and advice, display aerobatics were neither dangerous nor too difficult for any fighter pilot trained to the RAF's exacting standards. In many years of low-level displays, I only twice came close to putting myself (and others) in danger. To explain how this occurred, I first need to provide some background.

Aerobatics represent a key element of RAF training. Apart from being fun, practice in aerobatics allows a pilot to experience high g and unusual flight regimes, including how to recover from them, and is thus a useful prelude to other disciplines, not least air combat. While the RAF chose not to blow its own trumpet about its aerobatic and combat training, from my experience its training in these disciplines matched or bettered that of our allies and potential enemies. By way of example, RAF Hunters regularly won the NATO Central Region gunnery competition. This involved live firing on a towed target and cine attacks on another evading fighter, both disciplines calling for the accurate manoeuvring and spatial awareness developed in aerobatics and air-combat training.

My experience on exchange with the USAF adds weight to this argument. On my first flight in the F-102 Delta Dagger, a single-seater, I was accompanied by my mentor, an experienced USAF major in a 'chase' aircraft. When we reached a reasonable height, he invited me to lead him in whatever manoeuvres I wished. In about three minutes I had reversed our positions and was on his tail with my gunsight trained on him. When we landed, he shook my hand. I then realised that what was standard for me, an average RAF pilot, represented to him a rather impressive level of performance.

My first flight in the two-seat version of the F-106 Delta Dart was also revealing. The highly experienced major in the back seat invited me to investigate the capabilities of this fine machine. I carried out a loop and at the top felt a little twitching on the controls that could only have been caused by the other pilot. After landing I mentioned this to him. He answered that he was nervous because in many hundreds of hours on the aeroplane he had never looped an F-106!

Reflecting on my privileged experiences, and indeed those of others, I learnt a good deal about the business of display flying, and indeed the individuals involved. There is certainly no place for the gung-ho extravert who may sacrifice safety for showmanship, or who takes on the task without the requisite consideration and preparation. While above-average handling ability and judgement are prerequisites, even more important is the sort of stable and steady personality who will devote effort to preparation, and who will approach the task with safety as the paramount concern. Related to this key consideration are a few precepts I kept in mind and vowed never to violate. Some aerobatic pilots who killed themselves or others, destroying a fully serviceable and expensive aircraft in the process, would still be with us had they kept these precepts in mind. The potentially hazardous incidents I referred to at the outset stemmed from ignoring two of these key principles. Notwithstanding the overriding importance of tailoring a display to the prevailing weather conditions – cloud base, visibility, wind direction and strength, and even changeability – I saw four precepts as critically important:

- First, never start a vertical manoeuvre such as a loop at a lower speed than planned, i.e. use an entry speed that guarantees recovery at a safe height.
- Second, never start a rolling manoeuvre with the nose below the horizon; this applies in particular to hesitation rolls where the resulting and potentially dangerous tendency to descend is increased.
- Third, never insert a manoeuvre into a routine until it has been mastered at altitude.
- Last, but by no means least, never include a manoeuvre with the potential for dangerous misjudgement.

I put the Cuban eight in this last category. A horizontal eight with the plane at 90 degrees to the ground, it comprises two adjacent loops connected by a 180-degree roll while the aircraft is climbing vertically. I felt it was dangerous and never put it into a display because with no external references the exact point of rolling is hard to judge. Rolling too early could result in a low pull-out, in the worst case with the aircraft hitting the ground at high speed.

The dangers of breaking this, the last of what might be termed my golden rules, were tragically brought home in 1963 when I was on 111 Squadron at Wattisham. Here our sister squadron, 56's 'Firebirds', took over the formation aerobatic commitment from the 'Tigers' of 74 Squadron. These pilots, who had never done any formation aerobatics before, rose to the challenge and produced commendable displays despite their inexperience in the role. (It is a tribute to the training mentioned earlier that any normal RAF pilot was considered capable of carrying out this demanding task.) Meanwhile, two pilots from 111 Squadron, of whom I was one, alternated in the solo part of the Firebirds' display.

The nine 56 Squadron Lightnings lined up on the runway with two airborne spares behind and the solo man lined up at the back. The aircraft then took off at two-second intervals, including the solo man. It was rather unnerving to be behind 22 Avon engines in full reheat, with the aircraft bucketing around in the combined slipstream, and the shimmering heat obscuring the view. But it always seemed to work. After take-off, landing gear had to be retracted smartly before the aircraft reached the limiting speed of about 250kts, when the gear would not retract. At 240kts each aircraft snapped into a steep climb. The Firebirds and their spares cleared away from the display line to form up into the diamond formation with which they began. The solo man stayed behind to entertain the crowd in the four or five minutes it took for the main formation to assemble and position for their run-in. He also reappeared later in the display to fill in time after the main formation's 'bomb-burst' and subsequent reassembly.

My colleague used to follow the aircraft ahead into the steep climb, but straight ahead while the others turned away from the crowd. He continued the climb until he judged that he had enough height to roll over into a half-loop back down the runway line and continue with a few manoeuvres until the diamond nine formation returned. I, on the other hand, used to turn away under the other aircraft and carry out a tight, low Derry turn[25] to bring me back onto the runway axis for my other manoeuvres. The Firebirds' squadron commander asked me to do the same as my colleague. I politely refused on the grounds that it would have gone against the precepts outlined above. My colleague was later killed doing just this manoeuvre, on this occasion in a solo display where temporary entry into cloud was also a factor. He was a good friend, and to have my judgement vindicated in this way was no consolation for this sad and unnecessary loss.

Let me end on a more light-hearted note by returning to the incidents I mentioned at the outset – occasions when I made some embarrassing mistakes.

I thought one day that it might be effective to include in my display a manoeuvre that to my knowledge had not been attempted before. It was to be a hesitation Derry turn. The idea was to pause in the inverted position halfway through a Derry turn before completing the second half. The aircraft would be travelling away from the crowd, with its fiery aft end pointing at it, which I thought would look good. I practised it – but not enough – at high level and then put it in a practice low-level display witnessed by my long-suffering Wing Commander Flying in the air traffic control tower. I could not keep the nose up above the horizon and it dropped – nearly into a hangar at Wattisham. I had flirted with not only one, but two of my

---

25 A display manoeuvre developed by test pilot John Derry. It consists of a bank reversal during a steep turn where the aircraft passes through the inverted rather than upright attitude.

golden rules. A fully justified admonition from the tower ensued. After I landed, I heard a fellow squadron member comment that low-level aerobatics was truly a job for the bachelor!

The second cautionary tale comes from a display for the Belgian National Air Day at Beauvechain. King Baudouin and associated bigwigs were located on a dais right next to the centre point of the runway that constituted the display line. There was a very strong wind blowing at 90 degrees to the runway, directly into the faces of the king and his acolytes. My display at that time included a loop pointing directly at the crowd. I pulled up, underestimating the strength of the on-crowd wind at the top of the loop – which was, of course, considerably greater than that at ground level. So when the ground came into sight again in the second half of the loop, I was far too close to His Majesty. I put on maximum bank and pulled 7g to avoid an international incident. 'British Pilot Assassinates Belgian King' would not have made a good headline. On landing back at base, I reported this overstress (the Lightning's limit was 6g) to the squadron commander, whose personal aircraft I was flying that day. Gentleman that he was, he forgave me, but I am not sure that the ground crew, who had to do three days' hard and difficult work removing the engines to check the bearings, ever did.

However, a few days later I received a letter, which I still have on file, from the Belgian Chief of Air Staff which included the following: 'At the controls of his Lightning Flight Lieutenant Lucas produced one of the most impressive solo demonstrations ever witnessed, doing credit as much to his ability as a pilot, as to the power and handling qualities of his magnificent aircraft.' He had not guessed the real truth: that this 'piece of cake' was nearly a monumental cock-up.

If the aircraft of today are different from those that I displayed, their pilots perform before a similar audience: a public likely to be more impressed by speed, noise and the fiery glow of afterburners than by beautifully precise aircraft control. However, the precepts outlined above remain just as valid now as they did when learnt by a young officer making his way in an exhilarating world.

CHAPTER 8
SQUADRON LEADERS' LESSONS

SQUADRON LEADER 'CHING' FULLER

During a diverse career, mainly on fighters, Ching Fuller flew around 4,500 hours: 100 on the Vampire, 1,500 on the Hunter, 650 on the Lightning, 650 on the A-7D Corsair II and 650 on the A-4 Skyhawk. The latter two types were the result, respectively, of a tour as a USAF exchange pilot and early retirement; he emigrated and joined the Royal New Zealand Air Force. Between times he also managed a tour as a Gnat and Hunter QFI. Ching retired from flying for a second time in 2000.

IT'S AN ILL WIND

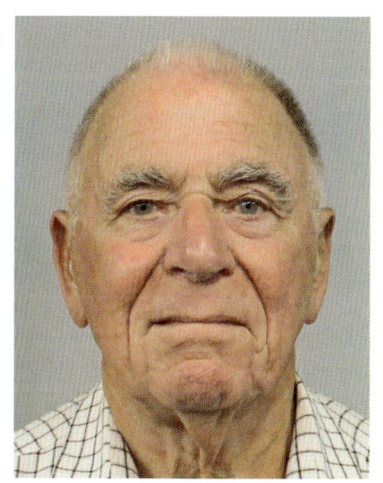

'Ching' Fuller.

The air defence lane system of the 1960s gave rise to one of the more stupid (and potentially dangerous) situations in which I have ever put myself. The episode started normally enough with a typical Friday night party from which I went to bed 'a bit puffed' as the navy say, at about 0330. Fighter Command pulled a major surprise air defence exercise at 0500 and I was airborne at 0600 heading out over the North Sea towards my 'gate', still in no condition to pass any kind of breathalyser test (it hadn't been invented then, of course). I was ill-prepared, without having seen a weather forecast and without a map, albeit not a particularly useful item over featureless ocean. But, more critically, I was without a serviceable navigation aid in the aircraft. No problem for a hungover 22-year-old, though.

I remembered the heading and distance to my gate and pressed on, but when I arrived I found another 19 Squadron Hunter already there. Then I remembered that the QRA aircraft had been scrambled before me – one of them had obviously been assigned to the same gate. There then ensued the following conversation:

"Have you got a map?"

"No."

"Well, have you got a DME (distance measuring equipment)?"

"Yes."

"We need 96nm from Acklington and 120 from Leconfield."

After this exchange my friend Brian Johnson completed another orbit then headed west for about three minutes, about 27nm in still air. During the orbit, rather than put on power he descended a few thousand feet towards the mintra[26] (contrail) level but we were still making contrails when we got to the real gate position. We were still trailing for the first orbit there, but then he put on power and once we climbed up to our assigned height the trails stopped. Unfortunately, shortly afterwards Brian got an indication of booster pump failure and descended, heading for base. I continued orbiting the contrail we had laid down during our first orbit and stupidly gave not a thought to the fact that we'd had to fly quite a way west to get there.

As there had been no other instructions, I followed the SOP and listened out on the radio frequency that provided broadcast target information for my lane while continuing to orbit, enjoying the 100% oxygen I'd selected on the regulator. After a while the broadcast started breaking up and finally went silent. The alternate frequency was equally quiet. Having been airborne for an hour or so, much of it doing a boring orbit in clear air, once the fuel was down to 650lbs a side and the Bingo lights came on I was happy to head west towards base. I then found I couldn't raise Patrington radar station on any of the possible frequencies. When I called the emergency fixer service, which would tell me where I was, I got a reply in a Scandinavian language that I couldn't understand. It was then that it dawned on me. I was probably a long way to the east of base, so I started to climb to the highest altitude I could attain to

---

26 The flight level below which exhaust/condensation trails will positively not form.

conserve fuel. Shortly after I reached 51,000ft I was happy to get a reply when I called Patrington again. They informed me that I was some 250nm to the east of RAF Leconfield. They had been worried about me (not as worried as I was!) and advised that there was a 220-knot jet stream blowing from west to east at between 35,000 and 38,000ft. I had been orbiting at 37,000ft.

By now the fuel was down to around 350lbs a side, but fortunately at 51,000ft I was using only about 25lbs a minute. However, allowing two miles per minute for the headwind gave me a ground speed of approximately seven nautical miles per minute, which meant I was going to run out of fuel four minutes before I reached Leconfield. I was starting to really worry. I advised Patrington I would be short of fuel and would require a priority approach and landing at Leconfield and asked them to advise me when 110nm from a point five nm from the touchdown end of the duty runway. When they did, I put the throttle to idle and started a gentle descent at Mach 0.9. As soon as I was below 45,000ft I selected positive pressure on the oxygen regulator and flamed the engine out.

The Hunter will glide 80nm from 40,000ft. I reached the five-mile initial point for runway 01 at Leconfield at 4,000ft, relit the engine and left the throttle at idle. I barrelled into the circuit at 450kts with less than 50lbs of fuel indicated, pitched out and landed from a gentle curve without advancing the throttle. I taxied in to the marshalling point and stopped for the 'groundie' to check the tyres. As soon as he'd finished I should have rolled forward another half-tyre distance, but I was unable to do so because the engine flamed out due to fuel starvation. The total time of flight was 15 minutes longer than that theoretically possible in a Hunter F6 with two 100-gallon drop tanks.

When I took my helmet off it felt as though my head would burst. As a result of my poor airmanship and lack of judgement I spent the next two weeks in the station sick quarters, suffering from what the doctor kindly called glandular fever.

The element of self-criticism here seems unduly harsh. Salvaging a difficult situation in this way represents airmanship at its best – an inspired piece of improvisation, arguably the product of a service that encouraged an adventurous, free-thinking approach. [Ed.]

* * * *

SQUADRON LEADER RICK OFFORD

'Ricko' Offord's operational career began with several tours on the Phantom, logging nearly 2,000 hours. After an F-18 exchange with the RAAF, he converted to the Tornado F3. In 1998, after 16 happy years, he left the RAF to join FRA (later Cobham Aviation Services), flying the Falcon 20. While with FRA he joined the Royal Auxiliary Air Force and continued to fly the Tornado F3, on which, as a part-timer he eventually logged 1,000 hours. Ricko retired from Cobham to run the Leeming AEF as a QFI.

OLD DOG LEARNS NEW TRICKS – DERRING-DO IN THE DESERT

After instructing on the Grob Tutor I joined Hawker Hunter Aviation (HHA) as a part-time Hunter pilot and QFI at Scampton. I hadn't flown the aircraft in my RAF service and found it a delight. Then in 2021 a fascinating prospect materialised: taking a Hunter to the UAE. I jumped at the chance, but got more than I bargained for. It makes quite a story.

The Abu Dhabi Defence Force Air Wing acquired Hunters shortly after its formation in 1968. It subsequently merged into the United Arab Emirates Air Force (UAEAF). To celebrate the UAEAF's 50th anniversary, a flypast on National Day was planned and they wanted a Hunter to participate. After much discussion and negotiation, a contract was agreed for HHA to deploy a camouflaged Mk 58 to the Al Dhafra Air Base in the UAE. The Mk 58 is basically the Swiss export version of the RAF FGA9. With four external tanks its range is around 1,200nm at 35,000ft; however, the absence of an autopilot effectively limits transit altitudes to below 29,000ft and range to 900nm. To avoid too many long oversea legs we settled on a route of Zagreb-Athens-Amman-Bahrain-Al Dhafra and were delighted when the UAEAF offered to send a C-130 Hercules to accompany me. The story begins on Thursday 25 November 2021 when I took off for Franjo Tuđman Airport, Zagreb.

The accompanying Hercules would obviously transit slower than a Hunter, so I left the crew to their own devices, arranging to meet at the end of each day. On board were two HHA engineers and a 'spare' pilot who would do all the 'trivia' (weather/NOTAMs/hotels etc.). Flying the HHA Hunter across Europe in the airways structure is a simple navigation task given the 'glassed' Mk 58 cockpit. Where the gunsight used to fit, HHA engineers had installed a Garmin GTN 750 multifunction display (MFD) that had all the civilian toys: you know exactly where you are and where other traffic is flying around you. It does, however, rely on a GPS signal (more of which later). With no autopilot, flying fairly long legs with four tanks can be hard work in a Mk 58; it is particularly 'twitchy' in pitch, so monitoring cleared height levels is a full-time job.

The covid pandemic added further risk to the whole enterprise. At every destination, once in the handling agent's lounge/office with coffee and customs sorted, the next event would be a doctor with a cotton bud to twirl around each nostril for what seemed like minutes. The good news was the result was instant and everyone stayed covid-free throughout. I then remained in the handling agent's lounge awaiting the arrival of the C-130 which, ideally (but not always) would park next to the Hunter. HHA had replaced the aircraft's original avpin[27] starting system with a specially designed start trolley which added another risk factor: no Herc, no start! Each leg the ground crew would see me off, then manhandle the trolley back to the Herc: easy if parked next door, but 'transports' were often parked on a different part of the airfield from fast jets.

After a rainy departure from Zagreb, the weather in Athens was gorgeous. As I wanted to reduce oversea transits, I hugged the Greek coast eastbound until heading south-east over Cyprus and headed for Jordan. All was going swimmingly until abeam Tel Aviv when the Garmin gave up on me: 'insufficient satellites, use other navigation source'. All I had left was a non-directional beacon (NDB), so I got out my old-fashioned map, dialled up the nearest beacon and tried to figure out an offset for the next waypoint – all the while trying desperately not to climb or descend. Once in contact with Amman, I requested 'direct', which was approved (phew – just point at the NDB). But the required procedural approach via a GPS waypoint meant more scrabbling around the cockpit for my approach plates. Luckily the cleared approach was straight-in via an inbound radial. Once I shut down in Jordan it was with a sense of relief, and the prospect of another long wait for the Herc.

Sunday 28 November was planned as the only two-leg day: Amman-Bahrain-Al Dhafra. I set off early for Bahrain – the longest leg – as the Herc couldn't overfly Saudi Arabia (a diplomatic issue), so had a long flight around Saudi airspace. Despite a stiff tailwind I had a long wait in Bahrain before the Herc showed up – and parked miles away in a different terminal. Eventually it was able to see me off for the last 40-minute hop to Al Dhafra. I arrived to see a gorgeous Middle East sunset. Time now to think about the reason for being here: the flypast.

---

27 The liquid used to fuel the Avon engine's starter motor. Also known as isopropyl nitrate (IPN), it is highly volatile.

While we had no detail on what the flypast entailed, I knew that the Al Fursan formation team with seven Aermacchi MB-339s were involved so assumed I would slot in behind them. Arriving on base on the Monday to learn more, we found the engineers fettling the aircraft under a sun shelter, supported by a small army of 'tradesmen' converting it to its old UAE paint scheme with the aid of numerous 'stick-on' panels. The base commander was thin on details of Thursday's flypast, but all would be revealed post-lunch when we met the F-16E/F Desert Falcon squadron boss and the Al Fursan formation team's Italian liaison officer. The Italian (callsign 'Coach') turned out to be a sharp operator who had a total grip on the flypast. He had flown multiple seasons with the Frecce Tricolori and was now advising Al Fursan, flying an extra jet with a professional photographer in the back seat. I was slightly surprised to discover that in two days' time I was to lead the entire 50th anniversary flypast in my 'UAE' Hunter – with an F-16 on one wing, a Mirage 2000 on the other and the Al Fursan team with smoke on in close trail. There were numerous sites to overfly, with one main TOT (time-on-target) commitment downtown Dubai. So, a ten-ship lead at 500ft? No pressure. I had once led a diamond-nine of Tornado F3s but that was many years ago, and with the help of a directional consultant (navigator). I was definitely out of currency in formation flypasts. Sensing a slight hesitation, Coach reassured me with the news that I had a practice day on Wednesday when I could fly part of the route over Abu Dhabi with the F-16 and M2000 in 'vic' and him taking photos; the Al Fursan team would then join in for the actual flypast on Thursday. Unfortunately, I couldn't practise the route over Dubai as its international airport would have to close whilst we buzzed the city at low level for 30 minutes; this could only happen on Thursday. Ho hum, time to get on to Google Maps and find out where I was going.

Wednesday was a gorgeous day and I got together first thing with the Mirage and F-16 pilots for a quick brief. We lined up on the runway in echelon, launched in a five-second stream then transited to the hold in vic to await the arrival of Coach at 1,500ft. The first problem was that the hold was only eight miles west of Sheikh Zayed International Airport, the second largest in the UAE. I had to talk to the airport approach controller to deconflict with their traffic on VHF whilst controlling my formation and arranging Coach's join on UHF; meanwhile, I was struggling to sort out timing and where I was. In most fast jets talking on two radios is a simple matter of a rocker switch on the throttle, but in the Hunter, using the Garmin MFD, you could end up in trouble – not listening to one frequency or worse, talking on the wrong one.

Once Coach arrived in his MB-339 we somehow departed the hold in good order on time. Luckily, we only had seven targets to overfly: the Sheikh Zayed Grand Mosque to Zayed Sports City Stadium then Capital Gate, Hudayriat Bridge, Qasr Al Watan, the Abu Dhabi Corniche and finally the Louvre Abu Dhabi. I had studied the route the night before and flown it on my PC Garmin trainer. The 'targets' were all so close together that it wasn't possible to plan traditional IP-target runs – just join the dots and memorise the route. I planned to reposition only once: oversea to line up for the Corniche. I needed an accurate run-in at 500ft to avoid the high-rise buildings either side of the estuary. I couldn't spend too long repositioning as the MB-339 photoship was tight on fuel. To say I was working hard would be an understatement, especially with Coach driving me left/right to get the best photos. He then departed back to Minhad while I led my three-ship back to Al Dhafra. I was seriously relieved to pop the Hunter canopy back when rolling down the runway. I was soaked and my flying suit was most unsavoury (lucky the Marriott had a decent laundry). According to the phone debrief with Coach, I was slightly abeam one target, Qasr Al Watan, but I reckoned six out of seven overflown exactly wasn't bad. Now for the big one.

The visibility next day, Thursday 2 December, looked hazy. I had chatted with Coach the night before to coordinate the join with Al Fursan post our flypast of Abu Dhabi. That part would be almost the same as the day before but with just four targets, finishing with another Corniche fly-by. Expecting to meet my F-16 and M2000 wingmen from the day before for a refresher brief, I was surprised to discover two junior pilots had replaced yesterday's experienced squadron commander types. Ho hum, all they had to do was hang on in vic so a simple brief would do: 'Follow me!' With hindsight, I suspect the F-16 boss had been checking me out before I was entrusted with the ten-ship lead on National Day.

Once we launched into the same hold as before, minus Coach in his MB-339, at 1,500ft there was a murky haze layer. I tried to negotiate a higher hold with Sheikh Zayed International but was denied due to airliner traffic above – traffic that meant my Garmin would default to the traffic alert and collision avoidance system page and not the 'north-up' navigation display that I needed. Who said it would be easy!? But all went well and we flew past the Corniche with a spirited amount of bank and headed north-east to meet with the Al Fursan team. Handed off from Sheikh Zayed International to Dubai International, I climbed my formation to 5,000ft in clear weather and headed for the rendezvous with the seven MB-339s, just east of the famous Dubai Palm (there are two). They showed up on time and I slotted in behind. For the first two targets my vic had to follow in close trail, staying slightly low as the

Rick Offord leads a mixed ten-aircraft formation over Dubai.

team would put 'smoke on' as they passed beside Ain Dubai, at 800ft the world's largest Ferris wheel, and then over the northern Palm.

Once past the Palm and oversea, I overtook the Al Fursan team and got them into close trail for the run-in towards the coast to fly past Ain Dubai again then Burj Al Arab, the iconic hotel shaped like a huge sail. Then it was inland, dodging skyscrapers, for a flypast over the Meydan Hotel, followed by the highlight: the Burj Khalifa, the world's tallest building at over 2,700ft. We climbed to avoid some tall buildings downtown then turned lazy left west to get the timing right past the Burj. The good news: it was poking out of the haze layer clearly, so impossible to miss. We went past with smoke on at 2,000ft and it still seemed to loom over and dwarf us. With radio communications slightly fraught throughout, I was certainly kept busy. Once past the Burj and out to sea, the Al Fursan team headed back to Minhad while my wingmen left for more fun: 1-v-1 combat – they had loads of gas. This left me on my own to enjoy a transit down the coast, just above the haze, enjoying the view and reflecting on an unexpectedly interesting two days.

The following day the locals removed all the UAE decals and repainted the Hunter so that it was almost the same as when it arrived. It was a day off for the HHA team: time to reflect on a splendid effort by the two engineers who ensured the jet remained serviceable throughout, and by my spare pilot who had done most of the planning.

The return began on Saturday and was the reverse of the outbound route – with less pressure. A quick hop to Bahrain then press on to Amman. Once again, this was the longest leg but this time into wind, forecast to be 60 but actually 100kts. No snags as there was an alternate, Al Jouf, 250nm short of Amman in western Saudi. I kept a careful eye on my planned fuel, but one snag with the Hunter is that you don't know how much fuel you actually have until you get down to 'wings and feeders'. The outboard external tanks just show a white 'dolls-eye' when empty after about 20 minutes. While the inboard drops have a float switch and a Perspex window on the front of the tank, it gives only a vague indication of how much is left. I came up

with a figure for how much fuel I required passing abeam Al Jouf and, sure enough, I didn't quite have that amount. But then the inboards normally show more once you've descended. Also, at the back of my mind was that the Hercules was routing around Saudi again, so if I landed in Al Jouf for fuel, I could be there for some time awaiting my start trolley. But the weather was good in Amman, so onward I pressed. As expected, the GPS dropped out nearing Jordan; then my

Job done – Rick celebrates.

planned range descent was denied due to traffic below me. Fortunately, I could see Amman from the top of descent and pointed at the runway with the throttle at idle. The gods had finished playing with my worry beads and Amman tower cleared me to land from a straight-in visual approach; I shut down with almost the planned fuel.

No more dramas to Athens on Sunday. However, with a storm expected to hit the UK on Tuesday, we went for a two-leg day on Monday via Genoa. Eventually airborne on the final leg after a minor delay, my heart rate calmed down as the Alps appeared in glorious sunshine with snow on all the peaks. I had a skiing holiday coming up, so all was well with the world.

Driving home from Scampton that night to North Yorkshire, reflecting on a busy couple of weeks, foremost in my mind was affection for the 62-year-old jet that had flown 12 sorties without even a minor hiccup. This was a feat I never achieved in the RAF flying the Phantom or Tornado! I had also worked harder leading the ten-ship downtown Dubai than at any other point in my flying career (except perhaps on the QWI course). And I had passed my ten-ship lead check.

Strictly speaking this is an ex-RAF story, but its unique nature more than justifies inclusion. [Ed.]

* * * *

SQUADRON LEADER DEREK SHARP

After two tours on Canberras, with 73 Squadron in Cyprus and 14 Squadron in Germany, Derek Sharp became a Chipmunk QFI before returning to the front line on 6 Squadron, flying the Jaguar. A further bout of instructing at the Hawk Tactical Weapons Unit (TWU) was interrupted by the loss of an eye in a bird strike.[28] Undeterred by this handicap, he spent the latter part of his career flying the VC10 from Brize Norton with 10 Squadron.

NEVER VOLUNTEER

I spent the first half of my RAF career as a fast-jet pilot. But after the Hawk accident that cost me my left eye, I moved sideways to the 'Queen of the Skies', the mighty VC10. It's been said that the life of a VC10 transport crew is long periods of boredom punctuated by short periods of excitement. Nothing illustrates this better than a

---

28 Half-blinded, Sharp was awarded the AFC for successfully recovering the damaged aircraft.

Derek Sharp.

sortie to Skopje to support the Balkan war effort in late 1995. I probably should have known better than to volunteer for a mission to the front line. There were warning signs right from the start – only one steward, and cargo comprising 35,000lbs of high-explosive artillery shells.

We were a few hours late leaving for Macedonia, but initially all went well. That was until we crossed the Adriatic. I wasn't really bothered about penetrating the no-fly zone, or the threat of cruise missiles bound for Serbia, nor even the prospect of thunderstorms ahead. But I was concerned to learn that we had rations for only six hours' flying. How could we possibly cope? Pulling myself together, I began to concentrate on avoiding the nastiest storms on the weather radar. More problems: lots of ugly blotches on the screen stretched far ahead. It was partial relief to learn from my wise old head of a navigator that they were mountain tops – but they were only 2,000ft beneath us. We could fly no higher because of the potential cruise missile risk. A quick glance out of the cockpit was enough to prove my navigator right. What luck to have a window seat. I'd certainly have to pick my way carefully through the cumulonimbus clouds, as well as those others with a hard centre in the shape of a mountain top.

As if there wasn't enough to worry about, a jagged fork of lightning appeared from an ominously dark cloud. We'd been hit. The aircraft shuddered and there was a strong smell of burning. My first thought was, thank heavens we're not carrying any passengers. Then I remembered the air stewardess who was sitting on the flight deck jump seat. Maybe it hadn't been such a good idea to invite her to observe a routine sortie as a way of helping to overcome her timidity, and even her fear of flying. It was only then that I recalled we were also carrying 35 tons of high explosives!

It seemed that the lightning strike fireball had rolled past the high explosives and left the aircraft at the tail. What now? Divert to somewhere other than a potentially hostile

VC10 at Bardufoss.

Macedonia, of course: a nice little holiday airport in Greece would do. And it did. Once we'd landed the engineers found only limited damage – some charring and a few holes. It certainly wasn't enough to stop us from continuing on to Skopje, where we landed uneventfully – except for the surface-to-air missile which fortunately missed us.

Once on the ground my mobile phone soon rang. Mother to wish me happy birthday? The boss perhaps? After all, I'd recently made a mess of my logbook (not my fault: computer error). Or was it an apology from in-flight catering for starvation rations? No, it was simply HQ to advise that surface-to-air missiles had been launched at incoming aircraft at our destination. Do not pass 'Go', do not collect £200. Too late, of course. We were well aware since we'd been the target. Not to worry though. We were safely on the ground having a cup of tea.

After hours of negotiation (to avoid spending the night in tents – decidedly not Transport Command practice), HQ was persuaded to let us return home. The decision owed at least something to the fact that refugees were still leaving in civilian airliners. At the end of what was already a long day we at last took off – but for Germany rather than home. The change of plan was thanks to another inbound aircraft turning back on learning of the likely dangers (cowards!). It thus became our task to deliver *his* passengers to RAF Brüggen. All went well, co-pilot landing apart (nothing unusual there) until we checked in with HQ. Because we'd been on duty more than 18 hours, we were grounded. Even worse: when we arrived at our hotel the bar was closed (nothing unusual there either – it was 0200). But we staggered off to bed, happy in the knowledge of a job well done. Tomorrow would be a better day – or so we thought.

As we lined up for take-off next morning, the army colonel to whom I'd offered the jump seat remarked on what he'd heard had been a difficult day for us 24 hours earlier. I reassured him that yesterday was an exception; today everything would run on rails. But it didn't. The flight engineer saw to that just minutes later with his call to abort take-off: "Fire, number one engine!"

Looking back, my guardian angel must have been on double time those couple of days. On second thoughts, she didn't prevent me from ignoring my father's advice never to volunteer. Nor did she persuade me to remain at Thessaloniki rather than press on to Skopje with a damaged aircraft. That said, she's done me pretty good service over the years. Like most who survive traumatic experiences, I've been pretty lucky.

* * * *

SQUADRON LEADER KEN SIMPSON

After completing the last Piston Provost[29]/Vampire course at Cranwell, Ken Simpson went on to fly Hunters in a variety of roles: with 14 Squadron, the last of the day fighter squadrons in Germany, 1 Squadron in the DFGA role and 1417 (FR) Flight at Khormaksar.[30] A Phantom conversion in the US was followed by tours on the OCU at Coningsby and subsequently 2 Squadron in Germany. He retired at his 38/16 point[31] to join British Aerospace.

A BIT OF A FLAP (1)

During my time in Aden, from 1965–67 I ferried 11 Hunters (including FGA9s, FR10s and T7s) to and from the UK. Sometimes it was via Jeddah in Saudi Arabia, and sometimes via Tehran, in what was then Persia. Every trip had a story of some kind. On this particular occasion I was leading a guy who I did not know and who did not have a great deal of Hunter time under his belt. After leaving the UK we stopped overnight in Luqa, Malta. The next day, landing at Nicosia, Cyprus, my number

---

29 The Percival Provost T1 as it was commonly known.

30 During his Aden tour he enjoyed the possibly unique distinction of earning both an AOC's Reprimand and a Mention in Dispatches.

31 The date on which an officer reaches the age of 38 or the day after the date on which he completes 16 years' reckonable service from the age of 21 to qualify for immediate retired pay.

Ken Simpson in Sharjah.

two forgot to lower full flap. He must have landed a bit fast too because just as I turned off onto the taxiway, he hurtled past and off the end of the runway – there was no safety barrier in those days – and into the desert, completely destroying a recently refurbished FGA9. He was told to wait at Nicosia until the Board of Inquiry concluded, while I had to wait until a Canberra could escort me the rest of the way to Aden. (Just in case there was a major emergency which might result in an ejection, for example, unaccompanied long-range flights in the Hunter were not permitted.)

Whilst in limbo we decided to go downtown one night and gatecrash a party we had heard about. It was very boring so my number two decided to push people into the pool. Needless to say we were ejected. Very early the next morning a flying officer (the adjutant) knocked on the door of our room in the officers' mess. We were told to report to the station commander's office immediately. The group captain asked about the previous night's mission downtown and told us the owner of the house where we had caused trouble wanted to see us – it was the German ambassador! Apparently one of the people who ended up in the pool was his daughter who, for medical reasons, was not allowed to go swimming.

We waited with knees shaking in the ambassador's office. When he arrived he came forward and shook us warmly by the hand and offered us a drink – of whisky. It seemed his daughter's supposed medical condition did not exist. She was very shy and for years had been using the excuse of an ear problem to avoid going into the water. What she really craved was attention – which she received in spades as she was pulled from the pool. The ambassador thanked us for helping his daughter break a lifetime's habit of shyness, wished us well and sent us on our way.

The station commander refused to believe our story and confined us to base for the rest of our stay.

A BIT OF A FLAP (2)

One evening in the officers' mess bar in Aden, I met a Gibraltar Shackleton crew who were on their way to Muharraq, Bahrain. We had a few beers and realised that we would be taking off about the same time the next day. The captain and I concurred that it would be great if we could take some pictures of each other, so we agreed a rendezvous point and time. Sure enough, we met up not long after take-off. Flying a Hunter FR10 with four external fuel tanks to match speed with the Shackleton flying flat out, I had to use full flap. But we did manage to take some amazing photos of each other. Just before we went our separate ways, I offered to bank away steeply so they could get some good underside shots. As I rolled away from them, inevitably I had to descend slightly. It was at this point I realised that the Shackleton had descended to about 500ft. The next ten seconds were some of the most frightening of my life – I very nearly hit the ground. Some phrases come to mind: unauthorised activities, improperly briefed, and I learnt about flying from that.

READ THE SMALL PRINT

In the early days of Tornado flying, shortly after taking off from Nörvenich, a German air force aircraft suffered a major hydraulic system failure. The crew consulted the emergencies checklist and found their failure required a landing as soon as possible.

A Hunter of 1417 (FR) Flight over the Radfan. (Ken Simpson)

Although the Tornado wasn't suffering any control difficulties, braking after landing and steering on the runway would prove difficult; the checklist therefore required an approach-end hook-wire engagement.

The crew returned to base, explained their situation to the control tower and prepared for an emergency landing. The Tornado had a hook similar to those on carrier-based aircraft; it could be used to engage the wires stretched across the runway at either end, i.e. for take-off and landing emergencies. With hook lowered, the crew made their approach and touched down just short of the hook-wire and waited for the Tornado to decelerate. But nothing happened. The aircraft continued down the runway at relatively high speed. The control tower advised that they could see sparks coming from the hook as it went down the runway, so clearly the hook was down. Approach-end engagements could sometimes result in the hook bouncing over the hook-wire. Assuming this to be the case the crew decided to rely on the hook catching the far-end/departure wire and informed the control tower accordingly. However, when they reached the far-end hook-wire nothing happened; there was no deceleration. With a large drop at the end of the Nörvenich runway, the crew had no alternative but to eject – which they both did and landed safely. Meanwhile the aircraft went down the embankment and was totally destroyed.

What went wrong? Although the crew had turned to the correct page in the emergency checklist, they hadn't noticed the small print at the end of the page. It said that to protect the aircraft from serious structural damage on making an approach-end hook-wire engagement, they needed to reduce weight by burning off fuel. The checklist then referred the crew to another page where they could calculate the maximum aircraft weight for such a landing. This they failed to do.

As a precaution the manufacturer had fitted the hook with a shear pin so that in the event of an overweight landing, the pin would break and the claw part of the hook would break off. The crew had caught the hook-wire on landing but because they were overweight, the shear pin broke and the claw part of the hook came away. It was simply the stub end of the hook that caused sparks to fly, as noted by the control tower team. The crew were unaware of this and assumed that the hook would still catch the far-end wire. Clearly, that was not going to happen. The simple moral of a story from my time with British Aerospace: read the small print.

Another ex-RAF story, justified in this case by the lesson drawn. [Ed.]

* * * *

SQUADRON LEADER BOB TUXFORD

A former Cranwell cadet, Bob Tuxford's first operational tour was on the Victor tanker. After a USAF exchange posting flying KC-135s and a QFI tour on the JP at Church Fenton, he returned to Marham, first on 57 Squadron and subsequently 55 Squadron. Much of 1982 was spent in the South Atlantic thanks to the Falklands War, after which he completed the Empire Test Pilots' School (ETPS) course; he went on to test all the RAF's large aircraft and introduce the TriStar into service. Retiring in 1987, Bob spent a further 24 years in civil aviation, logging over 18,000 hours on 72 different types.

AN AIR-TO-AIR REFUELLING MASTER CLASS

Sixteen days after Argentina invaded the Falkland Islands, on 18 April 1982 five Victor K2 tankers arrived on Ascension Island; a further four aircraft and crews followed next day. With some specially modified, they were tasked with photo and maritime reconnaissance and an array of air-to-air refuelling support missions, including what proved to be a record-breaking Vulcan attack on the runway at Port Stanley airfield – a mission that would involve a round trip of some 7,600nm.

On 29 April the mood on the island changed with the arrival of two sinister looking 'Tin Triangles'. Sitting squat on the apron, even to the uninitiated the bombers were obviously heavily laden. Next evening the plan was revealed. Three sections, comprising 11 Victors and two Vulcans, would make up the outbound wave. There would be four tankers in each of Red and White sections, whilst a further three in Blue section would support the two Vulcans. Seven tankers, two sections of three backed up by an airborne reserve, would make up the recovery wave. Launching approximately seven hours after the initial take-offs, two of these Victors were tasked to RV with the post-attack Vulcan some 450nm off the Brazilian coast, abeam Rio de Janeiro.

Bob Tuxford (centre) and crew at Ascension.

Even the most seasoned tanker men had never seen such a complicated fuel plan. To add insult to injury, it would be conducted at night in order to achieve a dawn strike seven hours after launch. This meant all the outbound refuellings would be undertaken at night. Furthermore, the whole outbound detail would be conducted covertly, with radio silence until the strike was delivered.

At 2230 hours local time on Friday 30 April, when the massed formation started their engines simultaneously, one of the Victors encountered an engine problem and was replaced in the taxi stream by a ground reserve. Thirteen aircraft – 11 Victors and two Vulcans – assumed their designated positions within the choreographed taxi plan. Under total radio silence, they took to the runway at one-minute intervals and staggered into the air.

Once airborne each tanker made a brief check of its centreline hose-drum unit. White 4 found to his horror that the hose would not trail and was replaced by Flight Lieutenant Steve Biglands (aka 'Biggles') from Blue section. Next, the primary Vulcan aircraft would not pressurise and it too had to extricate itself from the snake-climb sequence. The reserve Vulcan, manned by Flight Lieutenant Martin Withers' crew, would now take over the bombing role as Blue 2. Within ten minutes of getting airborne we were down to the bare minimum of tankers needed to support the remaining bomber.

The plan called for the Victors to pool their fuel resources through successive mutual fuel transfers in a cascading sequence. Alongside, the Vulcan would be kept topped-up at the designated refuelling brackets en route. The first was 700nm

Victor K2s at Wideawake airfield.

down-track, less than two hours into the mission. Two Victors of Red and White sections were planned to refuel to tanks-full from the other two aircraft in their sections. I positioned myself, as White 2, astern White 1 for an uplift of some 50,000lbs of fuel. Such a massive transfer would require a contact lasting 25–30 minutes – at night. Even as their tanks approached full, all receivers would stay in contact so that each would be full of fuel at the same time at the geographical end of each refuelling bracket.

On completion of the first refuelling, the four offloading tankers turned for Ascension, their job done. The rest of the formation continued southbound, unaware that the departing four Victors had all eaten deeply into their fuel reserves. They were down to barely half of the expected fuel remaining on arrival at Ascension and had to be cleared for consecutive straight-in approaches, there being no time for the preceding aircraft to backtrack along the runway and vacate for the following aircraft. The first three Victors had to position as close to the runway end as possible to leave sufficient room for the fourth to land. With each aircraft pulling up behind the next, there was the potential for a motorway pile-up in the event of braking parachute or wheel-brake failure; but luckily, all aircraft landed in sequence without incident. That said, it was already clear that there might be serious deficiencies within the complicated fuel plan.

At the second bracket, approximately 1,900nm south of Ascension, the five remaining aircraft began refuelling, after which two more Victors headed back to the island. Unknown to those of us pressing on towards the Falklands, one of these aircraft had developed a fuel leak. Facing the possibility that they might have to ditch in the South Atlantic, the crew put out a Mayday call: an urgent request for the launch from Ascension of a rescue tanker, otherwise known as a terminal airborne tanker (TAT).

Approaching the third bracket, around 40 degrees south, I was leading a formation that now comprised Flight Lieutenant Biglands' tanker and Flight Lieutenant Withers in the Vulcan. Some 2,700nm from Ascension, I transferred around 30,000lbs of fuel to the bomber. At that moment the weather deteriorated. There was no longer any clear horizon in the black night sky; we encountered increasing turbulence, momentary flashes of lightning and witnessed the erratic sparks of St Elmo's fire. With our radar kit deliberately selected off under 'silent' procedures, we had flown unknowingly into towering thunderstorm clouds. With the start of the bracket approaching, I flashed my lights to call Biggles astern. All three aircraft reacted like bucking broncos and my centreline hose flailed up and down around 20ft or so.

After several aborted attempts, Biggles eventually made contact with my unstable hose and fuel started to transfer. Shortly afterwards, however, he broke radio silence: "I've broken my probe!" With little time to consider the options, I decided to swap places with the other tanker and take back the fuel already offloaded. I then experienced the same problems as Biggles had just a few minutes earlier. After a number of failed attempts, I finally made contact and fuel started to flow. However, I was immediately aware that my control inputs were becoming increasingly aggressive and my flying was bordering on the dangerous. I had to break contact to take a brief respite and regain composure. After a short while the turbulence started to abate and I regained contact with Biggles' hose without too much difficulty. I settled into the normal position, relieved that my flying was somewhat more measured. Slowly, the horizon returned; the stars began to show through the dispersing clouds and calmer conditions prevailed for the remainder of the refuelling contact.

Biggles' broken probe meant he would be unable to receive fuel on his return to Ascension so I broke radio silence briefly to ask him to limit my transfer to ensure he would have sufficient fuel to recover safely. Once my fuel transfer was complete, Biggles turned left for 'home', leaving the remaining Vulcan on my starboard side as we pressed on towards the final refuelling bracket.

It had been some time since we checked our fuel remaining and compared it with the master fuel plan. Finding we were some 20,000lbs short, we now faced a predicament. Assuming we gave the Vulcan the planned transfer at the final bracket, we would run out of fuel 500nm short of Ascension on our return. My gut feel was to press on with the mission, trusting in the operations team on Ascension Island to solve this potential problem. Without declaring my hand, however, I asked each crew member how they felt about continuing. They were unanimous, so we pressed on.

At the fourth and last bracket we planned to transfer close to the scheduled fuel to the Vulcan, around 13,000lbs. It would leave us enough to return north to around 24 degrees south, RV with a TAT (provided one was available) and take on enough fuel to get us home. As we flashed the lights to indicate to the Vulcan that he had received his offload, aware that his tanks were not quite full, Withers remained in contact. After a short altercation, I started a left turn northbound. Astonishingly, the Vulcan started turning with us! In desperation and perhaps against my better judgement, I asked my nav radar to clear him for contact again and offer even more fuel. Almost immediately, he broke radio silence with another call: "We're off."

This left us somewhat perplexed. Was he off to the Falklands or Ascension? Just after that, we lost visual contact with him and I let the aircraft settle into a cruise-climb to meter out our fuel as efficiently as possible. The atmosphere in my cockpit was subdued to say the least. We calculated that the aircraft would run out of fuel some two hours short of Ascension. Having gone through the drills and checks a couple of times, we settled back in reflective mood, only for disappointment and melancholy to be replaced with elation 45 minutes later.

Listening on the HF radio, my AEO heard the codeword 'Superfuse' and announced it on the crew intercom. There was suddenly euphoria in the cockpit as we celebrated the fact that the Vulcan crew had successfully bombed the runway at Port Stanley airfield. The AEO was now able to break radio silence and call HQ STC and Operations Control on Ascension. First priority was to request a tanker to meet us on our return. Next we advised that the Vulcan could arrive at the Rio RV with less fuel than planned. It took the better part of half-an-hour to get these vital messages through but eventually we were able to confirm a TAT had been scrambled from Ascension to meet us. Around three hours later, with barely one hour's fuel remaining, we established radio contact with our TAT. The RV was faultless and the tanker rolled out two miles ahead of my aircraft. In the gin-clear morning skies, the sight of that beautiful crescent wing and trailing centre hose was one for sore eyes.

Once cleared for contact, I started a careful approach to the basket, knowing that four pairs of eyes were boring holes into the back of my head. This was no time to rush things or attempt a first-time contact purely to impress. As I cautiously set up to make the most-important contact of my life, the probe tip gently passed the basket at the three o'clock position – the best missed contact of my refuelling career. On the second approach, my probe tip slid precisely into the centre of the basket and settled into the reception coupling with a satisfying clunk. Almost immediately, the call, "Fuel flows", came over the radio and all hell broke loose as my crew whooped and hollered in unison. Meanwhile, I had to maintain my composure because nothing was assured until we had sufficient fuel to get us back to Wideawake airfield, still almost three hours away. Distancing myself from the celebrations around me, I waited the ten minutes or so that it took to complete the refuel. Once that milestone was reached, the raucous reaction started all over again.

With recovery fuel onboard and a suitable reserve to cater for any contingency, the remainder of the flight back to Ascension Island was uneventful. But there was time to begin reflecting on what, at over 14 hours, would prove to be my longest ever sortie, effectively the culmination of everything I'd learnt about flying – and about people – during all my time in the RAF.

In recognition of the part he played in Operation Black Buck 1, Squadron Leader Bob Tuxford was awarded the AFC. His crew – Flight Lieutenant Glyn Rees (co-pilot), Squadron Leader Ernie Wallis (nav radar), Flight Lieutenant John Keeble (nav plotter) and Squadron Leader Mike Beer (AEO) – were all awarded the Queen's Commendations for Valuable Service in the Air. [Ed.]

CHAPTER 9
JUNIOR OFFICERS' JAPES

FLIGHT LIEUTENANT JOHNNIE BAINES

Hunters were the core of Johnnie Baines' operational life during an eight-year short service commission. After a first tour on 54 Squadron he moved to 1417 (FR) Flight in Aden and thence to 4 Squadron at Gütersloh in Germany where he was part of 'Four's Four', a formation team. He retired in 1967 to join the civil aviation world and was still enjoying flying well into his 80s.

YOUTHFUL EXUBERANCE

It was 1959 and I was close to completing basic flying training on 147 Course – on the Piston Provost at Tern Hill. I had done well, thanks to my previous experience flying Chipmunks with Queen's UAS in Belfast. In fact I had won several of the trophies to be presented at the end of course prize-giving.

Johnnie Baines.

But wait. Not so fast. A week or so before said prize-giving I was in the officers' mess bar late one night, in the company of one of the instructors. The bar eventually closed and we spilled out into the passageway, right beside a notice board. The instructor took out his cigarette lighter and singed a couple of the notices. I thought this was a great jape and did likewise. The only trouble was that the notice I chose to embellish had been handwritten by no less a person than the station commander; it exhorted us all to use italic script. I only burned a corner, which we covered up with the large red 'immediate attention' notice. Alas, the subterfuge was to no avail. Monday morning brought demands to know who did the dastardly deed, or we would all be shovelling snow for a week!

I meekly confessed. Next came an 0900 appearance, hat on, before the station commander. I was marched in … left right, left right. The outcome: severely reprimanded, and all my trophies but one went to the student in second place. Thankful not to be ejected from the service forthwith, I was permitted to proceed to jet training on the Vampire, at RAF Oakington. From there, in 1960, I went to the Hunter OCU at Chivenor, and then on to 54 Squadron at Waterbeach. It's here that I learnt another lesson. I was on a 'fill the squares' routine three-leg low-level sortie. First leg was across the south of England, second leg north over the Brecon Beacons in Wales and third leg back to Waterbeach. It was very much routine stuff. 420kts, 250ft.

When I turned onto the second leg I saw that the Brecon Beacons were covered in cloud. I climbed to about 4,000ft, adjusted the airspeed accordingly to keep the stopwatch timing accurate, and sailed along using time and heading to navigate. (This was 1960 remember.) After a minute or two of this, I decided to ease down and clip the tops of the cloud, to at least enjoy a sense of speed. Shortly afterwards I got the shock of my life when a farmhouse flashed past – it was slightly above me! I was flying past a hill which had been obscured by cloud. It was a very chastened and subdued young pilot who completed the sortie back to base.

I wonder how many others made similar mistakes but never lived to tell the tale. It was a classic 'I learnt about flying from that' experience. I hate to think what the farmer experienced.

* * * *

LIEUTENANT CHRIS BOLTON RN

The first productive posting in Chris Bolton's unusual career was in 1966 as a creamed-off QFI, a JP instructor at Syerston. This was followed by tours on 208 Squadron, Hunters in the Middle East, then 6 Squadron, the RAF's first Phantom operational unit. An exchange tour with 892 NAS, flying the F-4K, led eventually to a second – via a brief period as an OCU instructor – as a lieutenant RN, the rank at which he retired in 1978 to join the airlines.

IN THE NAVY ...

With a good deal of Phantom experience already behind me, in 1974 I was due to begin an exchange tour with the Royal Navy. Having positioned by rail in Plymouth, my observer (no more navigator terminology) and I enjoyed a final meal ashore at a rather good restaurant. So good, indeed, that my astute observer spotted FOCAS (Flag Officer Carriers and Amphibious Ships), one Rear Admiral Desmond Cassidy, amongst the other diners.

The following morning we embarked on an RFA tanker to rendezvous with HMS *Ark Royal* for replenishment at sea. Closing alongside the carrier, lines were fired across between ships to take on the transfer hoses – and me. Jackstay transfer between ships was used for light stores (up to about 250kgs) and for personnel comprised a webbing seat, which was how I joined *Ark* for the first time. The rest of 892 NAS, 12 aircraft, had flown aboard the previous day. Having dumped my bags in my assigned cabin, down in the bowels, I made my way to Flyco (Flying Control), where my next couple of hours were spent observing flight operations under the supervision of an experienced US Navy exchange pilot. That completed the build-up to my first launch and subsequent recovery.

I was scheduled for first launch in the afternoon push: one of three F-4Ks to carry out air intercepts followed by two-inch rocket projectile practice on the

splash target towed 500 yards astern. Taxiing out to the waist catapult, my pulse rate was probably a little elevated. The pulse rate of my observer was clearly even more so. For him, it wasn't just another launch, it was a first launch with a rookie carrier pilot. We were expertly marshalled onto the catapult. Brakes applied, aircraft holdback unit engaged, brakes released, nose leg extended (by 40 inches) and aircraft tensioned. The area ahead of

Chris Bolton.

the aircraft was no longer visible over the nose. Having clutched the stick-positioning device (SPD),[32] I acknowledged correct stabilator angle as reported externally, checked internally and correct for take-off weight. Ground crew cleared away to starboard. The flight deck officer (FDO) waved his green flag over his head and I applied maximum cold power, followed by maximum afterburner. Significant noise, vibration, and adrenalin. Heavy breathing from the rear cockpit. No surprise there – you'd be the same!

All internal checks complete, I held my right hand up to the FDO. He checked for the green light from Flyco, and upon receiving it and checking all clear ahead, he lowered his green flag to the deck. This was the signal for the catapult operator to take his hands off his head and press the large circular plate in front of him to fire the catapult. I held power at maximum top-left corner lest the g-force retard the throttles, with stick back against SPD restraint, and head firmly against the ejection seat headrest. A seemingly interminable wait as half-a-ton of superheated steam at 600°C broke the hold-back unit weak link – a break-out force of about 60,000lbs. In reality it was about two seconds. Then the very rapid acceleration to about 4g. After the 195-ft take-off run of about two-and-a-half seconds, I was airborne – with a marked decrease in acceleration. Rotate from nine to a 14-degree climb angle. Gear up, flaps up, burners out at 250kts. That was fun wasn't it? A real thrill! Only 80 minutes to go and it would be time for my first deck landing.

So what did I learn of the differences between the RN and RAF? As will already be obvious, I found much of the navy flying more exciting as well as more demanding. Whereas I was consistently assessed as high or above average in the RAF, a personal assessment of my naval flying performance was a steady average. The RN also had fewer restrictions on flying, having seemingly resisted the urge to legislate after almost every incident. There was no 'closing the barn door' culture. In this context, I hadn't previously pushed the limits to the degree I was now expected to. My first carrier experience was at age 28. For RN pilots, it had mostly been 20 or 21. At my ripe old age, I was no longer the daring, irresponsible 'ripshit' I once had been. What caused that I wonder? Maturity? Responsibility? Belated recognition of danger and being only human? Perhaps related to this was a navy career structure that treated aviation as a sub-specialisation in a seaman officer's progress. It should be noted that promotion was limited to lieutenant commander if you were on the supplementary

---

32 A small, clutched reel of wire mounted low on the centre console and attached to the control column to achieve the correct stabilator angle for any given weight/configuration. It prevented the control column coming back under high g during the launch and consequent over-rotation.

892 NAS Phantom F4-K with 40-inch nose-leg extension.

list: good enough to lead a squadron, but otherwise career limiting. Squadron COs were a level below their RAF equivalents. Rank inflation hadn't yet hit the RN. That said, two of my COs were promoted in post, but continued for the allotted period.

Enough of these philosophical observations on the intangible. A major difference was social in nature. I described my first day of carrier ops. To expand on that, immediately after parking the aircraft in Fly One,[33] I stepped clumsily and gratefully out of the aircraft and walked back towards the island superstructure. Elation was certainly the foremost feeling, but desire for a quick cigarette and a bacon buttie in the all-ranks aircrew refreshment bar (ACRB) were right up there. But before that, there was a debrief from the landing sight officer, Peter Shepherd. He was the gent who'd earlier shown me horror movies of launches and landings aboard. I'd made two rollers and a hook-on. Without going into great detail, he considered my landing efforts to have been distinctly unimpressive. Of the colour-coded landing assessments available, mine was judged Red. It could only get better from here on. Blue was excellent with very few corrections; Green was good average; Yellow was agricultural.

---

33 When the ship was recovering aircraft they taxied out of the arrestor cables and parked in Fly One, one of four loosely divided parking areas on deck.

You guessed it: Red was dangerous. I'd caught One wire[34] after landing quite short. Did I look bothered? I'd made it, and incidentally thrilled all the 'goofers'[35] who'd assembled on the ship's superstructure to see the new boy make his first attempt.

And so to the ACRB, the snack bar within the island. Sweaty flying kit was de rigueur. A great spot to eat at any time during 'Flying Stations'[36] and banter with the other aircrew, of whom there were many. The Air Group comprised 39 aircraft – four other types in addition to the Phantom: the Sea King, Buccaneer, Gannet and Wessex.

To conclude this RN/RAF comparison, a few thoughts on non-flying aspects. After a flight it was time to lay aft, shower/change into rig of the day, and continue with life on board. Reading and writing letters were popular pastimes – there was no Wi-Fi, TV or radio in our cramped cabins. Initially, I shared with three others on six deck, two decks below the waterline. My bunk sat over a built-in chest of drawers with an adjoining desk. Sleep was easy. With lights out, there was complete darkness. The constant sound of ventilation, propeller shafts and water flowing through many exposed pipes, could be soporific. Unhelpfully though, the heads (toilets) and showers were one deck above.

Leisure time could also be spent in the wardroom, where board and card games were common. 1800 hours was the magic time. The bar opened. We were all expected to be there: 14 crews' worth of generally thirsty folk raring to go. Don't be late or you'll be banished to talk to the 'Chopper Pukes' (helicopter crews). The dining room being small, and the Air Group being big, we alternated early and late dinner sittings with the Buccaneer squadron. Every night was a dining-in night for our very close community. Drink was cheap and a matter of personal perspective. There was a limit of £20 per month for all aircrew. With vodka at 2p per shot and 12.5p for draught beer, spending your daily allowance on vodka could be a quick road to oblivion – as well as being within the rules. But, as the boss pointed out to me: "It's a limit, not a target." After dinner, we'd commonly gamble for who bought liqueurs. Being prepared for such a gambling loss, I had the foresight to 'borrow' my teetotal observer's bar number on one occasion. Sadly, it resulted in my trusty partner being chastised for his excessive consumption by the XO (executive officer), a somewhat dour Scottish commander who watched closely for any excess in the drinks department. It could

---

34 The first of four, spaced eight feet apart, starting some 60ft from the 'round down' (the stern of the carrier where the flight deck starts). Target for the F-4 was the third arrestor wire.

35 Slang for anyone who positioned themselves, usually on the island superstructure (which extended up to four levels above the flight deck) to watch flight deck operations.

36 Any time when flying operations were being conducted.

be punished by 'stoppage of wine bill' or, more seriously, stoppage of shore leave too. 'Stoppage of both' was a dire punishment indeed.

On reflection, it was a surprise to find that even as an experienced aviator, the carrier experience taught me so much about flying – and also about myself. At the end of a tour with the navy that severely tested my abilities, I was left to ponder how I'd have coped as a much younger man. Not well I suspect.

* * * *

FLIGHT LIEUTENANT JULIE GIBSON

Julie Gibson was the RAF's first operational woman pilot. She began her service life as an engineer at Wattisham, where her second job was as junior engineering officer (JEngO) on 74 Squadron, a unique unit equipped with the Phantom F-4J(UK). One of the first two women to complete basic flying training, her first tour was on 32 Squadron at Northolt flying Andovers. After converting to the Hercules she was posted first to 70 Squadron and subsequently 24 Squadron, both at Lyneham. When she retired in 2001 Julie had some 3,800 hours in her logbook.

FIRST OF THE FEW

I'd always wanted to fly. But until I was in my late twenties it seemed there was no way to fulfil my ambition. It wasn't for the want of trying. In an effort to beat the RAF system I'd written to my MP and even applied for a sixth form flying scholarship pretending to be a boy, disguising my signature so that 'Julie' looked like 'John', but nothing came of it. I suppose I must have been rumbled.

If I couldn't fly, I felt the next best thing would be to study aeronautical engineering. But when I spent a year in America as part of my university course and saw the opportunities available there for women in aviation, it simply added to my frustration. Over the years I even took flying lessons with the aim of gaining a private pilot's licence (PPL). But limited opportunities and the expense involved meant that continuity was poor and progress frustratingly slow. It was therefore a logical step to join the RAF as an engineer. There were no female pilots in those days, of course; it was the mid-1980s.

From my earliest days I took any and every opportunity to get airborne. During engineering training at Cranwell I even managed the odd trip in a JP. Occasionally the early morning weather check would have a spare seat which I was only too delighted

Julie Gibson at Finningley. (Julie Gibson)

(and privileged) to fill. Wonderful though these experiences were, in practical terms I was no nearer achieving my ambition.

But the service was changing. Rumours finally turned into reality and the door (as distinct from the flood gates) opened. I'd become aware that this might happen during my tour at Brawdy. A number of well-informed senior officers, there for refresher courses, said as much. So I was well prepared, and the day after the RAF announced that it would be recruiting female 'front-end' aircrew, I submitted my application for flying training. It must have been one of the first received because it was accepted almost immediately. I was hugely excited – but what was I letting myself in for? One thing was clear from the start. The publicity associated with being one of the first two women to tread this path – the other was Sally Cox – would have an intrusive and unwelcome effect on our progress. So would something else.

While it was reassuring to find that we were treated the same as any other student on the basic flying course, early on I found myself at a distinct disadvantage. It was quite a jump from a few hours in the Cessna 150 to the JP. All the others at Linton-on-Ouse had considerably more previous flying experience: UAS or elementary flying training. It wasn't the start I wanted. Here, though, I have to pay tribute to the instructors, all of whom went out of their way to be helpful to one for whom things didn't come easily, certainly at first. If that sounds patronising, nothing could be further from the truth. It was simply that Sally and I were made to feel 'one of the boys'. The last thing we wanted, and equally the last thing the others on the course wanted, was for us to be given any kind of special treatment. As it turned out, though, very early on we were.

Sally and I were progressing at roughly the same rate and were cleared for our first solos on the same day. It was no coincidence. Without either of us being aware on the day, the occasion was exploited as a PR exercise. With hindsight we probably should have anticipated something like this, but it was exposure we could do without. It was also a signal that we'd continue to be the subject of press interest as we progressed towards the award of those coveted RAF 'wings'. It wasn't until I joined my first operational unit that it became possible to exercise active control over an RAF PR machine that occasionally seemed all too ready to feed a voracious national press.

With hindsight, I should have realised that the wider world, and not just the RAF, would take a particular interest in the progress of the service's first two female pilot trainees. I was told this before the course began but it hadn't really sunk in; worse still, I had no training in how to deal with the resulting pressures. Here, and not for the only time, six years' previous experience as an engineer proved invaluable. It provided a firm grounding in dealing with extraneous issues – people and problems as well as the inevitable technical matters. Even so, press events to mark the announcement of our selection, the start of training and the aforementioned first solos (albeit staged the following day as a wise precaution) were unwelcome distractions – as were the hundreds of letters I received.

I went on to complete multi-engine training (MET), whereas Sally became the first woman to begin advanced training on the Hawk. The press was present at my wings ceremony too and while any pressure I felt certainly eased thereafter, it increased on Sally. Whether this was a factor in her leaving fast-jet training – she subsequently trained as a helicopter pilot – I'll never know, but it wouldn't be a surprise.

Once free of the training machine, in concert with the hierarchy on the squadrons with whom I served (more on which later), I was able to deal with requests for publicity in a less pressured way. Together we looked at opportunities for visits to schools and universities, for example, in a more considered fashion – almost as a secondary duty. Few such activities attracted publicity but it was a way of opening people's eyes to the opportunities there for those interested in aviation. As I simply loved flying, talking about it and seeing others' enthusiasm was reward in itself.

Given a choice I'd probably have opted to fly the Hercules after MET so I was mildly surprised, but in the end delighted, to find that my first operational tour would be flying Andovers with 32 Squadron at Northolt. Sadly, it was a truncated one in a couple of related ways: the aircraft was soon to be retired from service and, as a consequence, there would be no chance of moving on to captaincy – which was what I saw as the next flying goal. But if progress in this sense was delayed by conversion to a different aircraft type, it eventually led to seven very happy years flying the Hercules with 70 and then 24 Squadron at Lyneham. It also represented a chance to move beyond the European flying I was used to into a worldwide role.

My final tour as a Hercules captain was without doubt the pinnacle of my air force career. It was here that everything I'd learnt during my time in the service came together. I'd never claim to be a gifted pilot – truth be told they're a rare breed – but I was safe and reliable. Nor had I ever had to deal with any really tricky situations. The worst seemed always associated with bad weather: a recovery into Cyprus on three engines in a quite frightening lightning storm and the loss of the ILS system during a landing on the US eastern seaboard in equally appalling conditions. But thanks to superb instruction, a graduated learning process, and not least the faith and support of others, I like to think that the RAF turned me into a good Hercules skipper.

Looking back on 17 very happy years I have only one regret. I should probably have given more consideration to that specialist aircrew offer.

* * * *

FLIGHT LIEUTENANT MIKE GRIERSON

A navigator, Mike Grierson's operational career began in 1969 on Victor tankers with 57 Squadron at Marham. A change of role took him first to C-130 transport aircraft with 36 Squadron at Lyneham and later, after a spell as an OCTU flight commander, to 70 Squadron as a navigation instructor. The Met(eorological) Research Flight at Farnborough then VC10s with 10 Squadron at Brize Norton followed. He retired in 1993 with over 10,000 flying hours to become a Civil Aviation Authority (CAA) training standards inspector.

IT'LL BE ALL RIGHT ON THE NIGHT

Whilst a total eclipse may occur only once every 18 months, the timeframe to observe another eclipse at the same location is only once every 400 years. It is therefore not a major consideration for aviation – but the phenomenon did once figure in an interesting experience.

In June 1974 I was a Hercules navigator on 36 Squadron when my June schedule showed a trip to Australia. This was not a routine trip by any means and proved exceptional from start to finish. We were to transport a one-off heavy load from Abingdon to the Woomera test range. The load was both large and very heavy and fitting it into the freight bay of a C-130 was a challenge in itself. It meant only a single crew would be carried, accompanied by two ground engineers. Halfway round the world with only seven people was unique in the air support world. The usual route to the Far East wasn't feasible either, as we couldn't carry enough fuel for some of the longer legs; it would mean additional stopovers.

The task involved transporting this load to Woomera followed by a 48-hour rest

period in Darwin before taking the empty airframe to Hong Kong; from there two 36 Squadron crews would continue back to the UK westabout via the USA. At first sight, it appeared as though my crew had drawn the short straw.

Mike Grierson (left) with co-pilot Dave Harris, Masirah.

On 7 June we left RAF Lyneham with a Stonechat rocket motor that had been coaxed into the Hercules freight bay at Abingdon the previous day. With Akrotiri as the first port of call, the route took us to Sharjah, no longer an RAF base, to refuel and then on to Masirah. From there we followed the usual route via Gan to Singapore, where an aircraft unserviceability delayed our departure by a day. The leg to Darwin was flown on a bright moonlit night and I recall navigating by pinpoints all the way along the long chain of islands leading to the Timor Sea. Darwin was just a refuelling stop; after following the rabbit fence to Alice Springs we flew direct to Woomera.

We had been told that there was no accommodation available at Woomera; however, they did manage to find us something for one night in a club used by civilian workers there. The aircraft was unloaded and on the morning of 13 June we were scheduled to fly XV298 empty back to Darwin. The ground engineer asked how long the flight was going to be; I told him 4 hours 20 minutes. The engine magnetic plugs were due a check in four hours so the question was, does he check them at Woomera or Darwin? He decided to conduct the check before we left and on the number three engine plug found several metal objects. This meant an engine change; however, communication at Woomera was largely non-existent, a holiday weekend was due to start and there was no accommodation for the crew. Logic suggested a three-engine ferry to the RAAF base at Edinburgh Field, but our request for this was declined.

Finally, it was agreed the crew would travel to Edinburgh Field by other means to try and resolve the engine replacement issue. Transport was a Ford Transit van and the 300-mile journey to the RAAF base, on the outskirts of Adelaide, would take around seven hours to complete – in part because for the 50 miles between Woomera and Port Augusta there was no metalled road. On arrival at Edinburgh Field we managed to communicate with HQ Air Support Command at Upavon. The nearest C-130 engine was at Masirah and the nearest aircraft to deliver it was in Cyprus. The process was likely to take a week but at least we would complete the return journey to Woomera by train,

or so we thought. But unfortunately, two days earlier there had been a train crash and the line was closed, so we had to plan for a journey back by road. The highlight of another lengthy trip was passing a convoy of Austin Sevens travelling south as we drove north of Port Augusta.

Austin Sevens in the Outback.

On arrival back at Woomera after the seven-hour drive we faced a number of problems. First, there was no airfield lighting, so we had to depart before dark – around 1800. Then there was no fuel available; it had been in the train that crashed. Next, the aircraft was no longer empty and we had to transport the unserviceable engine and change-kit as well as conduct ground runs on the new engine, using up some of our valuable fuel. The final factor that concentrated the mind was that rare natural phenomenon, a total eclipse; it was due one hour before sunset, necessitating an airborne time no later than 1700.

Just as the sun started to eclipse on 20 June, eight days after we had arrived, XV298 took off from Woomera for a 4-hour 15-minute flight to Darwin. Looking at my logbook, I logged 50 minutes by day – an eclipse does not qualify as night flying. But I did manage to watch the eclipse through the sextant.

By way of a footnote, when I was working at the CAA in 1999, a solar eclipse was visible in the south-west of the UK on 11 August. A number of aircraft had planned to head in that direction to take advantage of the spectacle whilst airborne and this attracted the inevitable question: do you have to have valid night qualifications to fly during a total eclipse? Whilst a few of my colleagues hummed and hawed over the new European regulation,[37] I pointed out that the UK legal definition of night is the time from half-an-hour *after* sunset until half-an-hour *before* sunrise, sunset and sunrise being determined at surface level. The position of the moon – the cause of a solar eclipse – has nothing to do with it.

As in Australia 25 years before, there would be no entries in the night-flying columns.

* * * *

FLIGHT LIEUTENANT MARTIN SELVES

Martin Selves' flying career embraced a variety of types, starting with a first operational tour on the Javelin with 60 Squadron in Singapore. Hunters with 8 Squadron in the Middle East followed, then Phantoms at Brüggen on 31 Squadron. He then served as an instructor on the Jaguar OCU at Lossiemouth and the Hawk at Chivenor. He ended his RAF career as the QWI on 54 Squadron Jaguars at Coltishall.

---

37 In June 1999 the UK voluntarily adopted European standards with some law changes, including one related to night currency. To fly at night with passengers a pilot must have completed three take-offs and landings at night in the last 90 days.

A JUNIOR PILOT'S JAVELIN JOURNEY

My grandfather always teased that I would either be a blacksmith, like him, or a vicar. I didn't want to be either, or the bank clerk dad had his eyes on. The problem of my future was solved when out of the blue he took everyone to the Farnborough Air Show. Two things stuck in my memory: my first and best ever ice-cold Coca Cola and watching a Lightning take off, rotate to the vertical making a huge noise and then disappear. That looked like a lot of fun to me and the idea I might become a fighter pilot did not go away. A couple of years later I was on my way to Biggin Hill wearing a brand-new, tight-fitting charcoal Burton's suit that I hated, for pre-assessment. I passed, my suit was history, and I was asked to report to South Cerney a few months later.

Fast forward to flying training on the JP – a good trainer with heavy controls but reliable and aerobatic – and then the Gnat: tiny, extremely agile, with some testing characteristics. Crosswind landings were exciting with its tiny, narrow undercarriage; and the controls were so sensitive it was easy to overcontrol. It was light, powerful, and had wonderfully modern flight instruments. At the end of our course, postings were announced in the officers' mess bar: I was posted to Javelins. I knew nothing about this aircraft, so the next day I drove to WHSmith in Holyhead, bought *The Observer's Book of Aircraft* and looked it up. It said the aircraft was obsolete. Obsolete or not, it was nothing whatsoever like the two aircraft I'd flown so far.

Before joining the Javelin OCU I was posted to RAF North Luffenham. The base was responsible for fitting and instructing aircrew in the use of the partial pressure suits that kept the pilot conscious if cabin pressure was lost at high altitude. We learnt about the dangers of hypoxia and were exposed to sudden explosive decompression – 'banged' from around 30,000 to 50,000ft where we practised pressure breathing in the instant fog that temporarily appeared. You didn't have to breathe in; the pressure in your mask was fierce and you had to control it into your lungs.

No. 228 OCU was at RAF Leuchars in Fife, just south of Dundee and only a few

Martin Selves.

miles north of St Andrews golf course (more of which later). It was also home to the Lightnings of 23 and 74 Squadrons – the aircraft that so excited me years before. I never flew this aircraft but was always in awe of it. Leuchars was a long drive from Reading, where I lived, in my Borgward Isabella TS 75. It would have failed the MOT in every possible way, but it got me safely to the officers' mess on 5 September 1966.

My first impression of the Javelin was that it was big and imposing; it had a presence. The only way in and out was via a large ladder and it looked clumsy and ugly on the ground. But in flight from some angles it was a beautiful-looking aircraft. It was certainly very powerful, with four Aden cannons and four Firestreak missiles. It was quick to height and took only four minutes to reach 40,000ft, where it started to run out of puff. In the next four months I was to learn how to fly it and become a day/night fighter pilot.

The first job was to settle into the mess. Within a few days we all assembled in the bar, around 16 students, to 'crew up' over a few beers. Here I met Mike Bruce for the first time, and we decided to join at the hip for a course that would last four months. I chose well; he was sharp and learnt quickly. We were a good team and remained together on 60 Squadron at Tengah for another 13 months afterwards. Mike was destined for high rank and became a Phantom squadron commander later in his career. We found the course quite easy and were able to enjoy the ride, whereas

No. 60 Squadron in Tengah. Martin Selves is seated fourth from the left with Mike Bruce seated on the far right.

others had problems. Four pilots failed to finish the course. One didn't even reach the runway on his 'chop ride' – he departed the taxiway for the grass. The Javelin had odd toe brakes, with a time delay from brake application to seeing any effect. It was quite easy at first to overcontrol and follow a zig-zag pattern. When the initial application failed to produce a result, a second inevitably followed, which in turn led the pilot to make two larger inputs in the opposite direction.

Ground school took only a few days. The aircraft wasn't complicated but, as with the brakes, it did have some odd features. Another concerned the undercarriage. If you pressed the 'up' button with more than 40lbs, a pin entered the linkage (there was no warning light) and the undercarriage couldn't be lowered on the normal system when you came to land. This happened to me as a junior pilot in Singapore. It's worth a quick digression because I certainly learnt from a scary experience.

We were to practise medium-level interceptions over the sea west of the island. A strong weather front could be seen as we climbed to around 30,000ft under radar control. On the second or third set-up we were given a heading into a cloud that towered above us and our aircraft was struck almost immediately by a big flash of lightning. I lost one or two instruments, but that wasn't a problem as we found ourselves in clear skies very soon afterwards. I burnt off a lot of fuel and set off for Singapore which was clearly visible, as was the airfield at Tengah. The circuit was empty when I called "Downwind to land". But then I had another problem: the undercarriage failed to lower. It felt as though the 40lb undercarriage override pin had engaged. I wanted an undercarriage check and asked for the emergency lights to be turned on so the tower could let me know how things looked. The controller told us he was 'under instruction' but quite alone, so he went off looking for someone to help. This took a long time. Meanwhile we were burning off more fuel as we flew around the circuit. Time passed. The controller was as nervous as we were, but the lights came on in the end and after the flypast we were told the gear was firmly up. It was time to get a little alarmed as our fuel state was low, but just in time the CO arrived and talked over with us what to do next.

Landing wheels up at night had been done before, but I think the SOP was to fly to the east coast, by RAF Changi, and eject over the sea. Mike and I had talked this over already – it was an unpleasant thought – and now I began thinking about what the best height and airspeed would be for such an eventuality.

The boss now took firm control. He told me to pull the undercarriage override ring, which would remove the pin that would allow the normal 'down' button to work. When I did, the ring came away in my hand. Its connecting wire had broken.

We were seriously down on fuel now, down on our luck as well, but there was one last action that could save the day. We could blow the gear down with compressed air. Joy! The wheels came down with a crash, and three green lights were a very welcome sight. We really didn't fancy the alternative of premeditated ejection at night. The lessons were all too clear: think carefully before burning off too much fuel, and pay more respect to 'cunims'.[38]

Back now to what was a gentle course. I flew only some 43 hours on the aircraft and 12 in the simulator, a simple link trainer used primarily for navigators to practise interceptions. We had a lot to learn, particularly the navigators. They had to master the radar and the geometry/mechanics for each type of interception. We pilots simply had to respond quickly to the navigator's instructions and fly as accurately as possible – smoothly and safely too, especially when closing to within 200 yards or so of the target. At night over the sea at 1,000ft, believe me, 200 yards is close. You can see the red jet pipes glowing quite clearly in the dark.

We also practised 'overshooting' in case things got hairy. This happened for real one night when our overtake speed was very high. When Mike called "Overshoot" I said, "Which way?" An instant reply: "Doesn't matter." When I looked out during the turn we flew very, very close to the target aircraft's tail. No surprise that my instrument flying improved a lot over those four months. It was fun but hard work, particularly when targets were allowed to evade, and not a little dangerous at night at low level over the sea.

The course was designed around the navigator, but the pilots had to learn new tricks too. Circuit bashing was important, of course, but not that easy for the instructor in the back seat of the T3 who had little if any forward vision. He had to peer into a binocular-type system, linked to lenses either side of the front cockpit, to see ahead. We learnt skills like battle formation that we'd use for the rest of our flying careers. Then there was the mission to fly the Javelin supersonic, a difficult thing to do (and why would you want to anyway?). Hard though I tried, my particular aircraft wouldn't pass muster. Another unusual experience at the end of the course was firing our Aden cannons out over the North Sea. With a big, clunky trigger it took quite a squeeze to fire off the rounds and gave the airframe quite a shudder.

The aircraft itself was roomy and pleasant to fly, although the instruments were old-looking after the Gnat. Roll rates and aerobatics are best described as sedentary, while stalling and loops were prohibited. It was a missile platform really, and the

---

38 Cumulonimbus clouds.

Firestreak it carried was very impressive. Reheat was useful over 20,000ft, but below that it actually slowed you down. The fuel pumps couldn't deliver enough fuel for the engine and reheat together until medium level. This peculiarity was actually used tactically to frighten the 'enemy' at low level during the Indonesia-Malaysia confrontation, the long yellow exhaust flame appearing menacing to an insurgent on the ground.

The one outstanding feature of the aircraft was its airbrake system. Awesome. The airbrakes were so powerful that there was a speed switch to ensure that above 430kts the system would provide only half airbrake. This was to protect the navigator from injury as the deceleration was truly magnificent! If weather permitted, you could approach the runway at 20,000ft and call "30 seconds to break". Getting the aircraft nose down first helped a lot, and then with the airbrakes out both pilot and navigator hung in their straps during an exciting ride down. It was simply amazing. No other aircraft could do this.

I had just two memorable experiences during the course. The first was a ride in the back seat of a T3 at night. The captain was another student, and our job was to act as a permanent low-level target. All went well until we returned to Leuchars. A Lightning declared an emergency as we arrived; we should have landed and got out of the way, but my friend decided to orbit burning off fuel. Luckily, the Lightning landed quickly without taking the barrier and we prepared to land. Unfortunately, my friend made a very poor approach and we had to overshoot; he then did this three more times. He had speed-control problems and kept flying through the centreline, still way off the runway heading. With minimum fuel approaching I suggested I should handle speed control from the back seat while he did the rest. Even this went badly, although we did manage to land in the end. It was no surprise that he was 'chopped' a few weeks later.

The other problem occurred very early on when I landed with a right brake failure. I wasn't aware of this until I applied the brakes and ended up running onto the grass on the left side of the runway. Thanks to the Javelin's very effective rudder, I soon ended up back where I should have been, on the centreline, albeit wondering what to do next. My call should have been 'Barrier' and a net at the end of the runway would have been raised, but I didn't think of this. I could have told the tower I had a problem, but I didn't do that either. Instead, as I neared the end of the runway, I reapplied the brakes. Thanks to the one that still worked I went rapidly through at least 360 degrees before stopping. Help arrived, we climbed down the ladders and I noticed a pool of liquid under the undercarriage oleo. I put my finger in it, only to suffer a painful burn up to the first joint. It was that hot. To conclude this story with a related Javelin peculiarity, the huge rudder that saved my embarrassment wobbled dramatically on the ground – even after a safety modification resulting from one that detached a few years before.

No tale of the Javelin OCU would be complete without mention of a student friend (name withheld) who had an engine fire on his first 'solo' flight in early October 1966. The immediate actions included jettisoning the ventral fuel tanks directly under the Sapphire engines. But instead of pulling a lever this pilot pressed a button, thereby jettisoning wing stores rather than fuel tanks. A Firestreak missile, less warhead and propellant, instantly headed south for St Andrews golf course and landed almost vertical, close to the pin on the 18th green. A few golfers apparently thought it was a prank associated with Rag Week at the nearby university!

A lifetime's flying experience would follow my few short months as part of the last Javelin OCU course, but they're remembered with immense affection. The change from a modern, sophisticated trainer to an ageing fighter nearing the end of its service life might be seen as a retrograde step. But it was one that prepared a carefree 20-year-old for his first great adventure. And it reinforced a lesson for life: you never stop learning.

* * * *

FLIGHT LIEUTENANT DUNCAN WYLIE

In receipt of a sixth form scholarship, Duncan Wylie joined the RAF through Cranwell in February 1995. After training on the Tucano and then the Hawk, his first operational tour was on the Tornado GR1/4. An instructional tour on the same aircraft was followed by a return to the Hawk on 100 Squadron, where he was also the unit's display pilot. A ground tour as the aircraft's simulator acceptance manager then led to an unbroken sequence of tours flying the Typhoon, both operationally and as an instructor. Duncan retired from RAF service in 2023.

PRESSURE

I've learnt a lot about pressure. I'd already had one 'chop ride' at Valley when, on 17 February 1999, I was slated for another make-or-break sortie: a Cold War-style low-level mission, leading a pair with another instructor acting as the 'bounce'. I had to pass, or I'd be removed from the Hawk advanced flying training course. That I did, and would go on to amass over 4,000 hours on three different fast-jet types,

Duncan Wylie.

was down largely to some calm and reassuring instruction.

Aware that I'd only just passed the course, I now had to prove myself on a more complicated front-line aircraft. I was posted to the Tornado GR1 OCU at Lossiemouth, as a 'training risk'. Despite my acknowledged pure flying ability (I'd won the prize for 'Best Air Combat' at Valley), I found the more advanced, scenario-based sorties challenging – an area that would sometimes dog me, especially later on the Typhoon. That said, by the time I'd finished Valley, I'd subliminally absorbed the lesson of how to bring out the best from others. It would stand me in good stead when I later became an instructor myself. The fast-jet flying training system was geared to producing single-seat pilots, but crew cooperation was key to Tornado operations, a skill I needed to learn quickly. I enjoyed sharing the workload with someone else and my performance on the Tornado course was steady, but I found close formation flying tricky compared to the previous aircraft I had flown. The techniques I had been using were not working and I found myself being shouted at by my instructor in the back seat: "Get back on the references!"

It was poor instructional technique that didn't work for me, and I failed this trip twice. Granted a third (and probably final) attempt with a true gentleman who had a totally different approach, I passed this sortie. The moral needs no further explanation. I went on to enjoy working as a team with navigators/WSOs and, on completing the course, was sent to Marham for my first tour, with 2 Squadron. A second, as an OCU instructor, followed – a chance to put those instructing lessons into practice.

It was just over ten years between my first flight in the Tornado and my first trip in the Typhoon. At 34, with just over 2,300 flying hours under my belt, I still found the aircraft amazing. It's relatively easy to fly. You make traditional control inputs and the four flight control computers then decide how much control surface movement to give you. You can't stall, spin or overstress the aircraft under normal flight conditions. However, I found the later part of the course tough and started to doubt my ability in the dynamic, three-dimensional air-to-air environment. I had to process the information on the radar display, carry out simulated missile shots at the correct range, on the correct target, whilst transmitting various things on the radio. To make matters even more demanding, there was lots of aggressive climbing and descending. I was often working to capacity and had to repeat a couple of sorties. It didn't help that there was one instructor who I didn't like flying with – I didn't feel at ease with him shouting from the back seat. Mirroring that earlier Valley experience, the end-of-course check was flown with a very different character, laid-back and pragmatic. It went well. Next, it would be 11 Squadron at Coningsby.

Duncan Wylie in a Typhoon.

With the squadron heavily involved in combat operations over Libya, my CR work-up was a bit disjointed, which meant I couldn't take part. I didn't like not being involved. But I finally achieved Typhoon operational status in June 2011 and it felt good; I'd become a single-seat fighter pilot and was proud of what I'd achieved. My retirement point was now two-and-a-half years away. It was going to take me this long to get fully comfortable with operating the Typhoon, so I accepted an offer to become a 'professional aviator' or PA. Experienced pilots were being offered an extension of service up to age 55 (later it was 60). It generally involved staying in rank, and I was still a flight lieutenant. As such, I committed to a minimum of five years' service beyond 38, at which point I was posted back to the Typhoon OCU to become an instructor. I wasn't entirely happy to go but had no choice. This is the background to an astonishing incident.

In 2014, I spent four weeks with 3 Squadron out in Lithuania to support NATO's Baltic Air Policing mission. We were co-located with a Polish MiG-29 squadron. I'd sat loads of QRA in the UK and had a few scrambles, but nothing ever came of them. This was very different. I found myself scrambled at no notice; there was no 'heads up'. Then 15 minutes later my wingman and I were alongside four Russian aircraft stretched out over two miles: two Tu-22 'Backfire' bombers and two Su-27 'Flanker' fighters, one allocated to each bomber. They were all heading back to Kaliningrad but hadn't filed any flight plan or established communications with the Lithuanians. Our job was to report back the aircraft types and make sure their intent was not untoward.

The Russian fighters were very aggressive and got uncomfortably close as we took imagery of the bombers. I'd instructed my wingman to proceed to the back of the Russian formation and asked how he was doing. He sounded rather concerned but confident with it, telling me the fighter next to him had almost flown into him. We didn't know if this was intentional or not. We were near Swedish airspace and discovered that two Swedish Gripens had also come up for a look. I could imagine the dilemma of the Russian fighters, not knowing who to try and stiff-arm away and found it slightly amusing. They would sandwich themselves between the bombers and our Typhoons. Had I been able to reach out I could almost have touched the Russian jet. It was much closer than any formation we ever practised. One pilot, wearing a bright orange flight suit, was just a few metres away from me. But I thought to myself, they're just doing their job. Having stabilised in a position to photograph the bomber, I engaged the autopilot. I wasn't particularly close, but close enough for comfort and results. We were then instructed to shadow the Russian jets, which meant dropping behind a few miles until they approached their own airspace.

I drifted back and the Russians did the same; they didn't want me behind them. I gestured a goodbye signal to the orange-clad pilot, who did the same. It felt like the right thing to do. I had a big smile on my face as I got out of the jet and headed back to the operations room. It had been a good day out.

In February 2017 I was back on 11 Squadron, deployed to Akrotiri for Operation Shader. We were part of a wider coalition force conducting close air support operations over Iraq and Syria. I'd completed the work-up over the previous few months. Despite having flown fast-jet aircraft for over 18 years, I hadn't done anything like this before operationally. It had also been 15 years since I was in an aircraft carrying air-to-surface weapons in a hostile environment. We always operated in pairs and I was involved in multiple attacks against ISIS targets over the next 14 weeks. Sometimes friendly forces were as little as 90 metres away from the enemy, so we had to get it right. The year 2017 into 2018 was the busiest and most challenging one of my RAF career, but there was also lots of enjoyment and variety. I would spend over six months away in different locations. After Cyprus there were seven weeks in the Falklands (the fifth of seven such deployments), then a big multinational exercise in the UAE and, finally, Red Flag in the USA.

I hadn't been to Red Flag since 2001 – how different my role was this time. No more flying around at 100ft with all the fighters thousands of feet above. I was now in the thick of it, trying to make sense of the vast amount of information coming at me both internally, from the cockpit, and externally from the tactical control frequency. I began my four-ship lead tactical work-up in the prior UAE exercise but found it very challenging. The weapons instructors guiding me through were patient and understanding, and towards the end I was getting some solid results. Unfortunately, though, I didn't make the grade on my check ride. I was gutted; it was a real kick in the pants. I would repeat the check ride back in the simulator at Coningsby, but the pressure and the nerves got the better of me. I didn't pass. We were out of time and resource so my work-up stopped. This was one of the factors that swayed my decision to leave the RAF. At 43 now, I'd likely achieved all I was going to do on the Typhoon, so it was back to the OCU as an instructor.

I was now a QFI, accredited by CFS, and a better instructor as a result. There was much more explaining about *how* to do things, not just *what* to do. The airborne analysis and debriefs were better, drawing the best from those going through the course. Debriefs would draw out the key areas for improvement, what went wrong, why – and, critically, how to fix it. What are you going to do differently next time to make things better? It sounds simple, but this approach represented a significant progression from my previous instructional tours. I was popular with those going through the course and they felt at ease with me. In another progression from my experiences as a student, I found you could get the best out of someone in a high-pressure environment by utilising appropriate interpersonal skills and avoiding unsettling them. I was calm, relaxed, firm and fair. In short, I'd learnt a lot about instructing.

By early 2020 I'd gained my commercial flying licence and was set to leave later that year, then Covid intervened. A change of plan put the ball back firmly in the RAF's court. The service came up trumps. I completed an instructor upgrade and became one of only two CFS agents embedded within the Typhoon force, responsible to CFS for upholding standards of instruction. It was a very rewarding role; it brought high credibility, more variety and I became a better operator as a result.

Then came the Gulf connection: posted in 2021 to 12 Squadron, a newly formed, joint RAF and Qatar Emiri Air Force (QEAF) unit, to train QEAF pilots to operational status and later as Typhoon QFIs. It was like being back on the front line, with elements of the OCU thrown in. I continued my role as CFS agent and would often 'guest' back on the OCU to support instructor training and examination. I completed my final Typhoon flight on 30 March 2023. It had been 13 years and 2,055 airborne hours in the making. I'd spent more than half my 28 years' service embedded in the Typhoon force, the vast majority of them flying.

When I left the RAF on 15 May 2023 I'd come full circle. I'd learnt to cope with disappointment; I understood my limitations and I'd learnt to handle pressure. Importantly – rewardingly too – these were lessons I'd been able to hand on to others.

* * * *

FLYING OFFICER MICHAEL 'HARRY' GILL

Michael Gill, known as Harry in his early RAF years (he joined in 1957), trained on Piston Provosts at Syerston then Vampires at Swinderby. He was then posted to Hunters and in 1960 joined 43 Squadron, based at Leuchars. After his second tour, as a JP QFI at Acklington, in 1965 he retired to begin a lengthy career in civil aviation.

A DIRTY DIVE

This particular morning at RAF Leuchars the flying programme showed that I was to be one of a four-ship flight to undertake battle formation practice and air combat. Flight Lieutenant Chris Golds was to lead one pair with Flying Officer Mike Fermor

Michael Gill in Nicosia.

as his number two; Flight Lieutenant Derek Parry was leading the other pair with me as his number two.

At this moment my heart sank at the probability that it would be me buying drinks in the mess bar that evening. It was accepted that after flying, once the station armoury had developed the films from the aircraft gunsights, if on review the film showed a clear indication that one was firmly enclosed within another's gunsight diamonds, this lamentable reflection of one's air-combat abilities justified the provision of drinks all round.

My dismay was caused by the fact that Chris was exceptional at air combat and in reality few in opposition would have lived to tell the tale. Derek Parry was also a very good pilot but his talents were steered in the direction of squadron navigation officer and his air-combat abilities were not quite as exceptional as those of Chris.

Later, at 40,000ft the pairs parted, one under the control of Buchan Radar and the other being looked after by Boulmer. Fifteen minutes or so later after a series of directional changes the pairs were searching the skies for one another when Derek spotted Chris and Mike. We noted that we had a slight positional advantage and went in for the attack. Lo and behold, within no time Chris and his companion had carried out a vertical scissors and a couple of other mind-boggling manoeuvres which found me quite clearly being lined up in Chris's gunsight.

Realising my predicament, Derek ordered me to 'Break' and it was with relief that I rolled inverted, opened the throttle, dropped 20 degrees of flap to expedite a tight turn and plummeted earthwards. Passing around 25,000ft the rear-view mirror showed no one to be following me and so I deemed it safe to start pulling out and perhaps trying to rejoin the fray.

To my consternation there was absolutely no response to the back pressure on the control column. With a slight sense of disbelief, I moved the control column forwards and then backwards again. There was still no response. With the ASI now showing about Mach 0.93, I confirmed that I had definitely closed the throttle and that it had not accidentally stuck open; my only thought was that somehow the elevator had become disconnected.

I was still hurtling earthwards, now passing around 18,000ft. After selecting airbrakes out, I recalled being told that if going vertically downwards one should be prepared to eject no lower than 10,000ft or one might not live to tell the tale. I then began to tighten my seatbelts even more and ensured that I could reach the ejection handle just above my head. On passing 12,000ft I recall the aircraft pointing directly at a small loch, a few miles to the north-west of Dundee, and wondering if it would be in that loch where the aircraft would end up.

I had a final glance at the ASI to note my ejection speed and saw that the aircraft appeared to be gently curving upwards out of the dive. At that moment, passing around 9,000ft, I decided to remain with the aircraft. Eventually, it was fully recovered about 3,000ft above the loch. Just then Chris Golds came back on frequency and asked where I was, and whether I could try and rejoin the formation shortly over the Tay Bridge for a run-in and break back at Leuchars. This I did, and noted that in the circuit my hands were shaking almost uncontrollably, followed shortly by my body. By the time I had taxied back into dispersal, as the airman clipped the ejection-seat safety pin back in position, he took one look at me and asked if he could help me out – so white and sick did I appear.

Back on terra firma, Chris in his usual hearty manner shouted down the line. "OK everyone, inside, grab a coffee and into Room 3 for debrief." By this stage I was unable to control the tears which were running down my cheeks. Feeling very awkward over such unmanly reactions, I walked over to Chris and said that I would join the debrief later. I'd had a monumental scare and had to put myself back in proper order and needed to walk around to the back of the hangar alone for ten minutes or so.

When I joined the debrief, Chris asked me to run through in detail the precise actions I had carried out after breaking away from the air combat until the time I rejoined the formation. He asked when I had raised the 20-degree flap again. I said that I had done so when I noticed the sluggish rate of climb once I was climbing back to rejoin the formation. This produced a smile and a couple of guffaws. Wondering what all the amusement was about and slightly irked, I asked why my flap selections produced so much amusement. I was asked if during my conversion at Chivenor, any of the instructors ever briefed me on the use of flap at high speed. They had not and he explained that at speeds in excess of Mach 0.92 the use of flap produced an aerodynamic effect over the elevator which rendered it virtually useless; in these circumstances flap should be raised again immediately or the speed brought smartly down below Mach 0.92. It was fortunate that things ended as they did, otherwise this tale might not have been told.

Many months later, whilst on detachment with 43 Squadron at El Adem, I was sitting chatting to Flight Lieutenant Rod Moon, the duty pilot in the helicopter SAR section, when he received a call from air traffic to say that a Hunter, one of a pair, had been reported as diving vertically at high speed into the sea a few miles offshore from Tobruk and would he 'scramble'. I asked if I might join Rod on his search mission to assist as an observer, and off we went in a Sycamore with his winchman. Regrettably, all we found was part of a limb, still inside the G-suit of the USAF exchange pilot from another squadron. His leader told me that they had been engaged in air combat when suddenly his number two had disappeared, going downwards and that that was the last he saw of him.

I couldn't help but wonder if the American's demise hadn't been the result of an incident similar to mine. It's hard to believe that this characteristic of a superb and otherwise viceless aircraft remained the probable cause of fatalities late into its long service life. Weren't the pilots briefed, or did they simply forget in the heat of the moment? We'll never know.

CHAPTER 10
SALVOS FROM NCOs

CHIEF TECHNICIAN ALLAN HUNN

Allan 'Geordie' Hunn's RAF career spanned 26 years, from 1981 to 2006. It began on the Phantom Maintenance Unit (MU) at St Athan; next came Harriers in Germany, at Gütersloh. He then returned to the Phantom, serving on 74 and 56 Squadrons at Wattisham, 1435 Flight at Mount Pleasant in the Falklands and, ultimately, Aircraft Servicing Flight (ASF) at Wattisham. With the retirement of the Phantom, Allan moved to the Hercules, first at Lyneham and then the Support Authority at Wyton. His final tour was as at MoD Abbey Wood on the A400M Integrated Project Team.

The brief stories that follow reflect the fact that little in my RAF career mattered more than the bond with colleagues, my fellow servicemen – in particular that between aircrew and ground crew – and working with them through adversity, when it really counted.

A FRIGHTENING ENGAGEMENT

In Cyprus as a young corporal on my first armament practice camp, with 74 Squadron at RAF Akrotiri in 1987, I was much enjoying life. The detachment was going well both at work and socially, but the work element was about to change. The end of the working day was approaching when a radio call came through telling us to recover the last aircraft, which had just landed. A colleague, Senior Aircraftman 'Oscar' Brown, reasoned it had engaged the rotary hydraulic arrestor gear (RHAG) and was having trouble disengaging. I had never done a RHAG recovery before and was nervous about the disengagement process. However, Oscar reassured me and explained what needed to be done.

Allan Hunn.

After landing, engaging the RHAG and coming to a halt, the pilot usually applied a bit of power so that the aircraft put the RHAG under tension. When power was reduced, it allowed the aircraft to roll back and then the hook could be raised. For reasons unknown, on this occasion the hook had not been raised and therefore the aircraft could not clear the cable. The aircraft engines were shut down, which meant we would have to fit the hook 'gag', a piece of ground support equipment which could be operated manually to slightly retract the hook, which would clear the height of the cable and in turn allow the aircraft to be towed clear.

We drove to the runway and noted that the aircraft was at the far end where there was a blue flashing light. I naturally had a bad feeling in the pit of my stomach and anticipated we were going to be dealing with the unknown. I was very worried. As we approached the aircraft, we saw an ambulance and a group of about four people attending a figure lying on the RHAG, about halfway between the aircraft and the right side of the RHAG mounting platform. One of those attending was holding a plasma bag above the injured man.

When we stopped and began to survey the situation I noticed the pilot, Flight Lieutenant Paul Lightbody, looked particularly dejected. A figure in civilian clothes ran up to me and in an agitated state explained that a Cypriot firefighter had become entangled in the RHAG and that we needed to disengage the aircraft from the RHAG to release him from the tensioned cable. The cable normally stretches across the runway with both ends attached to a series of straps which form part of the retardation mechanism. The firefighter had been caught in one of these straps.

Surveying the situation my immediate thought was, do not do anything that would increase the tension on the cable as that might further injure or, even worse, kill the firefighter. Then I realised I had no choice but to increase tension on the cable to release him. The firefighter had probably been stood in a position to observe the aircraft coming in to land when a section of the cable strapping had snapped, wrapping itself around him and dragging him into the remaining cable straps that were now under huge tension.

The remaining firefighters had tried to stop the situation becoming worse and had thrown a chock behind the right-side main wheel. This unfortunately did not help because the aircraft was being pulled back onto a grossly deformed chock by a massively tensioned cable which was wrapped around the firefighter. The chock was effectively locking everything under tension and was apparently immovable.

We would have to remove the chock to release the aircraft, which in turn would allow tension on the cable to be released and then the firefighter could be cut free. We formulated a plan to inch the aircraft forward whilst I tried to kick the chock out of the way, and then slowly push the aircraft back to reduce the cable tension and allow the firefighter to be released.

The guys connected the towing arm and tractor to the aircraft, and I positioned myself at the chock to try and kick it free. Oscar accelerated the tractor to pull the aircraft forward, but the rear wheels started spinning, which was enormously frustrating. It felt like we would be unable to release the chock. Then what would we do? With others in the cab of the tractor jumping up and down to provide more grip for the tyres, Oscar kept trying to pull the aircraft forward, while I tried to boot the chock free by sitting down and kicking it with my heel. Around this time the SEngO, Squadron Leader Brian Harvey, arrived, saw we were doing as much as we could and found an aircraft hardpoint to push on and help the overall effort. Very slowly the aircraft started to ease forward sufficiently for me finally to boot the chock free.

The relief of freeing the chock was incredible. I rolled free of the chock and Oscar allowed the aircraft to slowly roll backwards and release tension until the cable settled. We then attached the hook gag to raise the hook above the cable and allow us to tow the aircraft free of the RHAG altogether.

When I stopped to take stock of the situation, I was dripping with sweat from head to toe and my right ankle was bruised from kicking the chock with all my strength. We then towed the aircraft down the runway to the dispersal. During the journey back all I could do was hope that I had not made the situation worse for the injured firefighter by increasing the tension on the cable. Very sadly, we later learnt he had died of his injuries and raised a glass to him that night.

Although it was a sad and sobering experience, I learnt a massive amount that day – helped enormously by Oscar's experience and presence of mind. The incident gave me the confidence to deal with many dangerous and dynamic runway situations later in my career. But almost every success also depended on others' support – and a bit of luck.

GIVE ME A BRAKE! (1)

When Tornados were due to replace the four Phantoms of 1435 Flight at RAF Mount Pleasant in providing the Falkland Islands' air defence capability, there were only two remaining Phantom units in the UK, 56 and 74 Squadrons. In 1992, serving with 56 Squadron at the time, I was the second to last airframe sergeant to be deployed there, which meant I would see the Phantoms' decommissioning. What I did not realise was that there was already a logistics support ramp-down taking place at Mount Pleasant. This would present a considerable challenge and ultimately would have a dramatic effect on Phantom operations.

Each evening in the SNCOs' 'swamp', my opposite number and I held a handover. On this occasion, after returning from shift he described having replaced a brake unit. However, he went on to say that there were no more serviceable brake units left at Mount Pleasant; all those that remained were time expired. The Phantom wheel, tyre and brake unit bay had been closed and there were no qualified personnel to maintain those brake units remaining. Any replacements required would have to be flown in on the airbridge, which could take days and reduce operational capability. The requirement to maintain operational readiness demanded that the brake unit change go ahead, and my colleague confirmed that the replacement unit had passed independent checks. He emphasised that he wanted to make me aware should any related issues occur. In fairness, I would probably have taken exactly the same decision.

The next day two aircraft launched without incident; however, on recovery, the first to land suffered a left-brake seizure and burst tyre. It had come to a halt in the middle of the main runway, blocking it, which left a Phantom and the Hercules tanker still airborne. The engineering controller instructed me to recover the aircraft 'blacking' the runway. I picked up one of the infamous Storno radios and a spare battery and tested it; all good. I instructed the recovery crew to hitch up the wheel, tyre and brake change recovery kit and a towing arm to a tractor and off we all went. On arriving at the aircraft I deliberately did not start the brake replacement as I needed to understand the status of the airborne Phantom and Hercules. I then saw that the Phantom was making an approach to the emergency runway, which was much shorter than the main runway and would require a RHAG engagement. I lost sight of the aircraft behind a small hillock but heard it engage afterburner and then take off again. This was warning of an escalating situation.

At this point a fire engine came racing towards us and stopped, with the supervisor warning that the Phantom had just snapped the RHAG and could no longer use the short emergency runway. This kicked several thoughts into my head. The Phantom and Hercules kept circling the airfield but there appeared to be no attempt to conduct in-flight refuelling. I therefore reasoned there was insufficient fuel onboard the tanker to refuel the Phantom, meaning both were potentially low on fuel. This meant any diversion to Chile was ruled out. Also, the runway at Port Stanley had been closed for several years so landing there in an emergency would be extremely risky. The only conclusion I could draw from this was that there was a serious risk of two crewmen having to eject and the loss of a Phantom. This meant we had to move the aircraft with the seized brake unit off the runway as rapidly as possible to allow the airborne Phantom to use the main runway.

At this point I lost radio communication with ATC. I was put on the spot. The decision-making process now lay with me. In the best interests of the airborne aircraft and crew, we had to risk trying to move the aircraft, albeit with a seized brake unit and burst tyre, using the tractor. But would it have the power? An engineering officer then arrived, looked very concerned, realised there was nothing he could do and drove off, leaving us to our own devices.

The tractor and towing arm were connected to the aircraft, and I just hoped the towing-arm shear pin would not fail due to the strain imposed. Should that happen I planned to use a general service screwdriver or extension bar in its place. In normal circumstances this was severely frowned upon, but needs must! I signalled to the tractor driver to try towing the aircraft. After a couple of failed attempts, with an increase in applied power the aircraft eventually started to move; what was left of the burst tyre began to slowly spin on the brake unit and then started to tear itself apart. However, brute force had worked and the tractor moved the aircraft to one side of the main runway.

ATC were clearly monitoring our actions and once the aircraft began moving, the remaining airborne Phantom was called in to land. It passed us on the runway only a few metres away at considerable speed. It was followed by the Hercules, which engaged reverse thrust and came to a halt in a very short distance nowhere near us. With the immediate situation resolved we then proceeded to replace the seized brake unit with another time-expired unit so that it could at least be moved off the runway. It was then towed back to 1435 Flight to better inspect the axle and complete the brake unit and tyre replacement, albeit temporarily until serviceable brake units were flown in on the airbridge.

Looking back at this event, to counter the negatives, not least the logistics element, there were also lots of positives. The first of these was demonstration of man's resourcefulness in difficult circumstances – where ensuring that only experienced personnel were deployed to Mount Pleasant was a complementary factor. From a personal perspective, the experience gained during a previous runway event also proved invaluable. It gave me the confidence to make difficult decisions involving the balancing of risks. In short, I'd learnt well.

GIVE ME A BRAKE! (2)

On 1435 Flight we were required to always maintain all four Phantom aircraft at full operational readiness; when aircraft were unserviceable this could be quite challenging. On one occasion there were three unserviceable Phantoms and therefore only one available for QRA. Inevitably, there was a scramble.

The only serviceable aircraft taxied out from the shelter towards the runway. After a brief visit from an excitable engineering officer, who exhorted the airframe tradesmen to get out and start fixing aircraft, the engineering controller then called me. There was a brake problem with the QRA aircraft. I drove out to the runway and recognised the pilot, Flight Lieutenant 'Hagar' Hargreaves (we had been together on another incident), and could see from his expression the urgency of the situation. I signalled that I was going to check the brake unit and he gave me a thumbs up; the inspection revealed nothing untoward. Then, using hand signals, I indicated, 'apply power, do a fast taxi, apply and test the brakes, then return and we'll take it from there'.

The pilot did exactly as asked, but as he returned I could still sense the urgency to get airborne. He gave me a thumbs up, closed the canopy and did the fastest 180-degree turn I have ever seen on a jet aircraft. He then engaged afterburner and took off.

In the circumstances, little else could have been done. But the incident reinforced something important to me as ground crew: the need to form a good relationship with the aircrew, one based on total trust. I came to understand there is a bond between ground crew and aircrew; 'we see them out and see them back'. Taken to the extreme, ground crew are the last people to look aircrew in the eye – aircrew who might not come back.

A NOD'S AS GOOD AS ...

In the mid-1980s I was based at Gütersloh as part of a Harrier Field Repair Team (FRT). We were drawn from Harrier Servicing Flight (HSF), which normally conducted scheduled maintenance on the Harrier GR3. The role of the FRT was to support the Harrier Force (HF) during field deployments by both 3 and 4 Squadrons, where rectification could even include engine replacements.

HF deployments generally lasted 12 days with a three-day intensive exercise period towards the end. The exercise names usually reflected the HF acronym; one I recall was named Hidden Fun! As with all exercises where the need is to train for war and expect the unexpected, they resulted in intense activity which led to limited, disrupted sleep patterns.

During one mid-summer HF deployment we had just entered the intensive exercise phase; the weather was scorching hot and activity was ramping up. We were wearing nuclear, biological and chemical (NBC) protective suits over two layers of clothing, which naturally meant we were extremely hot. Then there was a mock air attack, accompanied by a stream of mock explosions and smoke. In such an emergency the priority is self-protection: everyone donned their respirators, aka gas masks, which resulted in further discomfort.

With the implication that the flying site had been compromised and would be subject to further attack, the priority became scrambling to the reserve location. Once the aircraft left, ground staff 'crashed out' and moved to the secondary site. This was all carried out as a matter of extreme urgency.

We arrived at the new site and began setting up. The good news was that we no longer had to wear respirators (several people had collapsed due to heat exhaustion); the bad news was that we still had to remain in NBC suits. Then came notice of an engine replacement at a totally different site. Once again, the FRT packed up and set off. At this point we had been on the go for close to 48 hours with minimal sleep; rest was nicknamed 'combat kips'. We were now faced with a task that, including tie-down engine ground runs (EGRs), usually took 24 hours.

On arrival at the flying site for briefing, we found the Royal Engineers rapidly laying a pad on which to park the aircraft requiring an engine replacement. The procedure was to position the aircraft on the pad, jack it up and then retract the nose landing gear, lower the forward jacks to level the aircraft, remove the wing and replace the engine. Then reverse the tasks: refit the wing, raise the nose jacks, lower the nose landing gear then de-jack the aircraft, complete flight control functionals and, finally, EGRs.

The Harrier differed from conventional aircraft through its ability to move the four exhaust nozzles from the horizontal to the vertical position required for hovering. This had implications for the 'tie-down' procedure, which meant tethering the aircraft to the ground using chains and six-foot spikes. This satisfied the needs of EGRs with the nozzles horizontal; however, it did not satisfy the need to apply full power with nozzles in the vertical position. As a safety precaution, the aircraft was never taken to full power with the nozzles vertical as it would rip the spikes and chains from the ground.

The consequences of not being able to carry out a full-power EGR meant the aircraft must not, under any circumstance, take off or land vertically. It had to use the short field runway for a single flight back to main base, where a full-power tie-down EGR was carried out on a special platform which ensured the aircraft was safely tethered. In any event, the normal practice for field exercises was to use the short take-off runway to minimise fuel burn and then land vertically.

Returning to the engine replacement, working just under 12 hours took us to the point where the unserviceable engine was removed, by which time we had been awake almost continuously for some 60 hours. It was then midnight, and we were relieved by our sister FRT. The decision to engage this team was simply for them to gain experience, as during the last three years there had been no requirement for engine changes in the field.

We awoke to the aircraft being prepared for a 'tie-down' EGR, which was carried out smoothly and successfully. It was impressive to observe the EGR, especially with the nozzles vertical, albeit not at full power. The sight of a Harrier fighting to pull the six-foot stakes out of the ground to get airborne is quite something. At this point the exercise was deemed complete and we all reverted to normal working conditions.

With the EGR successfully done, the aircraft was handed back to the squadron to carry out the flight servicing and make it ready for flight. Also, and essentially, the aircraft documentation was handed back to the squadron – annotated to limit the aircraft to one flight back to base using the short runway for take-off and then a full EGR at base. The aircraft concerned was the last to leave the flying site and those who remained stopped to watch the take-off from the short runway.

It was a complete surprise when the pilot taxied to the vertical landing pad. He then took off vertically, held the aircraft in the hover at about 300ft, turned towards us and dipped the aircraft's nose. Finally, he reduced height, landed on the vertical landing pad, taxied to the short runway and took off for the flight back to base.

The pilot's actions that day represented an extraordinary display of trust, not just in the ground crew of the FRT but all those involved in providing the HF's deployed capability. There was nothing more he could have done to reinforce the important and essential bond between ground crew and aircrew.

* * * *

CHIEF TECHNICIAN GAVIN 'HARRY' MARSHALL

Known in the RAF as 'Harry', Gavin Marshall joined as an airframe mechanic in 1978. After working on Lightnings and later Bloodhound missiles, he eventually escaped to the Tornado F2/F3 force at Coningsby. He spent the majority of his time with fast-jet units, including an exchange tour with the RAAF at Williamtown that led eventually to a post as eng controller with the Red Arrows. Experience with Joint Force Harrier and the Typhoon followed and he finally retired from the RAF after 31 years in 2009.

A CLOSE CALL

I was trade manager on 29 Squadron's Tornado F3s up until the unit was stood down at Coningsby in 1999. In the last few weeks, when the squadron was still functioning as normal operationally, I was on night shift late one evening when one of the pilots came in to rectification (rects) control to debrief. He had experienced a noise in the cockpit from somewhere towards the rear right-hand side prior to take-off. The navigator had been unable to detect where the noise was coming from or what kind of noise it was. To that end the pilot suggested that following the completion of flying we take the aircraft for a high-speed run down the runway to see if I could detect and locate the origin of the noise.

I had wanted to become a pilot but late onset short-sightedness put paid to that. So as an engineer I eagerly jumped at any opportunity to fly or to gain experience. With flying concluded for the day, the pilot returned to rects and called air traffic to inform them of our plan to do a high-speed run and then return to the HAS site.

We taxied out the short distance to the threshold of runway 25; power was increased as for a normal take-off and brakes were released. Whilst we were accelerating down the runway, I was turning to look and listen over my shoulder in an effort to locate the noise. I happened to be looking forward just as the pilot shouted an expletive. At the same time I saw the rear quarter view of a fuel bowser exiting the runway, having crossed from left to right in front of us. We taxied back in relative silence and once in rects control again the pilot started a series of phone calls.

Unfortunately, I was posted to Australia shortly after and was never to see an incident report; so what had happened? When the pilot informed air traffic of our intentions to perform a high-speed run following the end of flying, he said that no other services would be required. The fuel bowser had been carrying out a refuel of the last of the flying jets on the south side of the airfield and was transiting back to the north. The driver had called air traffic for permission but no one had answered the radio. On looking at the air traffic tower it appeared all of the lights were out so the driver assumed the airfield was closed and proceeded to drive across the runway. Imagine his concern – if in fact we were visible to him – seeing an F3 at full chat bearing down on his bowser!

I would estimate we were less than 100 metres away as he exited the runway and travelling at over 100kts. A quite sobering experience. I didn't have full kit on; I was only wearing a headset and although strapped in, I'm sure the seat was still safe for parking, i.e. not live. It just goes to show that even the most mundane of tasks, done to aid an engineering diagnosis, can rapidly and uncontrollably go wrong.

I went on to amass over 300 hours in the Lightning, Tornado F3, Aermacchi MB-326, F/A-18 and Hawk, but it was the day we did just a quick test that was to prove the hairiest moment. On reflection, it's the one incident I might not have walked away from.

* * * *

CHIEF TECHNICIAN TONY SMITH

A Halton apprentice, Tony Smith's first posting was to Honington ASF on the rectification team, working on Hunters and Buccaneers. Tornados came next, followed by a move to the Strike Attack Operational Evaluation Unit (SAOEU) at Boscombe Down on promotion to sergeant. In 1999 he was posted to Coltishall, 41 Squadron, Jaguars, as a chief technician; he retired from the service two years later.

SAOEU

I was privileged to spend ten years of my RAF career on the SAOEU at Boscombe Down, a unique entity that supported several different aircraft types: Tornado GR1s, Harrier GR5s, GR7s and T4s plus a lone Jaguar GR1. The attraction from an engineering perspective, especially as I was dual trade (airframes and engines), was the opportunity to work on several different aircraft types every day, perhaps completing an engine change on a Harrier one morning, and then diagnosing a flight-control problem on a Tornado in the afternoon. With regular detachments, often to multiple US locations and for months at a time, there was never a dull moment, as these brief stories bear out. In compiling them, I'm indebted to erstwhile SAOEU colleagues for supplementing a failing memory.

THE 'TOP SECRET' HARRIER TRIAL

It was summer 1994 when, in concert with Thorn EMI, we were tasked with carrying out a Harrier whole aircraft radar signature trial at a 'top secret' location near Wells in Somerset. The aircraft itself would be mounted on a large turntable at the bottom of a disused quarry where various radar emitters were sited, some apparently repatriated from previous Soviet-bloc countries. The problem was how to get the Harrier onto the turntable. It couldn't be flown in because debris on the quarry floor would have posed an engine-ingestion problem. As it transpired, a trial with a whole aircraft lifting frame had been conducted several years earlier, so the plan was to airlift the GR7 from Boscombe Down as an underslung load beneath a Chinook – but first we had to reduce the Harrier's all-up weight. Accordingly, the ejection seat was removed and all demineralised water and fuel drained from the respective tanks.

It was my job, along with an electrician, to look after the aircraft in preparation for the move and, together with visiting SAOEU armourers, to fit and remove external stores as required for various elements of the trial. The first task in preparation for the move was to fit the lifting frame. There wasn't a huge amount of information available on its installation, so the torque figures for the attachment bolts were the first stumbling block – but we came up with a suitable number of 'white knuckles' to enable its fitment. With hindsight, proper torque figures would have been much better for my blood pressure: lesson number one. We tied an old aircraft tyre securely to the top of the wing to allow the lifting frame to rest on it and not cause any damage.

The Chinook arrived bang on time and stayed, rotors running, alongside the Harrier while we attached the lifting strop. The load was carefully lifted into the air, under the watchful eye of most of the squadron it seemed. There was a worry that the Harrier

would slowly rotate once lifted, but as soon as the Chinook started to move forwards, the GR7 aligned itself to the direction of travel very nicely – a function of aerodynamics no doubt. The Chinook wasn't going to make it straight to Wells, as it needed to stop overnight and refuel part way there. This gave the electrician and me plenty of time to hop in a Sherpa van and drive to the quarry to accept the unusual load the following day.

Tony Smith at the 'secret' Wells location.

Chinook with underslung Harrier.

At the quarry we were equipped with goggles and masks so we could get under the Chinook to detach the Harrier, which soon appeared above us. As the Chinook carefully lowered its load below the rim of the quarry, the rotor downwash stirred up a huge amount of debris – quite alarming when you're in the thick of it. The Harrier was carefully positioned close to the turntable (we couldn't get it onto the table, space was so tight) and we detached the lifting line. The Chinook then climbed out of the quarry and was soon gone. Meanwhile a large crane was waiting, ready to move the Harrier onto the turntable. However, the driver informed us that although his crane could happily lift 50 tonnes, a larger crane would be needed to allow sufficient clearance from the Harrier's wing for it to be positioned safely on the turntable. So, we had to wait until late that afternoon until a larger crane could make its way to the quarry. Lesson number two: ensure the precise lifting requirements are relayed in full to the contractor.

The larger crane duly arrived and we positioned the Harrier on the turntable. Once safely parked and suitably tied down, to make the aircraft appear to be in a flying configuration we had to hide the undercarriage legs using radar-absorbent material (RAM), which made them 'invisible' during the trial. Only when this job was complete could we hand the aircraft over to Thorn EMI personnel for the real work to begin. As the trial progressed, various different types of RAM were added in efforts to reduce further elements of the aircraft's radar signature. After a partial refuel we also carried out a 'dry run' of the engine, to examine the effect of rotating fan blades on the radar image. In a further effort to enhance reality, for many hours the electrician would sit in the cockpit on a wooden box in place of the ejection seat, wearing a pilot's helmet, again to mimic as close as possible flight conditions, all whilst rotating on the turntable. Armourers from Boscombe Down also arrived regularly to fit various underwing loads to the aircraft – fuel tanks and dummy bombs – again to provide different radar signatures.

After more than two weeks in the Somerset sunshine, occasionally less than busy it has to be said, the trial came to an end. The process of returning the Harrier to the SAOEU was effectively the reverse of how we got it to the quarry in the first place: defuel, crane to lift it off the turntable and a Chinook to return it to Boscombe. No problem though: we were old hands – and wiser for the experience.

TORNADO TALES (1) – BEWARE GROUND FIRE!

On this particular morning, one of the Tornado GR1s was on the flying programme for a range slot using the Mauser 27mm cannon. This was a rare event on the SAOEU, in fact it is thought this was the first time we had loaded an aircraft gun at

Boscombe Down. The aircraft, ZA446, was towed from the hangar down the hill to the arming pan, not far from the SAOEU. The aircraft was B/F'd[39] and the armourers loaded the gun, leaving it initially armed but electrically disconnected. The crew walked to the aircraft, accompanied by the 'lineys'. With the navigator in the back seat prepping the avionics, the pilot, Squadron Leader Joe Brough, commenced his external check of the aircraft, accompanied by one of the ground crew. After the walk-round and prior to climbing the steps, the final act was arming the Mauser cannon, which involved fitting the electrical connector to the gun, situated on the left-hand side of the aircraft, just forward of the cockpit.

There was a golden rule when on the arming pan, especially when an aircraft was loaded with forward-firing weapons: you should never stand in front lest something malfunctioned and a weapon left the aircraft.

The pilot already had his helmet on during the walk-round, in preparation for getting into the cockpit. He knelt down beside the panel where the cannon's electrical connector was. As he pushed the electrical plug into its socket, there was an almighty 'BANG!' as the Mauser fired an electrically actuated 27mm round straight into the revetment wall in front of the aircraft. Thankfully, as the pilot had his helmet on, it gave him some hearing protection; however, the junior technician beside him had his ear defenders on top of his head, not over his ears. Thankfully, the second liney was strapping the navigator in, so was not standing in front of the aircraft. But he jerked his head up so fast he hit the lower rail of the canopy, and still has the lump on his head to this day.

This was now a major incident. The sortie was cancelled and the area cordoned off, awaiting an investigation. The crew directly involved went to the medical centre for checks, together with the junior technician, who would suffer long-term damage to his hearing. The aircraft was impounded on the arming pan for several days, but was eventually made safe and unloaded. The team tried in vain to locate the bullet in the grass bank of the revetment, but eventually gave up. It was a lost cause. I don't believe that it was ever found.

When the aircraft was recovered back to the hangar, investigations were carried out to try and ascertain the reason for the gun firing. It was discovered that the electrical plug that had been connected to the gun wasn't actually the gun connector, but a now unused plug that had been installed on the aircraft many years before under a special trial fit (STF). The STF was for the introduction of automatic release point camera

39 Given a before-flight inspection (BFI).

equipment (ARPCE). During its time on the SAOEU, ZA446 was extensively used for JP233 trials at West Freugh. Due to the nature of the JP233 weapon, and to try and prevent inadvertent release of hundreds of bomblets outside the range area, the aircraft was fitted with ARPCE. The STF mounted a camera sensor into the aircraft in place of the ammunition tank for the gun, with electrical power connections similar to the gun system. On the edge of the range, sensors were installed so that the system knew when the aircraft was on the range – effectively the final stage in making the weapon system live, thus allowing the crew to release the JP233 weapon.

At the time of this incident, the majority of the STF equipment had long been removed; however, the wiring and switches etc. remained installed. Although the system was made 'safe', the associated electrical-supply circuit breaker was still set, as it was linked to another system. It was subsequently discovered that the ARPCE connector in the gun bay was identical to the Mauser gun electrical connector. When the pilot fitted the identical, but incorrect plug by mistake, despite all previously taken safety precautions, current was supplied direct to the gun and initiated a single round. Thankfully, the electrical supply was a constant 28 volt DC, which was understood to be why only one round was fired.

After the subsequent investigation, it was surely no coincidence that the practice of fitting equipment onto aircraft under an STF was curtailed. STFs were replaced with service-engineered modifications (SEMs), which provided for greater scrutiny prior to installation and included complete removal instructions. Everything was now clearly documented and configuration was easier to maintain. We thought Murphy was now firmly back in his box – but he proved something of a Houdini.

TORNADO TALES (2) – THROUGH THE ROOF!

There's a similar moral to another STF-related story. Around 1995, when a Tornado GR1 was in the SAOEU hangar being prepared for routine maintenance, armourers were tasked with removing both ejection seats. The technician working on the front seat had disconnected some of the lower attachments and was sitting on the windscreen arch; his feet were on the seat cushion while he worked around the seat's head-box. Located on the side of the head-box was a recently installed STF mechanism, a microswitch. Activated by the main gun sear cross shaft, in the event of an ejection it initiated a small explosive charge on the pilot's helmet to jettison NVG.

While the armourer was working on this NVG jettison system, he must have moved the cross shaft, linked to the seat main gun sear, which initiated the ejection sequence. An explosive charge drove the seat up its telescopic rail and it rapidly left the cockpit.

As it did so, the armourer was tipped upside down and pushed onto the cockpit floor, suffering major injuries in the process. The ejection seat meanwhile continued its upwards trajectory, breaking through the acrylic of the open canopy (which consequently hadn't been jettisoned), through a gas-heating pipe and on through the hangar roof panels, eventually landing on the grass at the back of the hangar.

The damaged canopy remained precariously perched in the open position on only one of its two operating levers – the other one was sheared off as the seat exited – so it had to be made safe before anyone could help the stricken armourer from the cockpit. He was tightly wedged on the floor and couldn't breathe properly; he had a broken knee, a fractured arm where he had hit the canopy, and was literally smoking from explosive charge burns. Meanwhile, some of those working around the aircraft ran outside in a state of shock. Although the ambulance took ages to arrive, the injured armourer eventually made a good recovery – but it took a long time.

TORNADO TALES (3) – WELL, BLOW ME DOWN!

In the summer of 1989, when the majority of the SAOEU were on block leave, a skeleton crew was carrying out routine aircraft maintenance. One of their activities was to test the emergency undercarriage 'blow-down' on a Tornado GR1, a nitrogen-charged system that lowers the main and nose undercarriage legs if the normal hydraulics were to fail. With the aircraft up on jacks and external power provided by a hydraulic rig, the wheels were raised using the normal selector lever in the cockpit. When the rigger selected the emergency blow-down switch in the cockpit, all three undercarriage legs came down and locked in place as expected.

Now it was time to reset the system: a simple procedure thanks to a shuttle valve in the starboard undercarriage bay which had to be manually pulled. On this occasion, the rigger decided to reach *between* the main undercarriage leg and the lock-down strut (the 'drag brace') to grasp the reset knob. Immediately after pulling it and activating the shuttle valve, causing the undercarriage leg to begin retracting, the rigger found himself trapped in the 'V' formed between the leg and the drag brace. The unfortunate result was a broken pelvis.

Fortunately, the Tornado hydraulic system quickly sorted itself out and the undercarriage legs dropped to their correct locked-down position again. Released from the trap of his own making, the injured rigger fell to the floor, where he remained until the emergency services arrived. He eventually made a full recovery. It was a salutary lesson to us all about the dangers of taking short cuts rather than following established procedures – especially when dealing with 3,000 psi of hydraulic pressure.

CHOCKS AWAY!

As if the foregoing stories weren't enough, after I'd left the SAOEU another salutary tale emerged, involving a Harrier in 2002. Originally a GR5A, it had been converted to the GR7 specification some years earlier. Once the pilot had started the engine and completed his checks, he was marshalled away by the ground crew. They then watched fascinated as he taxied down the slope from outside the SAOEU hangar towards the runway – and promptly lost part of his undercarriage. The main wheel lower assembly, wheels, tyres and the lower portion of the undercarriage leg, all detached from the aircraft.

Fortunately, the Harrier remained supported on its nose leg and the outrigger wheels beneath each wing. But there was no way of slowing the aircraft as it continued down the incline – the pilot had no brakes either. He eventually came to a halt by steering onto the grass, where he shut the engine down and climbed out.

The moral of this brief, final story relates to the length of time the aircraft was in storage after its conversion. During this period a non-destructive inspection of the main undercarriage leg had apparently been missed – a check specifically to look for cracks in the casting. And it was failure of the casting that led to the wheel assembly falling off. I can still hear someone saying: "The job's not done until the paperwork's complete."

★ ★ ★ ★

SERGEANT MIKE VEALE

Mike Veale began his 12-year RAF career as an electrical tradesman, soon qualifying as a fitter. After working on Vampires at Swinderby he moved to West Raynham, where he worked on 1 and 54 Squadrons' Hunters. Next came an overseas posting to 8 Squadron at Khormaksar. He retired after a final tour at Coltishall, maintaining Lightnings.

LOOSE ARTICLE HAZARD

My first posting to a real RAF station came at the end of my aircraft mechanic's training at Melksham in 1960. My destination was Swinderby, 8 FTS, home to several dozen Vampire T.11 aircraft. The airfield was situated midway between Lincoln and Newark and was a pretty pre-war station; a road separated the domestic site from the technical one and there were plenty of trees, shrubs and well-maintained lawns. Service life was fairly relaxed at Swinderby, certainly on the technical site. One of the main

Mike Veale at Melksham.

ways to walk to work was past the guardroom where the dreaded station warrant officer tended to lurk in the early mornings ready to pounce on any airman improperly dressed, or not marching in an approved military manner. There was a hole in the perimeter fence though!

Once I had arrived at the Electrical Section, on the corner of one of the main hangars, off would come my uniform collar and tie and I would put on a set of denim overalls; shapeless and brown, they usually reeked of aviation fuel. To add a bit of individuality in the winter, instead of wearing my beret to work in, I took to wearing a brown and green bobble hat that my mum had knitted for me. She didn't knit very much, apart from the occasional pair of socks for my dad, and the colours were a bit odd but it did keep my head warm. Of course, not having any badges it would not have caused any damage to the engine turbine blades if it had been sucked down an intake during engine runs. Anyway, 'Chiefy' Shore, my boss, never complained about it.

After a few months I achieved the dizzy rank of leading aircraftman (LAC) electrical. One morning I was given a job that involved reconnecting the electrical connections at the base of the pilot's control column in one of the T.11s. Pilot and instructor sat side-by-side in these aircraft, each having an ejection seat. Gaining access to the connections required removal of the aluminium floorboards and, to get these up, both ejection seats had to be removed by the armourers. This had all been done the previous day, a new control column had been fitted by the airframes people and all I had to do was connect the wiring. Resplendent in my shapeless overalls and bobble hat, I arrived at the aircraft, clambered into the cockpit and set about re-making all the connections. Even with the seats removed there wasn't much room, the work had to be done virtually standing on my head, but all went well and all the buttons and knobs on the control column worked as they should. The operation would, of course, be independently checked by my NCOs.

There was nothing else to do now other than put the floorboards back, go and sign for the work and arrange for the seats to go back in. Putting the boards back was very tedious as it involved lots of tiny screws, many of which had been out so many times in the aircraft's long lifetime that they were very worn and difficult to engage. Eventually it was done. I cleared up and accounted for all my tools. We used a tag and shadow board system to make sure that no tools were left in aircraft where they could interfere with the operation of the flying controls.

Back at the section I told Chiefy that all was in order and he gave me another job. This one involved walking out to the flight line where all the serviceable aircraft were in use. It was winter and I had put on an anorak before venturing out of the hangar. Halfway across the pan I realised that my head felt very cold and reached up to find no bobble hat. I was sure that I had been wearing it sometime that morning. I raced back to the section to check whether I had left it on the bench or on the coat hooks but there was no sign of it. Mentally retracing my movements that morning I realised that the last time I actually remembered wearing it was in the cockpit of the aircraft where I had done the control-column connections – and the seats were due to go back in any minute!

I raced to the tool shadow board, hastily exchanged my tags for the necessary tools and dashed over to the doomed aircraft. No sign of the armourers, thank God. I jumped in and frantically started to remove all those infuriating screws that had taken me ages to insert. Finally I had the floorboards up and there was my hat, resting on the elevator control chains. The first operation of the column would have drawn the hat into the cogs and gearwheels. Hastily I removed it, screwed the floor down again, checked my tools and disappeared from the scene as quickly as possible.

The episode taught me a vital lesson about flight safety. Any loose article in the cockpit represents a potential danger. While I don't think the presence of my hat would have affected the operation of the controls, the crunch would have come the next time the floorboards were lifted and a mass of brown and green wool was found and, in particular, the remains of a bobble hat.

* * * *

JUNIOR TECHNICIAN RAY DEACON

Photographer, author and authority on both the Hunter and Gnat, Ray Deacon packed a lot into a nine-year career, one that included plenty of flying. After entering the RAF in 1958 he worked on Vampires, Hunters, Varsities and Gnats before leaving in 1967 to join the Royal Aircraft Establishment at Farnborough.

DON'T MESS WITH AUTHORITY

Having alighted from a train at Kingham Station in the late afternoon, three of us plopped our kitbags on to the platform and asked the porter how to get to Little Rissington airfield. He pointed to a bus stop in the station forecourt. Our transport was a red and cream City of Oxford double-decker bus, operating on the second of two daily services between Chipping Norton and the airfield. Climbing through narrow, winding lanes and across the border into Gloucestershire, it felt like we had arrived on the top of the world. At 730ft asl, Little Rissington was the highest operational RAF airfield in the UK and it was covered in a blanket of snow.

A considerable number and variety of aircraft were allocated to the CFS during its tenure of Little Rissington between 1946 and 1976. In the early sixties, a force of some 650 airmen, with ancillary support from 70 airwomen, were tasked with maintaining a fleet of around 80 aircraft. I joined this happy station on 29 December 1959 following 18 months' Boy Entrant training as an air wireless mechanic at Cosford.

After completing the arrival procedures, I was assigned to Scheduled Servicing Flight and didn't get off to the best of starts. Most of the airmen who worked there were up for a laugh, but I had the misfortune to work for a dour, humourless senior technician, a real creep of a guy who was not much liked by the others. He got a kick out of bossing the new boy around but, being a red-head, I had no intention of putting up with that. Having completed a primary inspection on a Valetta, he told me to rub the aerials down to the bare metal, clean them up and repaint them ... again. That was enough; I knew I had done a thorough job and point-blankly refused. He stormed off in a huff muttering away to himself. A short while later I was summoned to explain my actions to my direct boss, Sergeant Pat Trumper, in the radio bay and he informed me in no uncertain terms that a senior technician had the same authority as a sergeant. With the threat of a charge hanging over my head so early in my career, he let me off with a stern warning and by way of punishment (!), transferred me to Handling Party (HP) duties. It was the best move I could have wished for; the next two years were great fun.

DON'T FORGET THE PINS!

In the early sixties CFS operated four squadrons, each with its own dedicated ground crews. Headed by a flight sergeant, sergeant and two corporals, 2 HP, where I worked supporting 2 Squadron's 20 Vampire T.11s, was staffed by 20 airmen. After a hearty breakfast and a ten-minute walk to the hangar, our first task was to pre-flight aircraft for the first sorties of the day. It was then all hands to the hangar doors. Each of these massive structures was opened using a large winding handle manned by two men, additional brawn being supplied by half-a-dozen bodies pushing on the trailing end. Each hangar had six doors at each end and for a bit of fun the middle pair were pushed as hard and fast as possible until they crunched at speed into the buffer stops, the objective being to see how far back along the tracks we could make them bounce. The doors weighed several tons and the consequences of one coming off the rails would have been catastrophic, but, hey, life was fun on the line.

The airmen on 2 HP were a mix of 'old lags', many of whom had served with front-line units overseas, and keen young airmen like me on their initial postings. Apart from a couple of oddballs, it was a good mix and we got along well together. Our boss, Chief Technician Tucker, kept himself to himself and Sergeant Jack Castle kept out of the way, leaving the daily routine to Corporals 'Tom' Thomas and Des Mutton.

Aircraft refuelling and tractor driving services were provided by civilian staff of Refuelling Flight, a great bunch of characters who were bussed in from local villages. A phone call from 'Chiefy' Tucker, would trigger a response from one of the drivers, racing their David Brown tractor down to the hangar. A second driver followed on with a line of trolley accumulators snaking out behind him. With ten or so T.11s lined-up on the apron, the aircrew were informed that flying could commence.

Corporal Thomas returned to the UK in the spring of 1960 after three years on the ranges at Woomera, Australia. He was a laid-back kind of guy who was happy to leave us to get on with our tasks. On one busy day, however, he decided to help out as starter crew for Lieutenant 'Dickie' Wren RN, one of the flight commanders, who was keen to practise his solo aerobatic routine. Having strapped him in, started him up and waved him off, fear struck Tom: had he removed the ejection-seat safety pin? He couldn't be sure. Dashing into the office, he phoned air traffic control and Dickie was instructed to abort his take-off. Tom walked out to meet the aircraft as it stopped on the peritrack (perimeter track) and the canopy opened. Nothing was said but we could see Dickie glaring at Tom as he took the pin out of the seat pocket, showed it to the agitated pilot, gave a thumbs-up, and restowed it in the pocket. Tom *had* removed the pin after all, but was absolutely right to admit to a possible error, no matter the potential embarrassment.

On Dickie's return, he had words with Chiefy Tucker, who in turn had a quiet word in Tom's ear. Next morning, the airmen were gathered around a T.11 where Tom, looking somewhat embarrassed, gave us a demonstration on how to remove and stow an ejection-seat safety pin. It was a lesson neither he, nor I, ever forgot: having the courage to admit to a possible mistake.

BE CAREFUL WHAT YOU WISH FOR (1)

Up until mid-1960 it was rare for ground crew to experience trips in a Vampire, but this changed with the arrival of our new CO, Squadron Leader Peter Hicks. On one occasion, while I was strapping him in, he started talking about life on the squadron, so I seized my chance and asked if it would be possible for airmen to gain some jet experience. He said he would see what could be arranged. He was true to his word and the first of seven trips took place on 9 September in XD383/VW with Flight Lieutenant Peter Broughton at the controls. Having taken us up to 20,000ft, Peter demonstrated the art of performing a perfect loop. Tipping the nose gently down until the needle touched 350kts, he pulled gently back on the stick and held it steady all the way over until levelling out at the bottom. "See that church in the distance?" he quipped, pointing the nose towards it, "I want you to perform a loop as I just showed you." So I did, and to my amazement we were pointing directly at

View from the lead aircraft of an eight-ship Vampire T.11 formation. (Ray Deacon)

the church on levelling out. "Very good, let's try a barrel roll." With my fingertips lightly holding the top of the stick, my QFI instructor tipped the nose down for a few seconds to build up a little speed then pulled back slowly on the stick while gently tilting it over to the right, and over we went. "Your turn Deacon. You have control." To my surprise, I performed what I thought was a perfect manoeuvre. "Have you flown before?" Pete enquired. "I gained my glider B licence at Hawkinge three years ago but no aerobatics or powered flight," I replied. And feeling rather chuffed with myself, we headed back to Little Rissington.

At the end of every course, the squadron would fly a formation of T.11s over local RAF airfields and, in appreciation for their hard work, eight airmen were invited to fly as passengers in an eight-ship formation. Two days before Christmas 1960 I joined Squadron Leader Hicks in the lead aircraft, XK586/VO, with the intention of taking some photographs; however, being in the lead made it difficult to turn far enough to get a decent shot. It was a dull, wet day and after going through a couple of points he said: "If we have a problem and I shout 'Eject, eject, go,' if you turn and say, 'What?' you'll be talking to yourself." Food for thought and something to remember forever. We took off in two box-fours and headed south-west in arrow formation. Taking us down to 1,000ft, we flew over Kemble before moving on to the USAF bomber base at Brize Norton. The formation then split into two groups of four and climbed up through the murk for some close formation flying, ending with an exhilarating vertical dive in dense cloud. All too soon, we were breaking in sequence for a stream landing at Little Rissington.

When aircrew reported that their aircraft had flipped uncontrollably onto its back while practising high-speed stalls, the station test pilot, Flight Lieutenant Peter Marsh, was summoned to fly an air test on it on 30 October 1961. It was possibly because WZ416/VF was relatively old – the third Vampire T.11 off the production line back in 1953. Nevertheless, I badgered Peter into letting me ride in the right-hand seat. He warned me that the test would be hairy, but I was determined to give it a go. Little did I realise that I was about to experience the scariest 30 minutes of my life.

Following a standard take-off, the aircraft was trimmed for a steady climb with a high power setting as Peter made a series of notes on his knee pad. During the climb he explained the fundamentals of a high-speed stall, as I had no idea what it entailed, and how he intended to recreate the reported problem, before quietly slipping in that if the problem did occur, he would need to check the aircraft's behaviour in a spin. Only now did it begin to dawn on me what I had let myself in for.

Some 20 minutes into the flight and with around 40,000ft indicating on the altimeter, we levelled out and accelerated to something approaching the Vampire's maximum speed. With Peter pulling ever harder on the stick we began a slow bank to the right, the g-force increasing until suddenly the aircraft began to shudder violently before flipping over to the left and onto its back, just as had been reported. Having regained control, a few notes were added to the knee pad and the exercise repeated with the same outcome. "I'll need to see what happens to the left," he said. And so off we went, two high-speed stalls to the left. This time, however, the buffet came on and the vibrations increased but the aircraft remained under control. More notes.

Now for the spins. Without knowing what to expect, the aircraft flipped over and headed downwards in a clockwise spiral at a disorientating and increasing rate. As Peter applied what I now understand to be out-spin aileron and opposite rudder to correct the spin, the effect of severe vibration combined with heavy stick forces prevented him from holding the column to the left with his right hand in order to extend the airbrakes with his left. Having tried unsuccessfully a couple of times, he told me to hold the column hard over, which I did without hesitation. By now I was deeply uncomfortable, anticipating the dreaded words, 'Eject, eject, go,' whereupon the airbrakes extended and the Vampire slowly shuddered into a controlled vertical dive. Yet more notes. "Is that it, Sir?" I enquired in a pleading voice. "No Deacon, it is not," was his sharp retort. "Each test has to be performed twice." So back up we climbed to repeat a spin to the right, with the same unnerving result. The final pair of tests comprised spins to the left, from which we recovered without incident or requirement for passenger assist, and we headed back to base.

It was a great relief to feel my feet on the pan. WZ416 was towed into a corner of the hangar to await rigging checks by my good friend Tom Thomas. Using a set of jigs, he determined that one tail boom was higher than the other and that this was the likely cause of the problem. A week or so later, Victor-Foxtrot was flown to St Athan, ostensibly for scrap, but records show that it was refurbished and re-issued to 1 FTS in 1963.

BE CAREFUL WHAT YOU WISH FOR (2)

Following a two-year tour on 8 Squadron (Hunters) in Aden, six months with 4 FTS at Valley and a further year on a fitters' course at Cosford, I could not believe my luck – a posting back to Little Rissington. My second tour on 'God's favourite airfield' commenced in October 1965 with a short stint on 2 Squadron (Varsities), but a request to transfer to C Flight (Gnats) was granted in early 1966.

Digging an 8 Squadron Hunter out of the sand, Sharjah, 1962. (Barry Potter)

The year before my return, it had become clear that trying to integrate an increasing number of Gnats with slow-moving, piston-engined aircraft and JPs in an already crowded circuit, could lead to serious accidents, and the decision was taken to operate the Gnats from another airfield. As the Americans had recently vacated Fairford, C Flight relocated to this extensive facility in November 1964, taking up residence in a large, modern, domed-roof hangar, almost hidden out of sight behind two 'tin' hangars. It was equipped with spacious office and ground crew accommodation, superb servicing bays and a long gallery linking first-floor offices, offering a panoramic view of activities on the floor below. A large concrete apron separated our hangar from the tin hangars, providing ample space for two Gnat flights.

Early in 1965 the Red Arrows' aircraft began arriving from the Kemble paint shop to share the hangar with C Flight. With no other aircraft to be concerned about, the team was able to practise over the airfield four times a day. As a junior technician, I was assigned to the Rectification Team and worked alongside Sergeant Chris Armes and Corporal Ron Turrell. In addition to maintaining the CFS Gnats, we were responsible for rectifying defects on the Arrows' aircraft on their return from weekends away. Mondays were particularly busy as the team's aircraft were needed for practice flying on Tuesday mornings.

Over the summer of 1966, with refurbishment work at Brize Norton unfinished, the first VC10s and Belfasts for the RAF entered service at Fairford, 10 Squadron in one tin hangar and 53 Squadron the other. As their numbers increased, the circuit became more active and following confirmation that the Concorde Trials Unit would occupy our hangar, the Gnat detachment prepared for another move – ten miles down the road to Kemble.

For anyone like me who had an interest in aircraft, Kemble was a dream. Home to 5 MU, it was one of two Hunter maintenance and storage units, with facilities for the refurbishment, repainting and storage of various RAF, Royal Navy and foreign air force aircraft. With no operational flying, Kemble was ideal for both the CFS course and Red Arrows operations. Two tin hangars on G site were prepared for CFS occupation, newly constructed office and servicing facilities provided within. C Flight was assigned to one hangar and the team the other; the move was completed on 26 September 1966. It didn't take long to settle in, one of the most important tasks being the marking out of a volleyball court. As a new aircraft pan was still under construction, flight lines were set up on the unused runway.

After trips in the Vampire, JP and Hunter, a flight in the Gnat was my next objective. In October 1966, Boscombe Down authorised the Gnat to be flown in formation with slipper tanks fitted. With a trip to the Middle East fast approaching, team leader Ray Hanna decided to fly all ten aircraft with tanks fitted on a fuel-flow exercise. Just my chance, I thought, and asked Tom if he could fix it. And he did – for me and several other airmen from our team. Flight Lieutenant Bill Langworthy, Red 3, was my pilot in XR993. After a formation take-off, the team opened into loose formation, flying fast and low towards Somerset. Climbing to 10,000ft or so

Smoke from Ray Hanna's Gnat partly obscures Derek Bell's aircraft. (Ray Deacon)

Ray Deacon about to enjoy a flight with the Red Arrows on his last day in the RAF.

above Ilfracombe, we sat back and enjoyed the delights of formation loops and rolls, but nothing more serious. On arriving back at Kemble, the opportunity was taken to give the civilian staff a foretaste of what they could expect in the years ahead. Slotting into line-astern with smoke on, the team performed a seemingly endless tail chase over the airfield. Oh, what fun!

With comparatively few aircraft movements, the circuit at Kemble was quiet, ideal for the team to practise. At the end of a practice session, one of the Gnats would sneak in, low and unseen across the line, covering everything in a cloud of diesel smoke. Ray Hanna, Henry Prince and Terry Kingsley were masters at this.

My last trip in a Gnat took place on my last day in the RAF, 2 May 1967. Ray Hanna agreed to let me fly on a practice sortie so that I could take some photographs, but as events transpired and unbeknown to me the practice was changed to a full display for an officers' passing-out parade at South Cerney. It was the first full show I'd done and the effects of loop after loop, roll after roll, continually changing from high positive to negative g, induced a stinking headache. The twinkle roll finished me off. Flight Lieutenant Frank Hoare was my pilot in XR993 and as we taxied out he warned me to stiffen my neck during the roll. It was exciting to watch this manoeuvre from the ground – but nothing compared to being in it. As the roll began, my helmet thumped hard against one side of the canopy, followed a split-second later by a whack on the other. Since my arms could no longer lift the camera, several shots were taken of the inside of the cockpit.

To my relief, the bomb-burst concluded the show. After an unnerving dash between the hangars and a steep climb-out, I asked Frank if he wouldn't mind dashing back to Kemble. "I thought you wanted to take some photographs, Deacon," he quipped. "I've got everything I wanted thank you, Sir," came my sheepish retort. I climbed out of the aircraft and sat on the grass for the hour it took for my headache to go. But what a great way to end a service career.

CHAPTER 11
PRE-SCHOOL PRANKS

NIGEL ADAMS

Between tours at Gütersloh and Binbrook that saw him accumulate 2,000 hours on the Lightning, somewhat ironically given the story below, Nigel Adams instructed ab initio navigators on the JP at Finningley. His flying career came to an end after serving as a tactical leadership programme instructor at Jever and Florennes. He retired as a squadron leader in 1992.

MAN IS NOT LOST

I'd nurtured an ambition to fly for a long time and when someone at Biggin Hill mentioned the possibility of getting a special flying award I leapt at the chance. I put in an application, which to my delight was accepted, and during the school summer holidays I took a flying course, financed by the RAF, at Cambridge Aero Club which in those days (it was 1965) operated the Cessna 150. Successful students were awarded a PPL.

We flew from grass strips and it took me a while to get to grips with landing the aircraft. My instructor was an ex-Second World War pilot who was surprisingly relaxed about my attempts to crash the aircraft. Eventually I went solo which gave me a great boost in confidence. All the exercises we now flew were in the local area, until it came to the point where I had to complete a triangular cross-country. This was different. Now I had to fly over unfamiliar territory, holding a map, and recognise landmarks at the expected time on the stopwatch. Alternatively, I could put the map away and follow line features such as roads, railways and even pylons. This had a certain appeal.

My route went from Cambridge to Oxford Kidlington, then up to Coventry and back to Cambridge. I planned to land and refuel at Kidlington, which was about

Nigel Adams in Cyprus.

70 miles away, and would take about 45 minutes. I decided to follow the major road to Oxford. After 55 minutes it was clear that I had no idea where I was. Fuel and confidence were diminishing fast. The map now covered the entire instrument panel whilst I tried desperately to recognise any feature on the ground. As I looked up I was surprised to see a glider in front of me taking avoiding action, the pilot shaking his fist.

Thoughts of making a forced landing in a field crossed my mind when, to my relief, an airfield appeared on the horizon. It wasn't Kidlington but it would do. I made an approach in what I thought was the correct direction, only to have my second near miss with an aircraft taking off from a different runway. Now I knew the runway to use and after landing I taxied onto the grass towards the petrol pumps I'd spotted from the air. To top a bad day, I became bogged down in the field over which I shouldn't have ventured had I bothered to read the signals square.

Feeling rather dejected, I shut down the engine and reported to air traffic control, where I discovered that I was at Gloucester Staverton airfield, some 45 miles from Kidlington. My attempt to file a flight plan back to Cambridge was met with raised eyebrows and I was told to go and have a cup of tea whilst a tractor towed my aircraft out of the mud. After some robust thoughts from the controller on what I should have done, I went to refuel the Cessna but found the keys to start it had been confiscated. I was obliged to stay put and await my instructor's arrival in another Cessna.

Returning to Cambridge I felt that was the end to my flying ambitions. It transpired that Kidlington had notified Cambridge when I hadn't arrived as expected and my instructor was relieved to find me safe and sound at Staverton. My blunders were luckily seen as part of the learning curve and I successfully completed another attempt at the same route. I obtained my PPL a year before I passed my driving test – which took three attempts but that's another story.

The RAF, amazingly, accepted me for pilot training in December 1966, not much more than a year after my abortive cross-country jaunt.

* * * *

JOCK HERON

During a 33-year career, after training on the Piston Provost and Vampire, Jock Heron flew a variety of aircraft, including the Hunter and several Mach 2 fighters: the Lightning, Mirage, with the French air force, and F-105 Thunderchief with the USAF. In Germany he flew the Harrier and Wessex and later commanded RAF Stanley in the Falkland Islands. Group Captain Heron retired from the RAF in 1987 to join Rolls-Royce in Bristol.

Jock Heron in a Piston Provost.

A FLIGHT CADET'S LEARNING CURVE[40]

In January 1955 I was one of 36 callow youths, schoolboys all, who began their RAF lives as flight cadets on 71 Entry at Cranwell.

My first flying experience was as a passenger in an Avro Anson, a seven-seat navigation training and communications aircraft. The one-hour sortie introduced us to basic air navigation and, for those of us who had never been airborne before, it gave us a taste of flying. I was so keen to repeat the experience that I persuaded the pilot to allow me to remain in the cramped cabin for a second sortie, during which I was sick somewhere over Boston. Later, in the early summer of 1955, I persuaded another staff pilot, who was conducting an air test in a Balliol trainer, which was powered by a derated Rolls-Royce Merlin, to allow me to fly in the second seat and thus to handle an aircraft for the first time and to experience briefly its famous engine.

It wasn't until September that we began our flying training on the Percival Provost. We were delighted to be trainee pilots and the aircraft, with its side-by-side seating, was a pleasure to fly, although bearing in mind our inexperience we would have flown anything. It was responsive and more powerful than its predecessors, the docile Chipmunk and the sluggish Prentice.

I was a student on A Flight, where my instructor was an ex-Lancaster pilot with a DFC. He was a kind man with a patient manner who assured me that the occasional need to throw up into a sick bag was not unnatural, but that I should always carry the appropriate greaseproof bag in a flying suit pocket to save embarrassment. It was good advice. During the first few weeks, prolonged aerobatics and spinning unsettled my stomach, but as I found the airborne equivalent of my sea legs the effect wore off and I gained confidence in my primitive flying ability. After about 11 hours of instruction, almost three weeks after my first dual sortie, my instructor climbed out of the cockpit and told me to fly a single circuit on my own. It was an experience which will remain with me for ever when, on a beautiful autumn day, I 'slipped the surly bonds of earth' on my first solo flight from the grass airfield at Cranwell North. For the first three months of our flying training we flew from this airfield but by January 1956 the base for our training had moved to Barkston Heath, a satellite airfield with its three asphalt runways laid out in the traditional triangular pattern eight miles south-west of Cranwell.

The main airfield at Cranwell South had been modernised to take the Vampire.

---

40 Adapted from The Rolls-Royce Heritage Trust book No. 45 from the Historical Series Book List, *From Schoolboy to Station Commander*, ISBN 978-1-872922-46-1, © The Rolls-Royce Heritage Trust – all rights reserved.

These jet trainers were due to arrive at the end of the year to replace the Balliol as the advanced training aircraft. The latter type had been based at Barkston Heath and was phased out fairly quickly to permit the two Provost training squadrons to be re-housed there. After the first few months the increasing demands of the training syllabus began to expose weaknesses in the flying aptitude of some trainee pilots, so our numbers began to dwindle. Although the system was designed to embrace the slow learner, and our instructors handled them patiently, it was not in the interests of these students in the long term for such perseverance to be prolonged. It was always a sad occasion to lose one of our small, close-knit community but, in retrospect, their lives may have been saved. Too often, suspect student pilots had been re-coursed, either because of the cost of the investment or from sentiment, only for them subsequently to die in an accident. Boards of Inquiry, quite correctly with hindsight, criticised these motives.

Following the move of our training to Barkston Heath we commuted daily by bus from Cranwell and I was allocated to a new instructor, an ex-Venom pilot who had been an exchange officer with the USAF in Korea, flying the Republic F-84 Thunderjet. He was aware of my early ambition to be a fighter pilot so he developed my limited flying skills in that direction. The 140-hour Provost syllabus comprised a conventional framework of dual instruction followed by solo consolidation on all the basic flying disciplines such as aircraft handling, aerobatics, practice emergencies, instrument flying, formation, navigation and night flying. The latter was restricted to take-off and landing practice, general handling and some limited navigation exercises. During a solo general-handling sortie I once nursed a Provost to 15,000ft, unwise without oxygen, just so that I could claim to have reached *Angels One Five*, the title of a film about the Battle of Britain made a few years before. The subsequent descent involved a 12-turn spin before recovering to routine flight at about 5,000ft, again an unwise manoeuvre, but an example of the overconfidence of youth.

In July 1956 I flew the Provost for the last time, another solo sortie described in my logbook as general handling and practice forced landings. The latter exercise simulated an engine failure with glide approaches to convenient fields without actually touching down. I took the opportunity to perform some unauthorised low flying at about 130kts which, unfortunately for me, was reported to the Cranwell authorities by an onlooker. Later in the day I found myself being interviewed by my squadron commander for annoying the public and asked to provide a reason for this unacceptable behaviour. I explained that I was attempting to simulate the higher approach and landing speeds of the Vampire jet trainer, which we were due to fly after the summer break, so that I would be better prepared for the forthcoming challenge. Despite the apparent severity of his tone I thought that I detected a smile around my interrogator's lips as I left the office. At least I'd come up with an original excuse.

Six weeks later we were installed in the main college itself. At the same time we were introduced to the de Havilland Vampire. Cranwell South was equipped with a fleet of new Vampire T.11 twin-seat trainers and single-seat FB9s, recently retired from the front line. The syllabus began with two weeks of ground school where we were briefed on the aircraft and its systems, the Martin-Baker ejection seat, the aerodynamic effects of high-speed flight and the significance of Mach numbers, together with the features of the jet engine and its fuel control system.

The T.11 cockpit was cramped and the installation of the two ejection seats side-by-side gave the impression of less space than the Provost, but we became used to the tight fit and thought no more about it. My familiarisation sortie in the T.11 was memorable in that I was determined to pull 6g, a figure which I thought was significant, and duly did so while flying some simple aerobatic manoeuvres to gain a feel for the aircraft. Gradually I began to feel sick and was forced to grope for the appropriate bag in my flying suit pocket and promptly filled it. Having spent almost nine weeks on the ground since I had last flown, my stomach was not in good condition; my instructor was amused and my pride took a knock.

By mid-October 1956, after about 11 hours of dual instruction which covered most of the Vampire's attributes, I was sent solo in the T.11; a week later I finally flew a single-seat jet aircraft, the Vampire FB9. The small cockpit of the single-seater lacked an ejection seat and was markedly different from the trainer. However, the handling of the aircraft and engine were similar and the systems were almost identical. We were not allowed to apply negative g to the single-seaters until a modification had been incorporated to vent fuel because of the risk of a flash fire. Dual handling and procedures were demonstrated in the T.11 while solo consolidation was conducted mainly on the FB9, although the existence of ejection seats in the T.11 meant that some particular solo exercises were conducted in the two-seater. The 160-hour jet syllabus followed a pattern of low- and high-speed handling, high-altitude flight, navigation by day and night, instrument flying, practice emergencies and an introduction to battle formation and fighter tactics. All these exercises demanded more from the pilot in the cockpit, not least acute awareness of fuel states because of the jet engine's thirst. Perhaps inevitably, more of my colleagues fell by the wayside as they failed to respond to these pressures.

By Christmas 1956 I had flown about 40 hours in the Vampire and, after a short break for the holiday, I returned to Cranwell to hear the sad news that my instructor had been killed in a T.11 whilst demonstrating a spinning exercise to his student on the senior course. Apparently the aircraft had failed to recover from the spin so he ordered his student to eject, which he did and survived. It appeared that the aircraft may have recovered from the spin, so the instructor attempted to pull out from the ensuing dive. With not enough height to recover he was killed instantly when the aircraft struck the ground. Although Cranwell had experienced four other fatal accidents in the previous two years, none had involved our entry or our instructors, so this was the first time we'd been affected directly.

The loss of such a popular man was a blow but I was allocated to another instructor, an ex-Sabre pilot who had been stationed at Jever in Germany. Cheekily, we graded our instructors into a number of categories. At the top of the list were the ex-fighter pilots, of whom the Hunter and Sabre men were the cream; next were the Meteor, Venom and Canberra men. Further down the list were the 'heavies', pilots who had flown Lincolns, Shackletons, Hastings and Varsities; finally, at the bottom of the pile, were the 'creamed-off' instructors who had gone straight from their own pilot training to CFS to undertake the QFI course. Our simple view was that our instructors brought a flavour of the front line to their job and that we would absorb their skills by osmosis, so we felt that QFIs who had never served on a front-line squadron wouldn't have anything to pass on to us – perhaps an immature and arrogant view, but one that prevailed at the time.

As we built up our experience on the Vampire during the autumn of 1956 events elsewhere created a tense atmosphere for British politicians and the armed services: the Hungarian revolution and the Suez crisis dominated the political scene. While they had no direct effect on our training, events shortly afterwards were to have profound consequences for all our futures. The 1957 Defence White Paper led to most future combat aircraft projects being cancelled; only the Lightning and the Canberra replacement survived, albeit eight years later the latter, in the shape of the TSR-2, would also be cancelled. The significance of all this was not lost on us, but we were assured that we would not be affected; Vampire training would continue. For our instructors, however, the matter was of immediate concern because, at a stroke, some 15 day fighter squadrons in the UK and in Germany were disbanded and the redundant pilots were competing for postings.

Later in 1957 we were reminded of Cold War activities by a summons from our Vampire squadron commander: all students were to visit his office, one at a time, to be shown a pink 'Secret' file. This was unusual as cadets were not normally exposed to material above a 'Restricted' classification. It contained a single enclosure comprising two sheets of paper, one of which was a brief note stating that if we saw the aircraft illustrated on the attachment we were not to fly near it, to say nothing on the radio and to report the fact to the squadron commander when we landed. The illustration was a three-aspect line drawing of an unusual shape which later we learnt was a Lockheed U-2. The reason was not explained to us at the time but according to information, since declassified, a few of these high-altitude reconnaissance aircraft were detached to the USAF base at Lakenheath in East Anglia. From there they flew highly classified missions gathering intelligence around and over the Soviet Union, under the guise of 'weather reconnaissance'.

In the summer of 1957, as an introduction to the 'real' RAF rather than our sheltered life within the training environment, we were given the opportunity to visit a front-line station. I chose to visit Leuchars, the home of 43 Squadron, 'the Fighting Cocks', whose Hunter F1 aircraft had been replaced by the F4 in 1956. One of the junior pilots was given the dubious responsibility of hosting my visit and he arranged for me to fly in the back seat of a Meteor T7, to spend a day at a nearby radar station and, as a special treat, to sit in the cockpit of a Hunter and to start the engine, just to whet my appetite further. Throughout my four days at Leuchars I was hosted sympathetically by the pilots who knew of my ambitions and they gave me a treasured memento as a leaving present, a 43 Squadron black and white chequered flying scarf. The visit made me even more determined to become one of the Fighting Cocks – on the several assumptions that I graduated successfully from Cranwell later in the year, that I would be posted to Hunters and that I would pass the course at the OCU at Chivenor.

The Fighting Cocks' aerobatic team had only recently completed the Hunter flying sequences for a Columbia film, *High Flight*, about a group of Cranwell cadets and their escapades during their time at the college and later as Hunter pilots at Leuchars. The whole cadet wing had been involved in filming some of the parade sequences earlier in the year at Cranwell and some of my entry had been used as extras. Although the film, with Ray Milland and Anthony Newley, wasn't due for release until the autumn, we looked forward to enjoying the Provost, Vampire and Hunter flying sequences and, as arrogant young experts, criticising the plot and technical accuracy. As it transpired when we were given a preview in the station cinema, we did indeed condemn much of the plot and the technical inaccuracies, but admired the spectacular flying sequences. Despite the criticisms, many years later

I was able to obtain a taped copy. Viewing it is a nostalgic reminder of three very rewarding and happy years as a flight cadet and, subsequently, as a Hunter pilot on 43 Squadron.

Of the 36 schoolboys who arrived at Cranwell nearly three years earlier, only 23 young men graduated as commissioned officers with their pilots' wings on 17 December 1957. Four were chopped for 'lack of officer qualities', eight for lack of flying aptitude and one, tragically, was killed when he abandoned his Vampire after experiencing a control problem; he drowned in the Wash.

Cranwell and its unique culture smoothed my transition from immature schoolboy to raw adulthood in a demanding environment. During what was effectively an apprenticeship for a service career, what I learnt there – not just about flying – would prove a template for life.

Superna Petimus[41]

* * * *

ANDREW ROBERTS

After Cranwell, Andrew Roberts became a JP QFI. He spent his operational career in the maritime world flying Shackletons and Nimrods. He qualified on 17 different types, including the Hunter, Canberra, Buccaneer and Jaguar, before retiring as an air vice-marshal in 1994. Subsequently, he flew cadets in the Chipmunk, Bulldog and Tutor.

A CADET'S CONUNDRUM

In 1955, as a 17-year-old RAF Combined Cadet Force cadet at Cranbrook, I was awarded an RAF Flying Scholarship, which covered 30 hours' flying in the Tiger Moth, culminating in the award of a PPL. This was carried out at the Surrey Flying Club at Croydon Airport (which dates me a bit). My instructor was the very heavily built, 6-foot 3-inch 'Tiny' Marshall – who could barely fit into a Tiger Moth; we reckoned the fuselage sagged in the middle when he got into it. He had a lovely sense of humour and spent much of the time telling me jokes, using the Gosport tube (a pipe leading from a funnel-shaped mouthpiece in front of one seat in this open-air, tandem-seated, cockpit to 'earphones' in the flying helmet of the person in the other seat – there were no electrics in the aircraft). I remember that one of his test questions

41 Motto of the RAF College Cranwell: We Seek Higher Things.

Andrew Roberts.

was, "What should be your first action when giving The Queen Mother a demonstration of a slow roll in a Tiger Moth and she falls out of the aircraft?" Answer: re-trim for loss of weight.

One of the early exercises we had to carry out was to practise forced landings after engine failure. For this, we used the then disused Redhill airfield, found by simply flying south down the Purley Way until one picked up the airfield visually. We would arrive over the airfield at about 2,000ft, close the engine throttle and not open it again until we were about 20ft or so from the ground and were sure that we would have been able to land successfully.

For some reason, Tiny regarded me as reasonably competent and sent me solo after only 4 hours 15 minutes of dual instruction. I certainly had less than ten hours' total flying when, walking out with another, more experienced, student to our respective aircraft one day, he suggested that we have a dogfight when we got to the Redhill area – quite unauthorised, of course. We duly met and had a good 'fight' for ten minutes or so, at the end of which I felt that I really did need to get on with my forced landing practice. I therefore closed my throttle and started my glide down to the airfield. Halfway down the descent, I noticed the signals square, used to indicate important airfield information to aircraft without radios. I remember being rather puzzled by this because I didn't remember there being a signals square at Redhill. Towards the end of the approach to land I thought: I wonder why the word 'GATWICK' is painted across the threshold of the runway. Realising my error, my first priority was to turn hard right at about 100ft to get safely away before the control tower could read my aircraft registration painted on the wings. At the time, my father was running the Southern Air Traffic Control Centre at Heathrow. He would not have appreciated the rumpus had my incompetence been detected and reached the press.

I should explain that I had not yet reached the point in the course where we started to receive instruction in navigation and therefore had no maps in the cockpit. Where the hell is Gatwick, and which direction do I take to get back to Croydon, I wondered. Well, a bit to the west of north should do it, so off I set. Wrong – Croydon is slightly to the east of north from Gatwick. Furthermore, there was an easterly wind blowing and I had completely forgotten about magnetic variation so, I was flying in the wrong direction in poor visibility. It can't have been more than about three miles.

However, I had once lived in Ashford, Middlesex, and recognised St Mary's and the Staines reservoirs when they hove into sight. Ah, I should now be OK, I thought – follow the railway line back to Croydon. Once I found the line from Staines, I flew up to Clapham Junction, turned hard right, took the first left and simply followed the line until I picked up the enormous cooling towers which then stood just to the west of Croydon airport. All I then had to do was to fly round the towers until I was in a position to be seen innocently approaching the airfield from the direction of Redhill.

I was never found out.

GLOSSARY

AB	Afterburner
ACRB	Aircrew Refreshment Bar
AEF	Air Experience Flight
AEO	Air Electronics Officer
AEW	Airborne Early Warning
AFB	Air Force Base
AFC	Air Force Cross
AFCENT	Allied Forces Central Europe
AFNORTH	Allied Forces Northern Europe
AMF(L)	Allied Command Europe Mobile Force (Land)
AOC	Air Officer Commanding
APU	Auxiliary Power Unit
ARPCE	Automatic Release Point Camera Equipment
ASC	Advanced Staff College
ASF	Aircraft Servicing Flight
ASI	Airspeed Indicator
asl	Above Sea Level
ASW	Anti-Submarine Warfare
ATC	Air Traffic Control
AWACS	Airborne Warning and Control System
BDLS	British Defence Liaison Staff
BFG	British Forces Germany
BFI	Before-Flight Inspection
C2	Command and Control
CAA	Civil Aviation Authority

CAF	Canadian Forces
CAS	Chief of the Air Staff
CAVOK	Ceiling and Visibility OK
CDS	Chief of the Defence Staff
CFS	Central Flying School
CO	Commanding Officer
Comms	Communications
CONOPS	Concept of Operations
CR	Combat Ready
CRM	Crew/Cockpit Resource Management
DC	Direct Current
DCB	Direct Commission 'B'
DFC	Distinguished Flying Cross
DFGA	Day Fighter/Ground Attack
DME	Distance Measuring Equipment
DZ	Drop Zone
ECM	Electronic Countermeasures
EEZ	Exclusive Economic Zone
EGR	Engine Ground Run
ESM	Electronic Support Measures
ETPS	Empire Test Pilots' School
FAC	Forward Air Controller
FB	Fighter Bomber
FDO	Flight Deck Officer
FGA	Fighter Ground Attack
FHT	Final Handling Test
Flyco	Flying Control
FOCAS	Flag Officer Carriers and Amphibious Ships
FR	Fighter Reconnaissance
FRA	Flight Refuelling Aviation
FRT	Field Repair Team
FTS	Flying Training School
GCA	Ground-Controlled Approach
GPMG	General Purpose Machine Gun
GPS	Global Positioning System
GR	Ground Attack/Reconnaissance

GTN	Garmin Touchscreen Navigator
HAS	Hardened Aircraft Shelter
HF	High Frequency or Harrier Force (context dependent)
HHA	Hawker Hunter Aviation
HLS	Helicopter Landing Site
HMG	Heavy Machine Gun
HP	Handling Party
HQ	Headquarters
HSF	Harrier Servicing Flight
IFF	Identification, Friend or Foe
ILS	Instrument Landing System
IMC	Instrument Meteorological Conditions
IP	Initial Point
IPN	Isopropyl Nitrate
ISTAR	Intelligence, Surveillance, Target Acquisition and Reconnaissance
ISR	Intelligence, Surveillance and Reconnaissance
JARIC	Joint Air Reconnaissance Intelligence Centre
JEngO	Junior Engineering Officer
KFOR	Kosovo Forces
LAC	Leading Aircraftman
LCR	Limited Combat Ready
MET	Multi-Engine Training
MFD	Multifunction Display
MHz	Megahertz
MoD	Ministry of Defence
MOT	Ministry of Transport Test
MP	Member of Parliament
MPA	Maritime Patrol Aircraft
MRAF	Marshal of the Royal Air Force
MRT	Mountain Rescue Team
MU	Maintenance Unit
NAS	Naval Air Squadron
NATO	North Atlantic Treaty Organisation
Nav	Navigator
NBC	Nuclear, Biological and Chemical
NCO	Non-Commissioned Officer

NDB	Non-Directional Beacon
NFZ	No-Fly Zone
nm	Nautical Miles
NOTAM	Notice to Airmen
NVG	Night Vision Goggles
OASC	Officer and Aircrew Selection Centre
OC	Officer Commanding
OCTU	Officer Cadet Training Unit
OCU	Operational Conversion Unit
OEU	Operational Evaluation Unit
OLF	Operational Low Flying
ORP	Operational Readiness Platform
PA	Professional Aviator
PPL	Private Pilot's Licence
PR	Photographic Reconnaissance or Public Relations (context dependent)
QEAF	Qatar Emiri Air Force
QFI	Qualified Flying Instructor
QRA	Quick Reaction Alert
QWI	Qualified Weapons Instructor
R/T	Radio Telegraph
RAAF	Royal Australian Air Force
Radalt	Radar Altimeter
RAF	Royal Air Force
RAFG	RAF Germany
RAM	Radar-Absorbent Material
RCL	Recoilless Weapon
RFA	Royal Fleet Auxiliary
RHAG	Rotary Hydraulic Arrestor Gear
RN	Royal Navy
RNAS	Royal Naval Air Station
RV	Rendezvous
SAF	Sultan's Armed Forces
SAOEU	Strike Attack Operational Evaluation Unit
SAR	Search and Rescue
SATCO	Senior Air Traffic Control Officer

SCT	Staff Continuation Training
SEM	Service-Engineered Modification
SEngO	Senior Engineering Officer
SF	Special Forces
SFC	Senior Fight Cadet
SNCO	Senior Non-Commissioned Officer
SOAF	Sultan of Oman's Air Force
SOP	Standard Operating Procedure
SPD	Stick-Positioning Device
STC	Strike Command
STF	Special Trial Fit
TACAN	Tactical Air Navigation
TAT	Terminal Airborne Tanker
TD	Tactical Director
TFR	Terrain-Following Radar
TIRRS	Tornado Infra-Red Reconnaissance System
TOT	Time-on-Target
TWU	Tactical Weapons Unit
UAE	United Arab Emirates
UAEAF	United Arab Emirates Air Force
UAS	University Air Squadron
UHF	Ultra High Frequency
UN	United Nations
UOR	Urgent Operational Requirement
USAF	United States Air Force
VHF	Very High Frequency
VID	Visual Identification
WSO	Weapon Systems Operator
XO	Executive Officer

INDEX